Monsters Are Attacking Tokyo!

The Incredible World of Japanese Fantasy Films

by Stuart Galbraith IV

ステュアート　ガルブレイス IV

Feral House

Research Associates, Yukari Fujii and Atsushi Sakahara

Monsters Are Attacking Tokyo! ©1998 Stuart Galbraith IV
All rights reserved

Feral House
2532 Lincoln Blvd. Suite 359
Venice, CA 90021

ISBN 0-922915-47-4

The publisher would like to thank Skylaire Alfvegren for improving and transforming this book.

Designed by Linda Hayashi
First edition 1998

10 9 8 7 6 5 4 3 2 1

Dedicated to

my mother and father,

Stuart (III) and Mary Galbraith

Acknowledgements

This book would not exist without the invaluable help of many individuals. Key among them **Atsushi Sakahara,** who was my interpreter during my primary visit to Japan. Atsushi came aboard literally at the last minute, and his generosity and kindness—at a time when I really needed it—will forever be appreciated. Besides his excellent skills translating questions about Japanese monsters and various Crazy Cats, Atsushi also taught me valuable lessons about finding one's way around Tokyo (no easy task!) and Japanese etiquette.

Many of these interviews wouldn't have taken place at all if it weren't for **Yukari Fujii,** who translated countless letters into suitable-for-framing Japanese and obligingly talked on the phone with people like Kyoko Kagawa and Senkichi Taniguchi in the middle of the night for me. Like most Japanese people, she couldn't fathom why I'd be so interested in Godzilla movies, Kurosawa and Tora-san when I was surrounded by so much wonderful American pop culture, but she was always patient with me, extremely dedicated, and hard-working.

The very generous **Brad Warner** let me stay in his Japanese-style pad, walking distance from both Toho Studios and where he works, Tsuburaya Productions. Brad kindly arranged interviews with most of the Tsuburaya-related people, and provided photos.

Writer **Steve Ryfle** and I traveled to Japan together in 1994 and 1996 (he also arranged and wrote several interviews included in this volume); Steve is an amazingly fun person, and I'm grateful we're able to share this crazy *kaiju eiga* passion. Hats off also to Steve's very talented wife, Joal Ryan, who never complains when Steve and I debate endlessly about such weighty matters as the merits of *Godzilla vs. the Smog Monster.* Thank you also to **James Bailey,** who kindly let me reprint his interview with the late Ishiro Honda, who is really the heart of this book.

I'm also grateful to **Adam Parfrey,** and also to **Linda Hayashi,** who made this book look really, really cool.

I would be remiss if I did not acknowledge those pioneers whose talent and tenaciousness paved the way for a book like this: Greg Shoemaker, Ed Godziszewski, August Ragone, Guy Tucker, and David Milner.

My thanks also to the following people without whom this book would be something less than what it is: Haruyo Moriyoshi (Daiei Co., Ltd.), Forrest J. Ackerman, Norihiko Asao, Buddy Barnett, Dennis Bartok, Linda Conrad, Mike Copner, *chambara* expert and writer Chris D (especially for the "Sonny" Chiba snippet!), Reiko Duba, Christopher Elam, Lisa Feerick (Pollison) and David Pollison, Yukio Fukushima (World Intelligence Partner), Kiyoko Goto, Don Glut, Rhonda and Jun Hanari, R.M. Hayes, Ryuji Honda, Ichiro Kadowaki (Daiei Co., Ltd.), Kyoko Kagawa, Regan Kibbee, Osamu "Sammy" Kobayashi, Tsuyoshi Kobayashi (Daiei Co., Ltd.), Akemi "Addie" Kohzu, Kurosawa Production, Bill Littman, Kate McMains (Ultracom), Tony Mostrom, Masanari Nihei, Seiji Okamura, Ted Okuda, Christopher Potter, Brian Reason, David Renwick, Donald Richie, Atsushi Saito (Tsuburaya Productions Co., Ltd.), the late Frankie Sakai, Tony Sol, Tomoko Suzuki (Watanabe Production), Senkichi Taniguchi and Kaoru Yachigusa [Taniguchi], Masayuki Tsuda, Bill and Beverly Warren, Takeshi Yagi (Tsuburaya Productions Co., Ltd.), Yuko Yoshikawa and Yoshifumi Hosoya, and Akio Yoshimura (Kyushu Asahi Broadcasting Co.).

And, of course, my deepest thanks to those who agreed to sit down and talk about this crazy, wonderful genre.

怪獣 東京大攻撃

Table of Contents

怪獣 東京大攻撃

For better and for worse, Japanese monster movies have become as much an icon of international pop culture as Kentucky Fried Chicken, Abba, and Disneyland's Pirates of the Caribbean ride. And amid much hoopla, Godzilla, the "King of the Monsters," died on December 9, 1995 at the age of 41 at the end of the last Japanese-made Godzilla movie to date. With *Godzilla vs. Destroyer* (1995), the long-running series had come full circle, pausing to reflect on the 1954 film that started it all and wonder how a giant, fire-breathing lizard could relate to the even more gargantuan changes that have taken place in Japan and around the world since. Meanwhile, in the United States, the producers of the first all-*American* Godzilla movie are hoping the picture's expensive computer-age effects and nearly unprecedented hype will sufficiently overturn America's campy/negative perception of Godzilla and his monster brethren. In the United States at least, Godzilla and Japanese fantasy films in general have come to represent cheap effects, bad dubbing, poor acting, mediocre scripts—and guys in rubber suits stomping miniature sets.

So while undeniably an icon, Godzilla is inevitably dismissed by nearly all "serious" scholars of Japanese cinema. And yet, this giant, radioactive dinosaur is also Japan's most recognizable movie star—everyone knows who Godzilla is—and he's probably the only "actor" aside from Toshiro Mifune, Yoshiko "Shirley" Yamaguchi, Sessue Hayakawa, Ken Takakura, Shinichi "Sonny" Chiba, "Beat" Takeshi Kitano and a few others to win any measure of fame in the West. (How many do you know?)

If you're reading this book, you're a fan of Japanese monster movies, called *kaiju eiga* ("kye-jew eh-ga"), or perhaps you've seen one or more of these films on the "Late, Late Show" and are wondering what they're are all about. *Kaiju eiga* have been around for more than 40 years, and are still popular in Japan today, but what made these this seemingly campy, cheap little films such pop culture staples? In one sense, their appeal can't be explained logically. It's a bit like asking someone why they fell in love with person A but not person B.

Nonetheless, *kaiju eiga* fans can be as obsessive as that other much-maligned fraternity: "Trekkers" (or, colloquially, "Trekkies"). From the various television shows to the movies, the appeal of "Star Trek" is universal—fans are drawn into its optimistic depiction of the future, its stories, and the appealing relationships between the various characters. It's that simple.

Kaiju eiga fans, on the other hand, are a far more splintered crowd. Surprisingly, there are fans who aren't especially enamored of the films at all. Instead, they're drawn to the imported toys, the model kits, the books and posters. They became collectors, for this merchandise is extremely appealing and collectable: the toys are cute and charming, the models are detailed and lifelike, the books and the movie posters are visually arresting. And because this merchandise has been so hard to come by in the United States, there's also a friendly (and sometimes not-so-friendly) air of competition among fans to be the first to own this or that action figure, with collectors paying exorbitant sums of money—sometimes of hundreds of dollars—for a single plastic monster. And the appeal of *kaiju eiga* is by no means limited to children; like "Star Trek," the most obsessive fans tend to be in their 30s.

A Symphony of Destruction

For some, the appeal of giant monster movies grew out of a childhood fascination with dinosaurs. Dinosaurs were, of course, real animals that actually roamed the earth, and yet there is also an undying air of mystery about them. How did these seemingly indestructible creatures become extinct? What would happen if dinosaurs and human beings co-existed in our modern world? We see their petrified bones in musty museums and can only imagine what they were actually like but, through the magic of the movies, better than any other medium, we can make them come alive. Audiences were amazed by Willis "Obie" O'Brien's stop motion creatures in the original *The Lost World* (1925) and, more than 70 years later, in Steven Spielberg's 1997 film of the same name. These films affected moviegoers in much the same way: for their audiences these dinosaurs seemed uncannily "real."

But there is something decidedly unreal, off-kilter and out of whack with Japanese monster movies. Part of our affection and fascination for them has to do with the very thing they are so often derided for: their weirdness, their goofiness, their inexplicability. By contrast the giant monsters in American movies usually are little more than cranky dinosaurs awakened from a million millennium slumber, or big bugs grown to out-of-control proportions courtesy Cold War nuclear testing. They do little more than stomp, bellow, and lumber about until dispatched at or near some famous urban landmark. By the time Japanese monster movies had reached the United States, the monster-on-the-loose genre here had pretty much petered out, both commercially and (especially) creatively.

What happened next can be likened to the rise of "Spaghetti" Westerns at about the same time. After years of mostly predictable oaters and literally dozens of

TV Westerns flooding the airwaves came these strange little movies from Italy breathing new life into the genre. The stars were familiar Americans (Clint Eastwood, Burt Reynolds, Charles Bronson), the stories and iconography were the same, but the direction, editing, music, etc. were unlike anything American audiences had ever seen. At first, American distributors tried to obscure the origin of these films by Anglicizing the names of Italian cast and crew members, but when these films proved to be blockbusters, Hollywood filmmakers even attempted, not very well, to imitate their unique style in films like *Hang 'Em High* (1968).

Similarly, after years of mostly bland monster-on-the-loose programmers like *The Deadly Mantis* and *The Beginning of the End* (both 1957), American audiences were drawn to these oddball monster epics from Japan. Even though American distributors would sometimes edit Caucasian

talent like Raymond Burr into the action, the films were obviously Asian-made. Moreover, these peculiar little pictures just didn't look like American monster movies at all. They were more colorful, ambitious, creative, ridiculous, and vibrant than anything being made stateside.

The first ones—*Godzilla, King of the Monsters!* (1954), *Rodan* (1956), *The Mysterians* (1957)—to a greater or lesser degree imitated American movies that had preceded them, but by the end of the decade this genre was becoming increasingly quirky. They became quirky partly because the giant monster genre is, by its very nature, pretty limiting to begin with and, probably out of desperation, Japanese filmmakers went to any length to give each film a new twist, no matter how outrageous. Consider, for instance, the first Gamera sequel, *War of the Monsters* (1966): A giant, fire-breathing, prehistoric, flying, frisbee-like extra-terrestrial turtle vs. a rainbow-emitting, four-legged rhino-like dinosaur with a jack-in-the-box-like, frost-shooting killer tongue?! The monsters, over time, also became more personable, more like "plain folks." The Godzilla of *Son of Godzilla* (1967) bears little resemblance to the Atomic Age metaphor-Godzilla of the first film. Godzilla purists here and in Japan cringed at these developments, and yet it's doubtful the series would've lasted more than a few films or be remembered as fondly as it is had Godzilla's persona not changed from the effective but colorless city-smashing Zamboni of the first picture.[1]

These movies, especially the ones made during the 1970s, were geared almost exclusively for kids and looked more like titanic wrestling

1. Since 1989, Godzilla's "character" has been pretty much the same from film to film, and the series has suffered because of it—Godzilla became boring.

matches than American monster movies, and that was exactly what some fans—especially those weaned on the burgeoning Japanese superhero TV shows—liked most. Relating to this is a kind of primitive fascination with scenes of destruction. Many *kaiju* fans grew up building model kits—then destroying them, creating massive train wrecks on their Lionel and Tyco sets *a la* Gomez Addams, and grew up watching disaster films like *Earthquake* and *The Towering Inferno* (both 1974) in theaters and on television. *Kaiju eiga* offered the best of both worlds: the destruction was always on a massive scale, but it was rarely graphic, comfortably toy-like and assuredly unreal.

Like Spaghetti Westerns, Japanese monster movies often aped the structure of similar films made in Hollywood, but virtually everything else remained singularly "Japanese." And just as the Italians had extremely talented artists like Sergio Leone and Ennio Morricone, the Japanese casts and crews were A-level talent, and during Japan's Golden Age of Filmmaking at least, in the hands of directors like Ishiro Honda, composers like Akira Ifukube and Masaru Sato, and special effects men like Eiji Tsuburaya, the Japanese created beguiling symphonies of mass destruction. Their collision-style editing of music, sound effects, special effects and live action shooting had a hypnotic effect on children and even some adults willing to suspend their disbelief.

If the best of these films are actually good—and this book contends that many of these films are very good—why then is this genre the fodder of stand-up comedians and television programs like "Mystery Science Theater 3000?" Partly this is due to the consumerism mode of spectatorship in American cinema today. We want our money's worth in the form of a quick, visceral fix of realistic sound and visual effects. We seem to be increasingly short on imagination, and want not to be **bothered** with suspending our disbelief. After all, what was the overwhelming motivation behind the commercial success of the otherwise mediocre *Jurassic Park* (1993)?

To see how *real* the dinosaurs looked. As writer Bill Warren notes, "For some in the West, [Japanese fantasy films] will always look 'fakey,' but of course, that's a culturally-based objection. It was rarely the intention of the producers of any kind of Japanese fantasy film, from the high art of movies like *Kwaidan*

Barugon's killer tongue wreaks havoc in "War of the Monsters" (1966)

(1964) to the lowest of the low-brow, such as *Invasion of the Neptune Men* (1961), to be 'realistic' at all. It simply is not a consideration in virtually any form of Japanese art, so directing that complaint at these movies is irrelevant."[2] However, many scholars of Japanese film argue just the reverse: that the work of Kurosawa and Ozu are to be admired *for* their "realism." Moreover, I was very surprised by members of Eiji Tsuburaya's staff who commented how much effort was put into making the special effects as "real" as possible. The Japanese (coming attractions) trailers bear this out: ads for *War of the Gargantuas* (1966), for instance, promise a picture "filmed in absolute realism!" Could it be that Americans and the Japanese have fundamentally different standards of what "realism" is and means? Are Japanese audiences simply less jaded than American moviegoers?

The reader will note that a great deal of space in this book, especially in the interview section, has been devoted to Japanese movies and filmmakers outside of the SF/fantasy realm. *This is deliberate.* Until now Japanese fantasy films have existed in a kind of vacuum. Indeed, most Godzilla fans never watch other kinds of Japanese

movies, while most "serious" students of Japanese cinema avoid *kaiju eiga* like the plague. And yet, the only Japanese films widely seen in the United States (beyond Japanese neighborhood theaters) are art films by filmmakers like Kurosawa, Ozu, and Oshima—*and* monster movies. But the postwar Japanese film industry, as big as any in the world save Hollywood, also made comedies (especially "Salaryman Comedies," light-hearted pictures centered around Japan's expanding white collar workforce), war movies, musicals, gangster films, domestic melodramas, and so on. To really understand Japanese science fiction films, one needs to have at least some idea of what was happening in the industry as a whole. Only then can one understand why and how actors and technicians freely moved from *Rashomon* to *Rodan,* from *Woman in the Dunes* to monster space chickens.

2. Stuart Galbraith IV, *Japanese Science Fiction, Fantasy and Horror Films* (Jefferson, NC: McFarland, 1993) xxii

Because the Japanese film industry was so strong, so successful, and so closely modeled after Hollywood, they had the resources and ambitions to produce these monster epics—resources the film industries of countries like France, Germany, and Great Britain just didn't have. (It's hard to imagine, for instance, Britain's Hammer Films producing anything on the scale of *King Kong vs. Godzilla*.). Even in Hollywood, few companies could have produced these SPFX-heavy features on the same scale; smaller firms like AIP simply weren't adept at pictures like this (as seen in their mediocre *Master of the World*, 1961), and major studios like Paramount and Warner Bros. saw big-scale sci-fi films as risky investments.

Nor did these countries have a special effects genius the likes of Eiji Tsuburaya (1901–1970), who pioneered the use of miniatures and men in rubber costumes and gave *kaiju eiga* their own unique look. Tsuburaya himself became a god-like figure in the industry, and he used his power and influence to define a genre he virtually owned; his special effects films were one of Japan's most lucrative exports, bringing in much-needed foreign monies from all over the world.

Stateside interest in Japanese monsters has swelled over the last decade, giving birth to a new generation of fans, and concurrent with a mini-Renaissance of *kaiju eiga* filmmaking in Japan. Though these newer films have had little, if any distribution in the United States, expensive, imported "garage kit" models, glossy, picture-filled Japanese magazines, and nifty little toys continue to pour in increasing numbers at sci-fi and comic book conventions. There's also been an explosion of "bootleg" videos. These early bootlegs were blurry copies-of-copies-of-copies, but for fans who hadn't seen a new Godzilla movie in years they were also thrilling,

even if these murky movies were in Japanese. Gradually, the bootleggers became more and more sophisticated: the picture quality improved, English subtitles were added and eventually the best bootlegs became virtually indistinguishable from the real McCoy. Some of the more ambitious bootleggers even traveled to Japan, camcorder in tow, and brazenly videotaped brand-new Godzilla and Gamera pictures inside Tokyo movie houses. Magazines and fanzines devoted to Japanese monster movies sprang up, notably *Markalite* and *G-Fan,* and by the mid-90s, Godzilla conventions were being held and monster suit actors like Haruo Nakajima even flew over from Japan.

One of the more frustrating aspects understanding Japanese movies is that there are almost no books on the subject outside of a half-dozen or so (mostly impenetrable) film theory works. A rare exception is Donald Richie and Joseph L. Anderson's recommended *The Japanese Film: Art and Industry,* but even its scope pretty much ends around 1960. And what books are out there are generally limited to so-called "art films." Monster movies, Yakuza thrillers, musicals, and slapstick comedies from Japan are dismissed or ignored altogether. Even something as fundamental as an English-language biography of the late Toshiro Mifune has yet to appear.

"Godzilla, the King of the Monsters!" (and inhabited by Haruo Nakajima). Even this still is something of an icon—several model/garage kits have been based on this shot

怪獣 東京大攻撃

The Japanese film industry patterned itself after Hollywood, and because the development of commercial television was about ten years behind American TV, their studio system lasted much longer. And while the Japanese could rarely match Hollywood's penchant for lavishness, their films were well-produced and their output enormous, with each studio making nearly 100 features per year at its peak.

And what of the men and women behind these movies? How did actors feel about starring opposite Godzilla, Gamera, and Girara, the extra-terrestrial space chicken? Were they embarrassed? What do Japanese effects artists think of the CGI revolution in Hollywood? What's their take on the rubber suits, the miniature cityscapes, and the bad dubbing of their movies in America?

Almost everyone reachable granted an interview for this book. There were some exceptions: Ken Utsui is apparently too embarrassed about his days as pudgy superhero Starman to want to look back his cape-wearing days. Similarly the actress Yumi Shirakawa, the heroine of *Rodan* and *The Mysterians,* told me she appeared in those pictures only because of her contract with Toho Studios and prefers not to talk about them. Actor Richard Jaeckel was too ill to be interviewed, while Russ Tamblyn, according to his agent, was busy writing his autobiography. Others, like Kyoko Kagawa (*Mothra's* female lead) and Kaoru Yachigusa (*The Human Vapor's* love interest) claimed not to remember working on these films at all.

Most, however, were happy and a little bit surprised by the attention. The majority had never been interviewed by an American before, and wondered why anyone in the United States would even be curious about them. A few, like "Starman" director Teruo Ishii and *Monster from a Prehistoric Planet* writers Gan Yamazaki and Ryuzo Nakanishi, weren't even aware their films had even been shown in the United States. The bulk of the interviews in this book were conducted in Tokyo in 1994 and 1996. We met in hotel coffee shops, in studio commissaries, and, occasionally, in their homes.

One interesting sidelight: Upon arriving in Japan, shortly before one of the first actor interviews was to begin, the actor's agent innocently asked, "How much would you like to pay Mr. So-and-So for the interview?" At this point my translator, Atsushi Sakahara, piped in, "In Japan, reporters generally pay around $200 per interview. You should also offer them cab fare." I was completely caught off guard and meekly explained that in the United States it's considered *bad* journalism to pay for interviews. Fortunately, very few agents expected this from an American, and most of the actors steadfastly refused their payoff when it was offered.

For people who were making films like *The Green Slime* and *Yog—Monster from Space,* these men and women were almost always sophisticated yet unpretentious, and most maintained a relaxed sense of humor about their monster-battling days. You'll also discover some strange and interesting quirks, such as the fact that most of the directors were influenced not by Hollywood films, but by French movies (though, interestingly, director Fred Zinnemann came up again and again). Read together, these interviews paint a portrait of what working in the Japanese film industry was like during the 1950s–1970s. Reading them you'll notice a studio-based camaraderie and loyalty that has all but vanished in Hollywood, and hopefully understand and appreciate why Japanese actors and craftsmen moved so freely between the high art of Kurosawa and Ozu, and that most disreputable of movie genres, the Japanese monster movie.

Stuart Galbraith IV
Hollywood, California
January 1998

AN IMPORTANT NOTE:

The names of the films and monsters discussed in this book open a can filled with worms. To wit: Toho Studio's 1965 Godzilla entry, *Kaiju daisenso,* translates to, literally, "Giant Strange Beast Great War." So it'll make a bit more sense, most would agree the best translation of this title would be, say, "Giant Monster War." Only when Toho was marketing this film abroad they didn't give it the English-language title "Giant Monster War," they called it *Invasion of Astro-Monster.* Forget "Giant Monster War," they didn't even call it *Invasion of THE Astro-Monster.* Anyway, when the picture was released here, its American distributor unleashed it as *Monster Zero.* However, when it was sold to television it was decided that *Monster Zero* was just a bit too vague, so it was retitled *GODZILLA VS. Monster Zero.* Did you get all that?

Simply Romanizing the original Japanese titles would probably be best, only that would drive every non-Japanese reader crazy: "after appearing in *Dai tatsumaki,* Natsuki made *San daikaiju chikyu saidai no kessen,*" etc. Alternate titles come and go—after 25 years, for instance, *Godzilla vs. the Smog Monster* suddenly (but officially) became *Godzilla vs. Hedorah.* English translations of the original, Japanese titles vary from source to source, and would be more confusing than useful. The myriad of Japanese names cited in this book are already pretty hard for the average reader to keep track of; to ask them to remember that *Big Duel in the South Sea* is the same film as *Godzilla versus the Sea Monster* is, to my mind, a bit much.

Therefore, for the sake of consistency and readability, the film titles used in this book are the original theatrical (or television, or home video) release title, which is why *Mosura tai Gojira* (1964) is called *Godzilla vs. the Thing* and not *Godzilla vs. Mothra,* and why *Gamera tai Barugon* (1966) is listed under its first television title, *War of the Monsters.* I've also used, whenever possible, the

name as it appears on the original title card (which is why *Godzilla versus the Sea Monster* is listed that way, instead of *Godzilla vs. the Sea Monster*). *Godzilla vs. the Cosmic Monster* (1974) was announced as *Godzilla vs. the Bionic Monster,* and posters for the film were prepared under that title but, for legal reasons the film was apparently never shown as such, which is why the former is used.[1] Common sense has been utilized for those cases where theatrical release was uncertain (and generally limited to Japanese neighborhood theaters, if actually shown here at all).

The years which accompany film titles reflect each film's **release date in Japan,** and not the American year of release, which is noted in the filmography. This has been done so the reader can get a sense of chronology with these films from the Japanese side of things. (The Godzilla films, for instance, were sometimes released out of sequence in America.) Although somewhat confusing at times (for instance, Myron Healey is in the 1958 *Varan the Unbelievable,* though his scenes weren't filmed until 1962!), this method seems to make the most sense.

Next, an even stickier issue: monster names. Godzilla isn't called Godzilla in Japan; in the land of his birth he's *Gojira* (say "Go-jee-ra," with equal emphasis on each syllable, while making the "ra" a kind of cross between "ra" and "la"; there, now you've got it).

Correspondingly, Rodan is called *Radon,* Mothra is *Mosura,* and so on. With some monsters, however, it gets a little tricky. The Son of Godzilla is named Minya in *Godzilla's Revenge* (1969), and in Japan his name is pronounced "Mee-nee-ra," and best spelled with Roman characters as *Minira.* However, sometimes publications in Japan use another spelling, "Minilla," as in "rhymes with vanilla." Of course, the Japanese don't pronounce it that way (they don't use an "L" sound in their vocabulary), and neither should you. After all, using this method, Mothra would be "Mosulla," Godzilla would be "Gojilla," etc.

Even the Japanese sometimes have a hard time reading the names of strangers, which is why Ishiro Honda's name has long been mistransliterated as *Inoshiro* Honda, and why Special Effects Director Teruyoshi Nakano's name has variously been listed in American credits as Shokei Nakano, Akiyoshi Nakano, et. al. In most cases the actual names have been confirmed one way or another, and are correct.

This book is a kind of oral history of the genre, told from the perspective of the men and women who were actually there. Except for director Ishiro Honda, whose words are excerpted from a 1991 interview with writer James Bailey, these interviews were conducted by the author or his associates between 1994 and 1997. Except where noted, all of the Westerners interviewed spoke English, while all of the Japanese people spoke Japanese, and their words have been translated into English. The film titles have been changed to standardize this book and, in some cases, their words have been condensed or slightly reordered for clarification purposes.

---

1. This also appears to be the case with *Mekagojira no gyakushu* (1975). Though advertising material was prepared with the title *The Terror of Godzilla,* (see page 176) I've yet to see it actually advertised in print as anything other than *Terror of Mechagodzilla.* And even if it were advertised as the former, it's possible, even likely, the film was exhibited with no title card at all (as appears in some home video versions of the film). In this book it's called *Terror of Mechagodzilla.*

Fantasy Films in Japan's Golden Age of Filmmaking

Shortly after the end of World War II, Japan entered what is fondly remembered as its "Golden Age" of filmmaking. During this period, Japanese movies like *Rashomon* (1950), *Ugetsu* (1953), *Gate of Hell* (1953), and *Seven Samurai* (1954) were recognized for the first time all over the world, and some its finest filmmakers—Akira Kurosawa, Kenji Mizoguchi, Yasujiro Ozu—were making masterpiece after masterpiece. At the same time, another uniquely "Japanese" movie genre emerged as famous—if much less respectable—as anything made by the country's great auteurs. It is, of course, the Japanese fantasy film, especially the Japanese giant monster movie *(kaiju eiga)*, a movie genre regarded, in America at least, as the lowest of the lowbrow.

These movies were generally lumped in and compared with American science fiction films from the same period, but in truth the Japanese fantasy film couldn't have been more different, even though the genre was, initially, clearly imitative of American sci-fi pictures. Though dismissed and likened to the kind of movies that are "so bad they're good," the Japanese pretty much dominated the sci-fi genre from the late-1950s until the late-1960s. Japanese monster movies from this period featured what were then state-of-the-art special effects, effects that far outmatched all but the most expensive American science fiction films, movies like *Fantastic Voyage* (1966) and *2001: A Space Odyssey* (1968). But those films were the exception and not the rule; most American sci-fi pictures were cheap affairs like *The Brain from Planet Arous* (1958) or

Invasion of the Star Creatures (1962) or, like *On the Beach* (1959) and *The Manchurian Candidate* (1962), avoided visual effects altogether.

In America, the sci-fi movie boom began in 1950 with the release of *Destination Moon* and *Rocketship X-M,* the first American features to take the concept of space travel seriously. The box-office success of these two modestly-budgeted films led to the production of a large number of sci-fi features for the first time. The majority of these films—*The Day the Earth Stood Still, The Thing (from Another World), When Worlds Collide* (all 1951); *War of the Worlds* and *It Came from Outer Space* (both 1953)—came from major studios and were budgeted in the high-B, low-A range. As these films were also successful, the studios were more financially and creatively ambitious, and during the 1954–1956 period, several large-budget science fiction films were produced. However, these films—*20,000 Leagues Under the Sea* (1954), *This Island Earth* (1955), *Forbidden Planet* (1956)—did not make back their negative cost. At the same time, the market for science fiction films in the United States was changing; the rise of the drive-in theater and its move away from family audiences to teenagers and children created a shifting market for science fiction films, one which was successfully tapped at the end of the decade by smaller production-releasing companies like American International Pictures (AIP). Their product, which included the likes of *I Was a Teenage Frankenstein* and *The Amazing Colossal Man* (both 1957),

frequently out-grossed big-studio science fiction releases.[1] As a result, the 1958–1962 period saw a creative decline in the genre, concurrent with a rise in the production of low-budget pictures from AIP and other independents, while the major studios either gave up on the genre altogether, or produced and/or acquired their own quickies to support double bills. By 1963, the American majors had all but given up on science fiction, which remained essentially the domain of the "indies" until the enormous and wholly unanticipated success of *Planet of the Apes* (and its sequels), and the hoopla surrounding Stanley Kubrick's expensive 70mm Cinerama epic, *2001: A Space Odyssey,* in 1968.

Conversely, sci-fi movies thrived in Japan during this period, and, to the Japanese at least, was not perceived as the second-class genre it was for so long in the United States. The genre's greatest commercial success, *King Kong vs. Godzilla,* was released in 1962, and seen by more than 11,200,000 Japanese during its initial release. Where the majority of American science fiction films from the 1958–67 period were in black and white, nearly all Japanese sci-fi features produced after 1955 were in color and anamorphic wide screen (i.e., variations of Fox's CinemaScope, though given names such as Nikkatsu Scope and Shochiku GrandScope in Japan). Toho, the leading producer of sci-fi features, also released several of its genre films from 1957–1965 in (Perspecta) stereophonic sound. Conversely, less than a half-dozen American science fiction during this same period were in color, 'scope and stereo.[2]

Studio trade ads from the 1960s. Note which genre dominates the Daiei and Toho ads; Honda films out-number Kurosawa 4 to 1

American sci-fi films of the 50s and early-60s starred B-movie actors (e.g., Richard Denning, Rex Reason), has-been leading men (Richard Carlson, John Agar), or rising talent waiting to be discovered (Steve McQueen, James Arness); its actresses generally were forgettable starlets riding out contracts or being eased into "bigger" roles (Diane Baker, Kathryn Grant).[3] Conversely, the actors and actresses in Japanese fantasy films were top stars. The 1950s saw American studios dumping its contract talent but, in Japan, then producing hundreds of feature-lengths movies per year—more than any other country in the world (including India)—studios could afford a large pool of contract players. At this time, the publication *UniJapan Film* featured publicity stills of each studio's top stars; Toho's Akira Takarada and Yuriko Hoshi, Daiei's Eiji Funakoshi and Kojiro Hongo, Toei's Hiroki Matsukata, etc., and **all** appeared in *kaiju eiga* at one time or another. Even the late Toshiro Mifune, Japan's biggest star, appeared in several films with fantasy elements, including Hiroshi Inagaki's *The Three Treasures* (1959), where the actor battled a multi-headed dragon, and *The Lost World of Sinbad* (1963), which featured witches, wizards, and other fantasy iconography.

But thanks to sloppy American dubbing, American film reviewers frequently and unthinkingly criticized the performances in Japanese science fiction films as amateurish. For instance, *The New York Times'* Howard Thompson criticized the cast of Toho's *The Mysterians* (1957), arguing, "not one of [them] can act."

1. Bill Warren, *Keep Watching the Skies!* (Jefferson, NC: McFarland, 1982) vii–xvi
2. Robert E. Carr and R.M. Hayes, *Wide Screen Movies* (Jefferson, NC: McFarland, 1988) 54–111
3. Warren, xii

Obviously the dubbing colored his opinion, for the cast includes some of Japan's best film actors, among them Takashi Shimura, Susumu Fujita, and Yoshio Tsuchiya, all concurrently members of Akira Kurosawa's stock company who also happened to be *kaiju eiga* regulars. Shimura was superb and deeply moving as the dying government worker in *Ikiru* (1952) and as the leader of the *Seven Samurai* (1954). Fujita essayed the title role in Kurosawa's first feature, *Sanshiro Sugata* (1943); he continued to play memorable roles in the director's films through the early-1960s. (In *Yojimbo,* Fujita is the cowardly-but-wise *samurai* who runs off before the big battle.) Tsuchiya played poor farmers whose wives are taken away from him in both *Seven Samurai* and *Yojimbo* (1961). The same held true for the other studios—Daiei's Eiji Funakoshi, star of Kon Ichikawa's superb anti-war film *Fires on the Plain* (1959) appeared in several Gamera movies, and even Eiji Okada, star of Alain Resnais' *Hiroshima mon amour* (1959) and Hiroshi Teshigahara's *Woman in the Dunes* (1964), toplined Shochiku's *The X from Outer Space* (1967).

Aesthetically, Japanese sci-fi films thrived during the 1954–68 period. As film historian Bill Warren rightly noted in his introduction to my book *Japanese Science Fiction, Fantasy and Horror Films* (McFarland & Co., 1993), these were sophisticated men working in a highly unsophisticated genre. The directors of American science fiction films from this period generally were hacks, culled from the ranks of serials, B-Westerns, two-reel comedies, and other secondary genres when the demand for those pictures died out in the early-1950s. In terms of camera placement, staging, directing actors—the kinds of things directors do—America sci-fi directors often displayed a

remarkable lack of imagination. In Japan however, even the schlockiest of schlock looked good. Even the most undistinguished of directors knew where to put the camera, position the actors, and splice it all together, no matter how mindless the resulting film.

Ishiro Honda, the genre's great auteur, had an altogether different background, and he brought to

kaiju eiga an intelligence and craftsmanship rarely matched in American sci-fi during this time. Honda was born in 1911, and joined PCL, Toho's predecessor, in 1933. There he began a lifelong friendship with Akira Kurosawa, and the two worked as assistant directors for several years, mostly for their mentor, a director of light comedies and war pictures named Kajiro Yamamoto. In 1938, Honda was drafted and

Mexican lobby card for "The Three Treasures" (1959), starring Toshiro Mifune

served in China; he spent several months as a prisoner-of-war, and when he was finally released, he passed through the rubble that was once Hiroshima. He didn't resume his vocation on a full-time basis until after the war. Back at Toho, he directed several documentaries, and served as an assistant director on Kurosawa's crime film *Stray Dog* (1949). Of Honda's work Kurosawa wrote, "Every day I told him what I wanted and he would go out into the ruins of post-war Tokyo to film it. There are few men as honest and reliable as Honda. He faithfully brought back exactly the footage I requested, so almost everything he shot was used in the final cut of the film. I'm often told that I captured the atmosphere of post-war Japan very well in *Stray Dog,* and, if so, I owe a great deal of that success to Honda."[4]

Honda's experience as a documentary filmmaker, to say nothing of his reliability, doubtlessly played a role when producer Tomoyuki Tanaka chose Honda as director and co-screenwriter for the very first Godzilla movie, the film that started it all, and called *Gojira* in Japan.[5] Honda had found great success the year before as the director of the very popular *Eagle of the Pacific* (1953), a Toshiro Mifune war film with extensive effects work by a man named Eiji Tsuburaya. Honda's compatibility with the perfectionistic, ingenious special effects director was also critical.

Gojira's huge international success proved both a blessing and a curse for the director. Despite the popularity of his non-genre films, Honda was soon typed as a *kaiju eiga* director, and though he was certainly one of Toho's biggest money earners during the 50s and 60s (the sum of his films quite probably outgrossing even Kurosawa's), the director's career seemed over by the early-70s. The Japanese film

Ishiro Honda, two months before his death in 1993

industry nearly collapsed, and Honda reluctantly moved into science fiction television, whose cramped screen shape and rigid story formulas ill-suited him.

However, he remained close friends with Kurosawa, who was facing severe personal and professional difficulties of his own. Then, according to Kimi Honda, a former script girl at Toho and Honda's widow, "One day Mr. Honda brought Mr. Kurosawa home with him after they had played golf. While the two were talking, Mr. Kurosawa suggested that they make a movie together. 'Why don't we make a film together just like the old times when we were very young assistant directors?' Mr. Kurosawa said."[6] And so, together these washed up, aging men, both in their seventies, made *Kagemusha* (1980) and *Ran* (1985), pictures that won accolades from all over the world and rejuvenated them.

Honda's collaboration with Kurosawa, which continued until Honda's death in 1993, was credited as "directorial adviser" or "associate director," but Honda's contribution was greater than is generally known, partly because Honda refused a larger billing, believing, according to Mrs. Honda, that there should be "one director for one film." At the same time, Honda's earlier work was finally beginning to be recognized in the West. During the production of *Kagemusha*, George Lucas and Francis Ford Coppola, producers of the American version, were surprised and delighted when they learned that the director of *Godzilla* was supervising *Kagemusha's* battle sequences.

4. Akira Kurosawa, *Something Like an Autobiography,* (New York: Random House, 1982) 174–76
5. The name merges "gorilla" and "kujira," meaning whale, and was the nickname of a burly Toho employee.
6. David Milner, "Ishiro Honda Interview," *Cult Movies* no. 9, pg. 50

And Martin Scorsese, who appeared in Akira Kurosawa's *Dreams* (1990), requested a meeting with the director when he learned of Honda's work in that film (he had essentially written and directed the autobiographical "The Tunnel" sequence, about a wandering soldier returning home; Kurosawa himself never went to war). During their meeting, Scorsese requested Honda's assistance in securing some of the *kaiju eiga* director's films for the Museum of Modern Art in New York.

Directors like Honda and Kurosawa grew out of the industry's remarkable assistant director program, which continues, though on a much smaller level, to this very day. In Hollywood, assistant directors rarely become full directors; they're trained to become unit production managers and producers, and the position itself is a respectable and challenging job all its own. In Japan though, ADs have always been considered directors-in-training. When you start out, you're little more than a grip, lugging equipment, running menial errands and other grunge work. As you move up the ladder, from 4th AD to 3rd AD and so on, assistant directors work more closely with their mentors, learning everything about filmmaking—writing scripts, cutting film, deciding which lenses to use, etc. After several years of this (sometimes even longer) assistant directors are finally promoted and, back in the "Golden Age," usually given a short feature (45–65 minutes) to cut their teeth. This system worked amazingly well—during the 1940s and 50s, literally dozens of superb filmmakers emerged from Japan.

Each studio also had some sort of "New Face Program" to recruit onscreen talent. These were essentially annual talent contests—anyone could enter—and the lucky winners were given studio

contracts. They were given acting, singing, and dancing lessons right on the lot, and gradually eased into their studio's pictures. At first their parts would be mere walk-ons, but slowly, if they had talent and/or proved popular, the size of their roles grew. Like the assistant director program, most of Japan's biggest stars started out this way.

Being big studio films, Japanese monster movies were, first and foremost, commercial pictures designed to make money for their studios. For years B-level movies were ignored by film theorists and historians. Recently the pendulum has swung 180-degrees; now even heretofore disreputable, "artless" films—the great Douglas Sirk melodramas, Sam Fuller's pulpy action films, Jesus Franco and Mario Bava horror movies—are enjoying major retrospectives at museums and repertory film theaters, and deservedly so. (As John *Pink Flamingos* Waters told an audience at a screening of his work at the pretigious L.A. County Museum of Art, "I feel so respectable I could shit.") But with their long-overdue appreciation has come a tendency to overanalyze and overpraise films as being more than they ever were.

Though much has been made of *Gojira's* integration

MIGHTY KING KONG! MIGHTY GODZILLA!

NOW AN ALL-MIGHTY ALL-NEW MOTION PICTURE BRINGS THEM TOGETHER FOR THE FIRST TIME IN THE COLOSSAL CLASH OF ALL TIME!

JOHN BECK presents

KING KONG vs. GODZILLA

IN COLOR

ALL NEW!

A Toho Company Ltd. Picture • A Universal Release

Universal Release

SEE!
King Kong Hurl an Entire Train to Destruction!
Godzilla's Radioactive Flame Burn Out Entire Cities!
King Kong Gouge Out A Mountainside!
Godzilla Snatch Jets From the Skies and Smash Them to Earth!
History's Most Gigantic Monsters In Combat Atop Mt. Fuji!

of Hiroshima- and Cold War-inspired nuclear fears, the actual filmmakers—Honda, Tanaka and others—saw the film's primary inspiration springing from the box office success of a modestly-budgeted American "indie," *The Beast from 20,000 Fathoms* (1953), itself inspired by the enormously successful reissue of *King Kong* the year

Before: Not the real Godzilla, but an incredible simulation—this paste-up uses the clay prototype of the Big G, and which doesn't appear in the actual film

before. The 20-year-old RKO film had outgrossed many first-run films, and had left an indelible effect on effects director Eiji Tsuburaya when *Kong* was first released in Japan. *The Beast from 20,000 Fathoms,* like *Kong,* revolved around a giant monster who ravages New York City. However, this monster, a "rhedosaurus," is

awakened by atomic testing and is radioactive, thus personifying the Cold War fear of nuclear terror. The film's unexpected success influenced not only Japanese filmmakers, but the sci-fi boom in America as well. More films featuring giant monsters unleashed via atomic testing were produced, including *Them!* (1954), *Tarantula* (1955), *The Deadly Mantis, Beginning of the End* (both 1957) and others.[7] In these later films, radiation was just a gimmick, present only because earlier, successful films had used the same idea, and screenwriters were reluctant to deviate from a proven formula. True, *Gojira* may have looked different, but "even after taking that into consideration," Honda argued, "the basic film is American."[8]

Tomoyuki Tanaka, who would later co-produce Kurosawa's *The Bad Sleep Well* (1960), *Yojimbo* (1961), *Sanjuro* (1962), *High and Low* (1963) and *Red Beard* (1965), as well as most of Toho's war movies and nearly all its *kaiju eiga,* had just seen his planned Japanese-Indonesian co-production, a project called *Eiko kage-ni* ("Behind the Glory"), shelved by the studio. With a cast and crew being readied with no movie to make, Tanaka quickly envisioned—on his flight back to Tokyo—a Japanese version of *Beast's* story, and even initially entitled the project *Dai kaiju no kaitei niman maru* ("Giant Monster from 20,000 Miles Beneath the Sea"), an obvious merging of both *20,000 Fathoms* and Disney's *20,000 Leagues Under the Sea.*[9]

And yet despite its uninspired inception, Honda and Tsuburaya were able to bring to the film both dream-like imagery and an uncanny realist look, partly culled

....

7. Warren, xii
8. Milner, 51
9. Ed Godizewski, "The Making of Godzilla," *The Japanese Fantasy Film Journal* no. 13: 17-18

from Honda's prior experience as a documentary filmmaker. "When I directed that film," Honda said, "in terms of society at that time, it was a surprising movie with all of its special effects. But, actually, when I returned from the war and passed through Hiroshima, there was a heavy atmosphere—a fear the earth was already coming to an end. That became the basis for the film." Through the character of Gojira, Honda sought to, in his words, "make radiation visual."

The horrors of radiation poisoning weighed heavily in the minds of the Japanese in 1954, not only in light of the international political situation, but also because of the "Fukuryu-maru ('Lucky Dragon') Incident" earlier that year. A fishing boat had accidentally strayed into a nuclear test site; its crew became seriously ill soon thereafter, one man died of radiation poisoning, and a nationwide recall of tuna was ordered.

In *Gojira,* several vessels encounter the monster (kept offscreen for the first half of the picture), and a group of stricken sailors reach an island community before succumbing to Gojira's radioactive residue. However, Honda and the screenwriters treated the nuclear references with kid gloves. "We skirted the issue, frankly speaking," Honda said, "because we felt that putting a real-life accident into a fictional story with a monster appearing in the midst of it wouldn't sit well in the world of a film entitled *Gojira.* That being the case, it was a matter of squeezing out the feeling I, as the director, was trying to cultivate, namely an intense fear that, having departed from the foundation of the atomic bomb and with scientific advances, having passed through various developments, has now become an environmental problem. Since those days I felt the atomic terror would hang around our necks for eternity."

In 1956, *Gojira* was released in the United States, retitled *Godzilla, King of the Monsters!* Toho licensed the film to a small corporation created by three large exhibitors. *Gojira* was extensively recut, and newly-shot footage featuring Raymond Burr was inserted, with the actor sometimes awkwardly, sometimes ingeniously

appearing to interact with footage shot nearly two years earlier. Some of the Japanese dialogue was dubbed into English; for other scenes Burr's character would ask his "translator" to explain dialog which, because of the extensive recutting, often matched the actual Japanese dialogue not at all.

After: Godzilla, in all his rubber-suited glory, makes a splashy exit from a devastated Tokyo, in the original "Godzilla" (1954)

Though a big budget, major studio film in Japan, the Americanized *Gojira* was released as an exploitation feature, the first such Japanese film to do so. The Japanese (coming attractions) trailer promoted the film as a prestigious production and highlighted its stars, Takashi Shimura (*Seven Samurai* having opened earlier that year), Akira Takarada, Akihiko Hirata, and

Raymond Burr, in the Americanized "Godzilla, King of the Monsters!" (1956)

Momoko Kochi. The mystery surrounding Godzilla and its human characters are emphasized, with the monster appearing in just a few fleeting shots.

Conversely, the American trailer is nothing but Godzilla, with its frenzied announcer promising "Dynamic Violence!" and "Savage Action!" Similarly, the paper advertisements for the two versions varied greatly. Though Godzilla's image dominates both campaigns, American movie posters make no mention

of the cast beyond Raymond Burr, nor the Japanese crew beyond Ishiro Honda (billed as "I. Honda" and as co-director with Terry Morse, who shot Burr's footage). Interestingly, the American version of *Gojira* was eventually released in Japan as well, as *Kaiju o Godzilla* ("Monster King Godzilla"), and Japanese posters for that version prominently feature Burr's image, something the *Godzilla, King of the Monsters!* one-sheet poster does not.[10]

Both versions of *Gojira* played all over the world, transcending language and cultural differences from Brazil to Poland. Of course a big part of the movie's appeal was its bevy of startling visuals by the undisputed king of Japanese special effects, Eiji Tsuburaya.

When he was a boy, young Eiji secretly used what we in America would call "bread money" to buy himself a toy film viewer. To hide the crime from his parents, he carefully studied its design, then destroyed it, and built a new one from scratch.

He became a cameraman near the end of Japan's silent era, but his technical wizardry steered him more and more toward special optical effects, especially those involving elaborate miniatures. In splashy war epics like *The War at Sea from Hawaii to Malaya* (1942), Tsuburaya produced visuals so convincingly real that the postwar Occupation Forces at first believed Tsuburaya's lilliputian planes and battleships were the real thing. Fearing reprisals, the makers of these propaganda movies destroyed the toy-like props while

---

10. And how did the monster's name become "Godzilla?" No one knows for sure, though back in the 1950s it was common to read the *katakana* character for "ji" as "dzi," while "ra" and "la" remain pretty interchangeable. Hence, Japanese audiences and Toho executives might just as easily pronounce the monster's name as "Go-dzi-la" as "Gojira."

Tsuburaya himself, having done perhaps too good of a job, was ostracized from the industry for several years.

But by 1953 he was back on course, again providing miniature planes and battleships because the real ones had all been destroyed—miniatures now *had* to be used. *Eagle of the Pacific* and *Farewell Rabaul* (1954), both directed by Honda, resuscitated the war movie genre. But it was the international success of *Gojira* that made Eiji Tsuburaya a star in his own right. At Toho he shot to a level of power and autonomy rivaled only by Kurosawa. In ads for his pictures his name was as prominent as the producer and director, and he was given a special title—*tokugi kantoku* ("Special Effects Director")—his name singled out among the opening titles and strategically placed just before the regular director credit. Toho and some of the directors who had to share billing with Tsuburaya disliked this formal acknowledgement of his stature, but the studio also correctly determined the name Eiji Tsuburaya would sell tickets. Over the next 15 years, Eiji Tsuburaya became as much a brand name in Japan as Walt Disney. Both men were born in 1901, pioneered their respective movie genres, produced ground-breaking, influential TV shows, were merchandising wizards, have amusement parks that bear their name—and both were irreplaceable.

Several months after the release of *King of the Monsters!*, and following a quickly-made, forgettable sequel, *Gigantis the Fire Monster* (aka *Godzilla Raids Again*, 1955), Toho produced its next major *kaiju eiga*, *Rodan* (1956), which again was patterned after American sci-fi, in this case Warner's *Them!* Both films featured giant insects lurking about underground passageways (giant ants in Los Angeles' storm drains in *Them!*, larvae-type insects terrorizing coal miners in

Rodan), monsters whose lair is discovered by a team of scientists searching from a helicopter (where, in both films, the skeletal remains of the monsters' victims are seen), etc.

Likewise, the American release of the film emphasized the more lurid aspects of the story, contrasting with the Japanese trailer which highlighted

its young stars ("Toho's Great Hopes for 1957!"), Kenji Sahara and Yumi Shirakawa, and the reputations of Messrs. Honda and Tsuburaya. Despite the box office success of *Godzilla, King of the Monsters!*, and the fact that *Rodan* was in color, the Westernized film was again distributed by a minor outfit, Distributors Corporation of America (DCA). And rather than integrate new footage of an American actor into the narrative, the producers of the American version cheaply hired a half-dozen

Starfish-like alien, actually man-size in "Warning from Space" (1956). Similar critters also turn up in the "Starman" movies and flail about like actors trapped in giant pillowcases

performers, some professional (such as the late voice artist Paul Frees), some amateur (a teenage George Takei, nearly ten years before "Star Trek") to cheaply dub the film into English. Some footage was cut, and stock footage of an A-Bomb blast was edited in.

In Japan, other studios began producing fantasy films as well, notably Daiei's *Warning from Space*

(1956), written by Hideo Oguni, who co-wrote *Seven Samurai,* and Shintoho's "Starman" movies (beginning in 1957), directed by Teruo Ishii. These pictures were beguilingly outlandish, featuring starfish-shaped aliens, outrageous stunt work, and wildly imaginative (if toy-like) special effects. American sci-fi films of the 1950s were almost always filmed in a flat, gray, even stodgy documentary-like style; by comparison, these Japanese films appeared to be the work of lunatics.

By 1957, Honda and Tsuburaya were also beginning to move away from the influence of American sci-fi movies. *The Mysterians* (1957) and its tale of alien invasion, borrows certain elements from *Forbidden Planet* and *War of the Worlds,* but Honda's use of color and scope, and especially its pounding score by Akira Ifukube and Tsuburaya's miniatures

predicted the move away from American sci-fi cinema, a move that would fully blossom with *Battle in Outer Space* (1959). Unlike American directors, Honda and nearly all Japanese filmmakers embraced the wide screen revolution of the 1950s. For Honda, the CinemaScope format (which the studio dubbed "Toho Scope") offered a wide canvas on which to explore character staging, the use of color and props as structuring metaphors, and other elements directors of American sci-fi had little time or talent for.

With *The Mysterians, Battle in Outer Space* and especially *Gorath* (1962), Honda explored the theme of international conflict and cooperation through science for the common good. "The interest I have embraced in directing, and the angle in which I perceive those films, has never changed. It comes through my own interests in science, and also a deeper regret that the nations of the world cannot trust one another, even when they take each other's hand. That's why even in my films after *Gojira,* I've made it an established practice to have the scientists of the world get together for the sake of cooperation."[11]

In many ways Honda's career echo that of producer George Pal, who made *War of the Worlds, Conquest of Space* (1955), and *The Time Machine* (1960). Like Pal, Honda was perhaps naïve about such matters and possibly too nice and too accommodating to make his films more personal, less compromised than they are. (Kurosawa, by contrast, was a notorious autocrat.) Still, Honda was certainly no less than a superb craftsman, and his work often rose well above that.

At the same time, Tsuburaya's effects became more and more dreamlike. In *Battle in Outer Space,* alien

---

11. Milner, 51

invaders unleash a flying saucer capable of sucking up Tokyo like a giant vacuum cleaner. The visuals of this sequence—the flying, intricate miniatures combined with Ifukube's great score, and Tsuburaya's Eisensteinian editing are quite unlike anything produced in America.

Interestingly, contemporary reviewers, even those who disliked Japanese science fiction—and many critics openly dislike science fiction films in general—usually lauded the special effects work. For example, *Variety* liked *Godzilla, King of the Monsters!'s* "excellently-lensed" special effects, and later said of *The Three Treasures*, "Western audiences will have to admire the artistry and painstaking photographic mastery of the craftsmen who designed and manufactured this film ... these Japanese artisans have set a new standard for themselves ... Kazuo Yamada's lenswork is agile and alert, but it is Eiji Tsuburaya's special effects that steal the picture." Similarly, *The New York Times'* Howard Thompson admired—albeit condescendingly—the American version of *Battle in Outer Space*, especially "the fetching assortment of obvious but effective miniature settings and backgrounds. Some of the artwork is downright nifty ... the Japanese have opened a most amusing a beguiling bag of tricks."

Indeed, Tsuburaya's perfectionism and power at Toho was such that his effects department was, until *2001* at least, state-of-the-art. Toho was, for several years, the only studio in the world besides Disney to own an Oxberry 1200 optical printer. And when American war movies like *Midway* (1976) needed footage of Zero fighters and Japanese battleships, their producers often turned, always without credit, to footage of Tsuburaya's miniatures from Toho's war movies, some dating back to the early-1960s. The year

Toho made the effects-filled *Frankenstein Conquers the World* and *Monster Zero* (both 1965), both of which feature elaborate, intricate miniatures and often startling matte work, the Visual Effects Oscar went to *Thunderball*, a James Bond film costing more than the two Japanese films combined. And yet *Thunderball's* optical effects and miniatures are clearly no better

than—and often inferior to—Tsuburaya's work.

While Tokyo residents saw their sci-fi epics in big, lush theaters owned by the major studios, Americans were being exposed to Japanese monster movies at the drive-in, decaying movie palaces downtown and similar venues, and their appearance in the United States was due, in part, to the decline of the Hollywood's own studio system. Spurred by the rise of television, anti-trust laws, the Baby Boom and new-found leisure activities, weekly movie theater attendance had plummeted from 90 million in 1946 to half that by the early-50s. Accordingly, mainstream Hollywood became very conservative: the studios made fewer pictures, and these were almost always adapted from already proven

Mothra before ...

material such as a hit play or novel (*The Seven-Year Itch, The Robe*, etc.)—even popular television dramas like *Marty* and sitcoms like "Our Miss Brooks" were turned into films. The studios contracted their facilities to independent production companies whose films they often co-financed and distributed, and they hedged their bets by teaming new stars with old ones, resulting

in some rather awkward casting.[12] To distance themselves from television, more and more pictures were made in color and released in wide screen formats like CinemaScope and Vista Vision, sometimes with the "added wonder" of stereophonic sound. They became bigger—how could television compete with star-studded epics like *Around the World in 80 Days* (1956), *The Ten Commandments* (1956), and *Spartacus* (1960)? They moved out of their backlots and shot portions of their films overseas in such exotic locales as Rome, Hong Kong, Paris, and Tokyo.

Conversely, films from abroad began turning up here as well. American men and women who hadn't traveled 50 miles from home were suddenly whisked off to Europe and the Pacific Theater during World War II, returning with a new-found fascination for these far-off countries and their exotic cultures. This gave rise to an interest in foreign films, including landmark Japanese films like *Rashomon, Ugetsu, Seven Samurai, Samurai* (aka *Musashi Miyamoto,* 1954), and *Street of Shame* (1956). The average theater owner, however, wasn't interested in booking *The Bicycle Thief* or *Rashomon*—he wanted something, anything playable, and Hollywood's output had been reduced to a mere trickle. Soon enough upstarts like American International Pictures (AIP), Distributors Corporation of America (DCA), Astor, and Allied Artists carved a profitable niche making or distributing cheap pictures with lurid and highly misleading ad campaigns (often created before the films were even made).

12. Audrey Hepburn, for instance, was almost always cast opposite men decades older than her—Fred Astaire, Gary Cooper, Cary Grant, while Clark Gable appeared opposite Grace Kelly, Doris Day, Ava Gardner and Marilyn Monroe—women decades younger.

Their biggest clients were the drive-in circuit and decaying downtown movie palaces, places where Japanese monster movies seemed especially appropriate. Though the stories were outrageous and the voices never quite matched the lip movements, audiences didn't care. The films were bright and colorful and filled with city-smashing monsters attacking Tokyo and other elaborate special effects. In short, these pictures were fun, and by the early-1960s the Japanese fantasy film had evolved into a genre all its own.

Honda's *Mothra* (1961), about a giant, unstoppable moth, had many of the trappings of American "giant insect" movies of the 50s, but was overtly and singularly "Japanese" in its fantasy elements, such as the monster's Polynesian-esque priestesses—two 12-inch women who speak in unison. *Mothra's* screenplay also marked a trend in these films to include bits of satire (a shameless "Rolisican" [read: American] entrepreneur kidnaps the priestesses for his Andrew Lloyd Webber-like stage show). Despite these surprising elements, the film was seen as just another big bug movie in the United States, and Columbia, the film's U.S. distributor, advertised "a fearsome monster [that] ravages [the] world for tiny beauties!"

Certainly the concept of a colorful, impossibly large moth whose flapping wings create hurricane-size wind storms capable of knocking down buildings and sending automobiles flying into the air is vivid and imaginative but, perhaps, a bit bizarre for American audiences. This move away from the semi-documentary, flat-lit style of American sci-fi films and toward attractive and/or grotesque, dream-like images continued with Honda's *Matango* (1963), an exquisite horror film about a corrupt group of urbanites shipwrecked on a foggy, rainy island. Like William

Golding's *Lord of the Flies,* the social order breaks down, and the castaways become animal-like savages. In Honda's film, they also succumb to the surprisingly sexual allure of the exotic mushrooms found on the island, symbolic of the social decay of the story's characters, who turn into moldy monstrosities which dissolve into the fauna.[13] The U.S. version, like so many

... and after a determined metamorphosis in Toho's wondrous "Mothra" (1961)

13. The makeup design was condemned by a Hiroshima/Nagasaki survivors organization, which has, to date, successfully prevented the film from being released on laserdisc in Japan. Toho's *Prophecies of Nostradamus* (1974) had similar problems, but the group has apparently never complained about *The Mysterians* (1957) or the first *Godzilla.*

Japanese genre films, was given a wildly inappropriate title, *Attack of the Mushroom People,* and released directly to television, where it remains a cult film.

Honda did find humor in *King Kong vs. Godzilla* (1962) and *Godzilla vs. the Thing* (1964), in which corrupt businessmen and politicians try to "cash in" on the monsters' appearance. For *Dagora, the Space Monster* (1964), Honda spoofed the then-popular gangster genre. In the film, a hapless band of jewel thieves is continually thwarted by a jewel-absorbing space monster. The humor in these films, unfortunately, was equally thwarted by their American distributors, who apparently didn't get the joke. Incredibly, the American version of *Dagora* takes the gangsters and their actions seriously, while *King Kong vs. Godzilla,* clearly a light-hearted monster movie in Japan, was heavily recut, with utterly inane footage of English-speaking actors inserted, and much footage of actor Ichiro Arishima (a fixture in Toho's comedies) deleted, leaving his scenes jarringly incongruous with the rest of the film. Most of Akira Ifukube's evocative score was replaced with stock themes from *Creature from the Black Lagoon,* giving the American version a B-movie feel that sharply contradicted the production values of the Japanese version.

The huge success of *King Kong vs. Godzilla,* and the relative failure of far more ambitious (and better) films

Shochiku's "The X from Outer Space" (1967)

like *Gorath* (1962) signaled both the beginning of an actual "Godzilla" film series, and the end of the genre's period of tremendous creative growth. Also during this 62–68 period, Honda and Tsuburaya's handling of the monsters, though varied from film-to-film, moved toward anthropomorphization. The monsters became, over time, rather cute and (intentionally) amusing. Godzilla, for example, does a victory jig in *Monster Zero* (1965) and "argues" with Rodan and Mothra in *Ghidrah—The Three-Headed Monster* (1964). In *Ghidrah,* Godzilla and Rodan even do double-takes worthy of Laurel and Hardy. While some fans of the earlier pictures were horrified by these shenanigans, it was also inevitable. The 60s films gave the series a new direction with avenues never explored in American giant monster pictures.

Toho also had to compete with other studios which, by 1965, realized their was money to be made (and, more importantly, money to be made abroad) in the giant monster trade. Every major studio made at least one: Toei made the delightful *The Magic Serpent* (1966), Shochiku produced the peculiar *The X from Outer Space* (1967), and Nikkatsu filmed the derivative *Monster from a Prehistoric Planet* (1967)—even nearby Korea got into the act, with *Monster Wangmagwi* and *Yongary, Monster from the Deep* (both 1967). But by far Toho's biggest threat came from Daiei, which created its own *kaiju eiga* series starring a flying, fire-breathing turtle named Gamera. Filmed in black and white, *Gammera* [sic] the *Invincible* (1965) was a competent if uninspired rehash of the first Godzilla picture. It differed, though, in that it featured a little boy as a major character. To this point, children in Godzilla movies were never central characters, and rarely turned up at all. And while Gamera gleefully roasted *adults* he had a strong affection for little kids, and little kids ate it up. The later Gamera films, while never quite up to the level of Toho's monster movies, knew what kids were about, how their minds worked, and what they wanted to see; these films had a child-like logic about them, and only make sense when viewed from that standpoint. Toho responded, belatedly, by producing Godzilla films where children had central roles. First among these was *Godzilla's Revenge* (1969) which, like Daiei's Gamera films, saved money by recycling a goodly amount of stock footage from previous entries. By the early-1970s, the Godzilla series was also geared almost exclusively for kids.

As the 60s wore on, production costs began to rise at an alarming rate while theater attendance in Japan was in sharp decline (due primarily to the growing popularity of commercial television). Toho began co-producing its *kaiju eiga* in association with American companies, but, as with Toho's product of the 1950s, the major Hollywood distributors were reluctant to participate. Instead, minor outfits like United Productions of America (UPA), Rankin-Bass, and Allied Artists co-financed Toho's more ambitious product of the 1965–69 period, and provided American "stars" like Nick Adams and Richard Jaeckel to boost stateside marquee values.

By the late-60s though, even the drive-ins were on the skids, and drive-in owners, who had built their outdoor theaters in the far-off sticks in the late-40s and early-50s, found themselves in a burgeoning, bustling suburbia 20 years later, and happily sold their now valuable property at a healthy profit.

And so big, Japanese-made monsters moved into small, Japanese-made television sets. They made regular appearances on "The 4 o'clock Movie" and

Discover the incredible space-age world of tomorrow... 15 miles straight down at **LATITUDE ZERO** beneath the sea!

Discover!
The life perpetuation machine.
The underwater metropolis.
The battle of the flying subs.
The lazer beam hand gloves.
The attack of the giant mutants.
And transplanting a live woman's brain into the body of a beast.

National General Pictures Presents LATITUDE ZERO Starring Joseph Cotten · Cesar Romero
Co-starring Richard Jaeckel · Patricia Medina and Introducing Linda Haynes as Dr. Anne Barton Story and Screenplay by Ted Sherdeman Based on his stories of "LATITUDE ZERO" · Produced by Toho Company, Limited · Directed by Ishiro Honda · Color [G]

Ad art for "Latitude Zero" (1967), a Japanese-American coproduction

"The Late, Late Show." Kids (and some adults) embraced these pictures, and pioneer *kaiju*-scholars like Greg Shoemaker and Ed Godziszewski wrote about them with great affection in the informative and fun fanzines *The Japanese Fantasy Film Journal* and *Japanese Giants,* respectively.

But then the bottom fell out. Effects master Eiji Tsuburaya died in 1970 and his demise coincided with the death of Japan's "Golden Age" of cinema. Daiei went bankrupt (thus shelving *Gamera vs. the Giant Monster Garashapu*) while Nikkatsu switched to "Roman porno" (i.e., soft-core porno) movies. Most of Toho's contract talent were let go and budgets were sharply reduced. Ishiro Honda moved into TV and Haruo Nakajima, who had played Godzilla since 1954, turned in his rubber suit.

New Godzilla pictures were made, but the 70s films proved cheap, uninspired, and juvenile. And if the Godzilla movies were poor, the non-Toho monster movies were even worse: Tsuburaya Productions' *Space Warriors 2000* (1974) and Toei's *The "Legend of the Dinosaurs"* [sic] (1977) were so atrocious as to be virtually unwatchable. What's more, these new films had to compete with bigger and better entries from the 1960s being reissued as part of Toho's "Champion Matsuri" packages; for a few hundred yen, kids could see a(n edited) Godzilla film, an Ultraman short and a couple of cartoons all in one fun-filled afternoon.

With two or more *kaiju eiga* being reissued annually, as well as one new Godzilla film every spring—and the endless giant monster TV shows flooding the airwaves—the market became over-saturated, and by the time Ishiro Honda and composer Akira Ifukube were brought back for the 15th Godzilla film, *Terror of Mechagodzilla* (1975), the growing number of imported American films and the rise of Anime seemed to defeat Godzilla more thoroughly than any *kaiju* could.

However, the series was revived—after a nine-year absence—with *Godzilla 1985* (simply *Gojira* in Japan, and released there in 1984).[14] Made by new generation of writers and directors, many of whom were children when the first Godzilla films were produced, these new films breathed life into the genre—at first. There's a communal sense of wonder in *Godzilla vs. Mothra* (1992), while *Godzilla vs. King Ghidorah* (1991) proved a surprisingly introspective look at modern Japan. But these films also borrowed heavily from American movies (*Godzilla vs. Mothra* featured an Indiana Jones-type opening while *Ghidorah* lifts elements from the *Terminator* films), and by the mid-1990s the series began imitating itself, with each film looking more and more like the last one. Special Effects Director Koichi Kawakita, who so impressed audiences with his innovative visual scheme for *Godzilla vs. Biollante* (1989), appeared to lose interest in the series, and his new designs became progressively wrong-headed; his recent work has been dispirited, dull, pastisched, and uninvolving. A flurry of non-Godzilla fantasy films appeared at this time, including *Gunhed* (1989), *Ultra Q—The Movie* (1990), *Zipang* (1990), *Zeram* (1991; a sequel followed), and *Yamato Takeru* (1993). Though some of these were likewise influenced by Hollywood films (and, in some cases, *Hong Kong* pictures), and some (like *Zipang* and *Yamato Takeru*) were generally ponderous, there are also interesting films—or bits of film—emerging from this new generation.

As I write this, principal photography has been completed on the first all-*American* Godzilla movie.

---

14. *Godzilla vs. Biollante* (1989), *Godzilla vs. King Ghidorah* (1991), *Godzilla vs. Mothra* (1992), *Godzilla vs. Mechagodzilla* (1993), *Godzilla vs. Space Godzilla* (1994), and *Godzilla vs. Destroyer* (1995) all followed. Only the first film has been released so far in the United States, and many Americans aren't even aware these films exist.

Produced and directed by Dean Devlin and Roland Emmerich *(Stargate, Independence Day)* and starring the almost always good Matthew Broderick, *Godzilla* will doubtlessly be an epic, visually awesome monster-on-the-loose movie with state-of-the-art special effects. But in their concerted effort to eradicate the campy image most Americans have of the big monster, can they also avoid also wiping out the very essence of what made Godzilla so popular in the first place? Their Godzilla, according to published reports, bears little resemblance to the Godzilla known all over the world. Their Godzilla, now essentially an overgrown iguana, runs away on all fours when attacked by the military, lays eggs, and doesn't even breath radioactive fire. Dean Devlin boasts, "We wanted ... to reinvent [the character], so when you think of Godzilla, this is the Godzilla you'll think of for the next generation."[15] But what will make this *Godzilla* distinguishable from a big scale remake of *Gorgo* (1961), *Reptilicus* (1962) or, for that matter, a 1998 redo of *The Beast from 20,000 Fathoms?* If it has nothing in common with the original Godzilla, why call it "Godzilla" at all, except to crassly cash in on a presold name?

Meanwhile, the appeal of Japanese movies in general seems to be growing: witness the popularity of Masayuki Suo's charming romantic comedy *Shall We Dance?,* released to rave reviews and enthusiastic audiences in the fall of 1997. The year also saw two Japanese films win two of the most prestigious of international film awards: Shohei Imamura, the veteran filmmaker who made *The Insect Woman* (1963), *Vengeance Is Mine* (1979), and *The Ballad of Narayama* (1982), won the Palm d'Or at the Cannes Film Festival for his film *Unagi* ("Eel"), while cult filmmaker "Beat" Takeshi Kitano nabbed the Grand

Prize at the Venice Film Festival for *Hanabi* ("Fireworks"). Hayao Miyazaki, the animator behind the delightful *My Neighbor Totoro,* recently signed with Disney, while another animated feature, *Princess Mononoke,* became Japan's highest-grossing film ever, spurring a major U.S. distribution deal.

Back in Japan, monster movie makers young and old quietly crank out new films. Director Shusuke Kaneko and 30-something Special Effects whiz Shinji Higuchi together made two new Gamera films in 1995 and '96. These films capture the flavor of the great *kaiju eiga* of the past while deftly addressing contemporary issues, something sorely lacking in Toho's recent Godzilla series. They're also surprisingly well-produced, even when compared to Hollywood films costing 20 times more. Made for about $3 million apiece, the Kaneko/Higuchi Gamera epics look like $50 million movies.

The Renaissance of Japanese monster movies in the 1980s and early-90s coincided with the massive success of the Japanese economy, and special effects artists were faced with a problem—new skyscrapers had dwarfed the giant monsters. Their solution was simple: make the monsters taller. And so it can be said both literally and figuratively—Japanese monsters are bigger than ever.

---

15. Excerpted from an interview posted on the Sony Pictures web site.

Witnesses

WITH THE EXCEPTION OF ISHIRO HONDA, WHO WAS INTERVIEWED BY JAMES BAILEY FOR THE *TOKYO JOURNAL,* AND A FEW OTHERS, THE FOLLOWING MEN AND WOMEN WERE INTERVIEWED ESPECIALLY FOR THIS BOOK. WHAT FOLLOWS ARE THEIR IMPRESSIONS, MORE OR LESS IN CHRONOLOGICAL ORDER, OF WORKING IN THE SCI-FI/FANTASY REALM, AND IN THE JAPANESE FILM INDUSTRY IN GENERAL.

Chiba, Shinichi "Sonny" (b. 1939)
Action star best known for his violent "Streetfighter" films, Chiba began his career as the young hero in *Invasion of the Neptune Men* (1961), *The Golden Bat* and *Terror Beneath the Sea* (both 1966). And he occasionally returns to the genre: Chiba is featured in Kinji Fukasaku's disparate *Message from Space* (1978) and *Virus* (1980).

Dunham, Robert (b. 1931)
Born in Portland, Maine, Dunham struck out as a Hollywood actor but found fame, of sorts, by moving to Japan and appearing in scores of Japanese films and TV shows. He played everything from extra and bit roles to major supporting parts in a wide range of pictures. When a Japanese film or TV show needed a Western actor (for an airport scene, a big meeting at the U.N.—you name it), they called aspiring actors like Dunham. In most cases, good acting wasn't required; as long as they spoke their lines in English, who'd notice the bad acting anymore than someone speaking Japanese in a Hollywood movie? Dunham was decent in Ralph Meeker-types roles (he'd have made a good Mike Hammer), and he spoke excellent Japanese,

which gave him an edge over many of his peers. Indeed, one of his very best roles came in the sci-fi satire *Dagora, The Space Monster* (1964), in which the actor (billed as "Dan Yuma" in the Japanese version) nearly steals the film as a "diamond G-Man" more Japanese than the Japanese! Dunham also appears in *Mothra* (1961), fought *The Green Slime* (1968), and donned a toga as the leader of the Seatopians in *Godzilla vs. Megalon* (1973). In the mid-1960s, he even wrote, directed and starred in *The Time Traveller,* an excruciating but amiable *Outer Limits*-esque featurette he filmed in Japan.

Fujiki, Yu (b. 1931)
The egg-loving reporter in *Godzilla vs. the Thing* (1964), Fujiki is one of Toho's best-loved comic actors. He did a series of films with Tadao Takashima, his co-star in *King Kong vs. Godzilla* (1962) and *Atragon* (1963), and later appeared memorably in numerous Crazy Cats comedies. Also an accomplished actor of dramas, Fujiki appeared in Ozu's *Early Autumn* (1961), and several films by both Akira Kurosawa and Mikio Naruse. His other credits include *Samurai II: Duel at Ichijoji Temple* (1955), *The Lower Depths* (1957), *When a Woman Ascends the Stairs* (1960), and *Las Vegas Free-for-All* (1967).

Fukasaku, Kinji (b. 1930)
Closely allied with Toei Studios, Fukasaku could always be counted on to deliver fast-paced and intelligently-directed action films.

He's worked in just about every genre, including science fiction and fantasy; his wildly diverse fantasy credits include the campy, John Waters-esque *Black Lizard* (1968), the lively, absurdly tacky *Message from Space* (1978), and the thoughtful, relevant *Virus* (1980). However, the director is best known in Japan for his violent, nihilistic but ground-breaking *Battles without Honor and Humanity* (aka *The Yakuza Papers,* 1973) and several of its sequels. He replaced (with Toshio Masuda) Akira Kurosawa as director of the Japanese half of *Tora! Tora! Tora!* (1970), and is probably best remembered in the U.S. for his goofy outer space adventure *The Green Slime* (1968). Fukasaku presently heads the Japanese equivalent of the Directors Guild.

Fukuda, Jun (b. 1923)
Something of a second-string director at Toho, Fukuda specialized in B-level thrillers like *Witness Killed* (1962) and *The Weed of Crime* (1964), but he also made several popular "Young Guy" movies with Yuzo Kayama and, occasionally, sci-fi features as well. Fukuda helmed two of Toho's best (and most underrated) Godzilla movies—*Godzilla versus the Sea Monster* (1966), *Son of Godzilla* (1967)—and, in the 1970's, three pretty bad ones: *Godzilla on Monster Island* (1972), *Godzilla vs. Megalon* (1973), and *Godzilla vs. the Cosmic Monster* (1974). He also directed the lukewarm *The Secret of the Telegian* (1960), the rollicking Bond spoof *100 Shot 100 Killed* (1965), the obscure comedy *Great*

Space Adventure (1969), *ESPY* (1974), and the abominable *The War in Space* (1977). When the author requested an interview, Fukuda wrote back, "I think my films are terrible, but since you wrote such a nice letter I guess I should meet with you." A lifelong chain-smoker with a face like fine-tooled leather, Fukuda is a sophisticated, intelligent man who dismisses almost everything he's made. Much of the interview consisted of the author arguing that some of the director's movies really *are* good, something Fukuda seemed to enjoy immensely.

Funakoshi, Eiji (b. 1923)
Longtime star at Daiei studios, Funakoshi was a handsome leading man in the 1950s who then moved into character parts in the 60s and 70s. He has worked in virtually every genre: modern-day comedies, period love stories, sexually explicit and graphic horror films, and kiddie sci-fi monster epics, including two Gamera pictures, *Gammera the Invincible* (1965) and *Attack of the Monsters* (aka *Gamera vs. Guiron,* 1969), playing the main scientist in both films. He is best known in the West for his long association with directors Kon Ichikawa and Yasuzo Masumura. For Ichikawa, Funakoshi played the lead in one of Japan's best postwar films, *Fires on the Plain* (1959). For Masumura, the actor starred in *Passion* (1964) and *The Blind Beast* (1969).

Hama, Mie (b. 1943)
Best known in the West as "Kissy Suzuki" in the 007 feature *You Only Live Twice* (1967), this former Bond Girl was a big star at Toho Studios, and a fixture in Hitoshi Ueki comedies like *The Age of Irresponsibility* (1962) and *Las Vegas Free-for-All* (1967). She appeared in a handful of fantasy features, notably *King Kong vs. Godzilla* (in the Fay Wray role, 1962), *The Lost World of Sinbad* (1963), *King Kong Escapes* (1967), and the Crazy Cats comedy *Monsieur Zivaco* (1968). Hama also starred opposite Akira Takarada in the Bond-like *100 Shot, 100 Killed* (1965), and Tatsuya Mihashi in *International Secret Police: Key of Keys* (1965), the picture that became Woody Allen's *What's Up, Tiger Lily?* (1966), and the arty *The Night of the Seagull* (1968). In her fifties Hama is still an incredible sexy woman, but rarely appears in films, her last role to date being 1989's *Kitchen.* Just the opposite of the ditzy characters she specialized playing, Hama is in fact an intelligent, well-spoken woman, who now spends most of her time as an environmental and political activist.

Honda, Ishiro (1911-1993)
The Orson Welles of Japanese monster movies, Honda brought solid craftsmanship and intelligent direction to the sci-fi genre, beginning with the landmark *Godzilla, King of the Monsters!* (1954). His sci-fi credits include: *Half Human* (1955), *Rodan* (1956), *The Mysterians* (1957), *The H-Man, Varan the Unbelievable* (both 1958), *Battle in Outer Space* (1959), *The Human Vapor* (1960), *Mothra* (1961), *Gorath, King Kong vs. Godzilla* (both 1962), *Attack of the Mushroom People, Atragon* (both 1963), *Godzilla vs. the Thing, Dagora the Space Monster, Ghidrah—The Three-Headed Monster* (all 1964), *Frankenstein Conquers the World, Monster Zero* (both 1965), *War of the Gargantuas* (1966), *King Kong Escapes* (1967), *Destroy All Monsters* (1968), *Latitude Zero, Godzilla's Revenge* (both 1969), *Yog—Monster from Space* (1970), and *Terror of Mechagodzilla* (1975). Honda is the human star of this book. **Kimi Honda** (b. 1923?), a former script girl at Toho Studios, is Honda's widow, and was interviewed approximately three years after the director's death.

Horton, Robert (b. 1924)
American television star who came to Japan to battle *The Green Slime* (1968). He is best remembered as Flint McCullough on TV's "Wagon Train."

Hoshi, Yuriko (b. 1943)
Wholesome star of Toho romances, especially as Yuzo Kayama's girlfriend in Toho's long-running "Young Guy" film series. Hoshi starred opposite Akira Takarada in *The Last War* (1961) and *Godzilla vs. the Thing* (1964), then opposite Yosuke Natsuki that same year in *Ghidrah—The Three-Headed Monster.* Her film credits also include the fantasy comedy *It's Crazy! I Can't Explain it Way Out There* (1966), and several Hiroshi Inagaki films,

beginning with *Daredevil in the Castle* (1961), and including *Chushingura* (1962) and *Kojiro* (1967). She now works primarily on the stage and in television.

Ifukube, Akira (b. 1914)
He created Godzilla's roar and remains the premiere composer of Japanese fantasy film music. His credits include *Rodan* (1956), *The Mysterians* (1957), *Varan the Unbelievable* (1958), *Battle in Outer Space* (1959), *Atragon* (1963), *The Little Prince and the Eight-Headed Dragon* (animated, also 1963), *Frankenstein Conquers the World* (1965), *War of the Gargantuas* (1966), the entire "Majin" trilogy, *King Kong Escapes* (1967), *Latitude Zero* (1969), *Yog—Monster from Space* (1970), and 12 "count 'em" Godzilla movies: *Godzilla/Godzilla, King of the Monsters!* (1954), *King Kong vs. Godzilla* (1962), *Godzilla vs. the Thing* and *Ghidrah—The Three-Headed Monster* (both 1964), *Monster Zero* (1965), *Destroy All Monsters* (1968), *Godzilla On Monster Island* (stock themes only, 1972), *Terror of Mechagodzilla* (1975), *Godzilla vs. King Ghidrah* (1991), *Godzilla vs. Mothra* (1992), *Godzilla vs. Mechagodzilla* (1993), and *Godzilla vs. Destroyer* (1995). Ifukube's themes were also used in several Godzilla sequels. His 150 other film scores (!) include such classics as *The Saga of Anatahan* (1953), *The Burmese Harp* (1956), Toei's entire *Musashi Miyamoto* series, numerous "Zatoichi" films, *Buddha* (1961), *Birth of the Japanese Islands* (1965), and *Sandakan 8*

(1974). In his eighties Ifukube has reconciled his relationship with the King of the Monsters, and in recent years has entertained visitors from all over the world in his large (by Tokyo standards), Russian-influenced home, where he graciously answers questions from Debussy to Dagora.

Ishii, Teruo (b. 1924)
Director best known in Japan for his tough action films starring the Nipponese Clint Eastwood, Ken Takakura, and for his macabre "Women's Prison" films. Here in the U.S., however, the director is infamous for helming four "Starman" movies: *Atomic Rulers, Invaders from Space* (both 1957), *Attack from Space* (1958), and *Evil Brain from Outer Space* (1959). Ishii's other credits include *Nude Actress Murder—Five Criminals* (1957), *Story of Showa Chivalry* (1963), *Abarashi Prison* (1965), *The Joys of Torture* (1968), *Horror of a Malformed Man* (1969), *Story of a Wild Older Sister—Widespread Lynch Law* (1973), *The Executioner* (1974), and *Field of Villains* (1995). Great titles, huh?

Kochi, Momoko (b. 1932)
The heroine caught between male leads Akira Takarada and Akihiko Hirata in the original *Godzilla* (1954), Kochi abandoned films for the stage in the late-1950s, but not before appearing in two other *kaiju eiga*, the mutilated-in-the-U.S. *Half Human: The Story of the Abominable Snowman* (1955), and *The Mysterians* (as Hirata's fiance, 1957). She

reprised her most famous role, Emiko Yamane, in *Godzilla vs. Destroyer* (1995), some 41 years (!) later. Today Kochi is still very active, mostly in television.

Kotani, Tsugunobu "Tom" (b. 1935)
Longtime assistant director on Toho's "Young Guy" film series whose English, shaky though it may have been, won him the support of producers Arthur Rankin and Jules Bass. Rankin/Bass, who needed help on their ill-fated musical about Kubla-Khan, *Marco* (1973), which Kotani co-directed. Then, in 1977, Kotani helmed his *kaiju eiga* masterpiece, *The Last Dinosaur*. The Rankin/Bass-Kotani team made two more fantasy features, *The Bermuda Depths* (1978) and *The Ivory Ape* (1980), both disappointments, but *The Last Dinosaur* remains a peculiarly likable work.

Kubo, Akira (b. 1936)
One of the genre's most recognizable players. He was the reporter looking for a story in *Son of Godzilla* (1967), the astronaut battling evil Kilaaks in *Destroy All Monsters* (1968), the nerdy inventor in *Monster Zero* (1965), and the sole survivor of *The Attack of the Mushroom People* (1963). Kubo was a child actor in industrial films before starring in an adaptation of Mishima's *The Sound of the Waves* (1954). He became an important star in youth-oriented films in the Yujiro Ishihara mode and in war movies. Kubo played the Malcolm role in Kurosawa's take on *Macbeth,*

Throne of Blood (1957), as well as one of the naïve *samurai* in *Sanjuro* (1962). He played the brash young space cadet in *Gorath* that same year, and also stars as the photographer in *Yog—Monster from Space* (1970). Kubo returned to the genre after many years as a ship's captain in the prologue to *Gamera— The Guardian of the Universe* (1995).

Kurosawa, Akira (b. 1910)
One of the greatest filmmakers ever, Kurosawa joined PCL, the predecessor of Toho Studios, as an assistant director in 1936, and soon began life-long friendships with ADs Ishiro Honda and Senkichi Taniguchi; all three often worked for director Kajiro Yamamoto. Honda and Taniguchi were called to service during WWII, but Kurosawa stayed behind and made his directorial debut with *Sanshiro Sugata* (1943). He has directed 30 features, of which a half-dozen or so are undisputed masterpieces of world cinema, and another dozen are merely superb. His best films include *Drunken Angel* (1948), *Stray Dog* (1949), *Rashomon* (1950), *Ikiru* (1952), *Seven Samurai* (1954), *The Lower Depths* and *Throne of Blood* (both 1957), *The Hidden Fortress* (1958), *The Bad Sleep Well* (1960), *Yojimbo* (1961), *Sanjuro* (1962), *Red Beard* (1965), *Dodes'ka-den* (1970), *Dersu Uzala* (1975), *Ran* (1985), *Rhapsody in August* (1991), and *Madadayo* (1993).

Matsubayashi, Shue (b. 1920)
Educated to be a monk, Matsubayashi instead became a film director, though his religious teachings have clearly effected his humanist work. His sole sci-fi effort was the end of the world saga *The Last War* (1961), yet Matsubayashi frequently collaborated with that film's effects director, Eiji Tsuburaya, on a series of navy spectacles. Indeed, these films — *Submarine E-57 Never Surrenders!* (1959), *I Bombed Pearl Harbor* (1960), *Attack Squadron!* (aka *Kamikaze,* 1963), *Imperial Navy* (1981)— frequently outclassed even the Godzilla series in terms of production values and special effects, and their prosperous collaborations were rivaled only by the Honda-Tsuburaya team. The director himself is a veteran of the Imperial Navy, as evidenced by his white beard, which admirals during the war were prone to wear. (Matsubayashi himself wasn't an admiral, but grew it determined to shave it off only when Japan won the war. Japan lost, and the beard stayed.) Besides his war movies, Matsubayashi is best known in Japan as the primary director of Toho's lucrative *Shacho* ("Company President") film series; he directed 22 of the 42 features made between 1956 and 1971.

Matsumura, Tatsuo (b. 1914)
Actor who, after a long career in the theater, made his screen debut in 1959, when he was already 45 years old. He worked mainly at Toho in the early days, specializing playing college professors and mid-level management types in musicals like *Young Generation* (1962) and in salaryman comedies. A decade later Matsumura became popular as Tora-san's uncle in the long-running Shochiku film series (he was the second of three actors to play the part in its almost 30-year history). Matsumura played the scientist who explains the big red berries in Ishiro Honda's *King Kong vs. Godzilla* (1962), and worked with the director again some 30 years later on Kurosawa's *Madadayo,* playing yet another professor, in what was certainly the best role of his career.

Medina, Patricia (b. 1920)
Screen siren who won many fans typecast as the quintessential bad girl, the vamp, in Hollywood costume pictures of the 1940s, 50s and 60s. She starred with her husband, Joseph Cotten, in *Latitude Zero* (1969). Now retired.

Mitsuta, Kazuo "Pete" (b. 1937)
A disciple of effects genius Eiji Tsuburaya, Mitsuta (pronounced "meets-ta") was the main director on many of Tsuburaya Productions' best TV shows, including "Ultraman," "Ultra Seven" and "Mighty Jack." He produced many of the company's most popular shows in the years since, and co-directed the feature *Ultraman Forever* with Hajime Tsuburaya's son, Masahiro, and as this book went to press he began work on three "Ultra Seven" direct-to-video features.

Mizuno, Kumi (b. 1937)
The sexy star of *Attack of the Mushroom People* (1963), *Frankenstein Conquers the World, Monster Zero* (both 1965), *War of the Gargantuas* (1966), and *Godzilla versus the Sea Monster* (1966), Mizuno, remains a huge cult figure with *kaiju eiga* fans both here and in Japan. Partly this is due to her chemistry with American actor Nick Adams, Mizuno's co-star in three films—*Frankenstein Conquers…* , *Monster Zero,* and the frustratingly elusive spy film *The Killing Bottle* (1967). Though married at the time, Adams was understandably attracted to Mizuno's mesmerizing exoticism, and Japanese tabloids asserted that the two were having an affair. Adams' mysterious death, generally regarded as a suicide, just one year after *The Killing Bottle's* release only furthered rumors of Mizuno's relationship with the troubled American. And unlike virtually all *kaiju eiga* actresses, including Momoko Kochi, Yuriko Hoshi, and even Mie Hama, Mizuno displayed a raw earthiness rare for Japanese women in general, let alone fantasy film stars. In every fantasy film in which she appeared, Mizuno brought an refreshing sensualness to a heretofore nearly sexless genre. Today, Mizuno works primarily on the stage and in television.

Nakanishi, Ryuzo (b. 1932)
Nikkatsu screenwriter who, with Gan Yamazaki, penned the studio's sole *kaiju eiga, Monster from a Prehistoric Planet* (1967), as well as Toho's *Star Wars* rip-off *The War in Space* (1977).

Nakano, Minoru (b. 1939)
Protegee of Eiji Tsuburaya who worked on several Toho monster classics, including *King Kong vs. Godzilla* (1962) and *Godzilla vs. the Thing* (1964). When Tsuburaya formed his own production company in 1963, Nakano became head of the optical effects department on such programs as "Ultra Q" and "Ultraman," for which Nakano also created their famous opening titles. He now operates his own effects house, and served as a consultant on *Gamera—The Guardian of the Universe* (1995).

Nakano, Teruyoshi "Shokei" (b. 1935)
Following the death of Eiji Tsuburaya and the departure of Teisho Arikawa, Nakano became head of Toho's Special Effects Group. (He had been an assistant director under both Ishiro Honda and Tsuburaya during the 1950s and 60s). Nakano (no relation to Minoru Nakano) worked during the film industry's leanest years, yet brought a certain amount of audacious fun to such generally mediocre films as *Godzilla vs. the Smog Monster* (1971), *Godzilla on Monster Island* (1972), *Godzilla vs. the Cosmic Monster, The Last Days of Planet Earth* and *ESPY* (all 1974), *Terror of Mechagodzilla* (1975), and *The War in Space* (1977). When he was given time and money, he was capable of impressive work, as seen in the epic disaster film *Submersion of Japan* (1973) and *Godzilla 1985* (1984). *After Princess of the Moon* (1987), he left Toho and now designs amusement park attractions.

Natsuki, Yosuke (b. 1936)
Handsome leading man of two back-to-back monster movies: *Dagora, the Space Monster* (1964) and *Ghidrah—The Three-Headed Monster* (both 1964). He played detectives in both of these films and was no stranger to crime movies, having appeared in many of director Jun Fukuda's thrillers around this time. He also co-starred in many war pictures (including the lead in Shue Matsubayashi's *I Bombed Pearl Harbor*) and *jidai-geki* like *Yojimbo* (1961) for Kurosawa and *Chushingura* (1962) for Hiroshi Inagaki. He played Toshiro Mifune's brother in "Shogun" (1980) and replaced an ailing Akihiko Hirata as the lead scientist in *Godzilla 1985* (1984).

Okamoto, Kihachi (b. 1924)
Looking a bit like a seasoned airplane mechanic (which he once was), Okamoto arrived for his interview dressed in a denim jacket and dark slacks. His hair thinning on top, with long gray hair on the sides, Okamoto smoked endlessly throughout the interview, gingerly depositing long bits of cigarette ash into a nearby tray. He specializes in war pictures, crime films, and *jidai-geki,* including *The Sword of Doom* (1966), and *Red Lion* (1969). His pictures deftly (and sometimes jarringly) blend comedy and tragedy. This is certainly true of the light-yet-tragic *Desperado Outpost* (1959) and its sequels, and the *Yojimbo*-esque *Kill!* (1968). Like many directors of his generation Okamoto's films became increasingly stylized,

less "studioized" and more personal; his incredible, way-ahead-of-its-time thriller/black comedy/spy-spoof *The Age of Assassins* (1967) is probably his crowning achievement. Okamoto spent most of his career at Toho, first as an assistant director under Mikio Naruse and Masahiro Makino; he made his debut feature there in 1958, and been been going strong ever since.

Omura, Kon (b. 1931)
Familiar Daiei star now working out of Osaka, Omura is remembered in the United States (and Japan) for his comic roles in two Gamera pictures, *Attack of the Monsters* (1969) and *Gamera vs. Monster X* (1970). He played stock characters in both, the hyperactive minor authority type, roles played at Toho by Ichiro Arishima, whom Omura vaguely resembles. His big break came in the early-1960s, when he starred in the salaryman comedy *A Manager and His Apprentices* (1960) and its two sequels. After Daiei went bankrupt, Omura appeared in several films for cult director Hideo Gosha, including *Tracked* (1985) and *Burning Yoshiwara* (1987). Omura remains a fixture of Japanese television commercials. His son is a writer/director living in Hollywood who recently appeared opposite Jodie Foster in *Contact* (1997).

Reason, Rhodes (b. 1930)
The lookalike younger (not twin) brother of actor Rex Reason *(This Island Earth, The Creature Walks Among Us),* Rhodes was the

American star of *King Kong Escapes* (1967). Like his brother, Reason has done some interesting genre work, notably an episode of "Thriller," a couple of "Time Tunnels," and the Boris Karloff film *Voodoo Island* (1957). And shortly after *King Kong Escapes,* Reason guest-starred in the "Bread and Circuses" episode of "Star Trek." Reason's career was somewhat more eclectic than his older brother's: Rex had been under contract to Universal, and was, to a large degree, at the mercy of the roles assigned him; he grew weary of the acting game and abruptly retired and went into real estate in the early-60s. Rhodes, working independently, had a wider, more satisfying range of parts, particularly on the stage and in television. He went to England to shoot the syndicated "White Hunter," and starred in the interesting, sometimes controversial television anthology "Bus Stop." Some of his best notices (and Reason's greatest personal satisfaction) came at the end of his career, playing Daddy Warbucks on Broadway and in the touring company of *Annie.*

Ross, William (b. 1923)
Founder of Frontier Enterprises, a company that dubs Japanese films into English for overseas release. Using the part-time voices of businessmen, musicians, students and other Anglos living in Tokyo, Ross has dubbed more than 465 feature films, plus countless TV shows and cartoons since the early 1960s. Among these pictures were a number of classics (e.g., Kurosawa's *Yojimbo, Sanjuro* and *The Hidden Fortress*) and numerous popular favorites, including the first 32 features of Shochiku's "Tora-san" series (Ross essayed the voice of Tora-san, and Robert Dunham was Tora's uncle). Ross also dubbed the international versions of *The Lost World of Sinbad* (1963), *War of the Gargantuas* (1966), *Son of Godzilla* (1967), and *Destroy All Monsters* (1968), several of which have appeared stateside in recent years. He was an associate producer on Toei's *Terror Beneath the Sea* and *The Green Slime,* and he was the dubbing director for Nikkatsu's *Monster from a Prehistoric Planet* (1967). Ross has several genre acting credits as well, including a bit in *Message from Space* (1978) and speaking parts in *The Last Dinosaur* and *The War in Space* (both 1977).

Sahara, Kenji (b. 1932)
A leading player in more Japanese sci-fi films than any other actor, Sahara was the handsome leading man stricken with amnesia in *Rodan* (1956), the hero whose girlfriend is kidnapped by aliens *The Mysterians* (1957), a scientist who uncovers the secret of *The H-Man* (1958), and the inventor of the super-strong wire in *King Kong vs. Godzilla* (1962). As he got older and his features filled out (and his star failed to rise much beyond the genre) Sahara moved into key supporting roles, playing villains in *Atragon* (1963), *Godzilla vs. the Thing* (1964), and *Yog—Monster from Space* (1970), and miscellaneous parts in *Destroy All Monsters* (1968), *War of the Gargantuas* (helping scientists Russ Tamblyn and Kumi Mizuno, 1966), and *Ghidrah—The Three-Headed Monster* (1964). He starred in Tsuburaya Productions' "Ultra Q," an "Outer Limits"-type TV program made just prior to the more familiar "Ultraman," and has appeared in most of the recent Godzilla films, playing military/government leaders. His long association with the genre dates back to the very first *Godzilla* (1954): he was an extra, a young lover aboard a passenger ship threatened by Godzilla.

Saperstein, Henry G. (b. 1919)
American producer/distributor whose United Productions of America (UPA) co-financed the first *kaiju eiga* co-productions, *Frankenstein Conquers the World, Monster Zero* (both 1965) and *War of the Gargantuas* (1966). Saperstein also distributed (though didn't finance) many other Toho titles and licensed the Godzilla character for many years. He also produced the animated feature *Gay Purr-ee* (1962), several rock 'n roll classics, including *The Big T.N.T. Show* (1966), John Boorman's *Hell in the Pacific* (1968), and Woody Allen's *What's Up, Tiger Lily?* (1966). He recently served as executive producer on the feature *Mr. Magoo* (1997).

Sato, Masaru (b. 1928)
Film composer of some of the best film music ever written, including the scores to *The Bad Sleep Well* (1960), *Yojimbo* (1961), *The Sword of Doom* (1966), *Goyokin* (1969), and *Hunter in the Dark* (1979). His fantasy film work is often no less brilliant—his music for *The Lost*

World of Sinbad (1963), *Godzilla versus the Sea Monster* (1966), *Son of Godzilla* (1967), and portions of *Godzilla vs. the Cosmic Monster* (1974) are splendid too, and a sharp contrast to the wonderful but heavy melodies of Akira Ifukube.

Seijun Suzuki (b. 1923)

With his white goatee, stringy white hair, and horn-rimmed glasses, director Suzuki looks exactly like a Japanese Colonel Sanders. Slight of build and eccentric, he's been dubbed the "Sam Fuller of Japan," and has emerged as a major cult director in the United States. This is due primarily to the discovery by bootleg video dealers and their audiences of *Branded to Kill* (1967), an outlandishly bizarre gangster melodrama/satire starring Jo Shishido and considered so strange and non-commercial that the director was fired by his longtime studio, Nikkatsu, and essentially blacklisted and unable to direct for some 10 years. After one feature he returned to prominence with the very strange *Zigeunerweisen* (1980), which beat out Akira Kurosawa's *Kagemusha* as Best Film of the Year at both the Japanese Academy Awards and in that country's leading film magazine, *Kinema Jumpo*. (Notably, none of Suzuki's earlier films ever cracked *Kinema Jumpo's* Annual Top Ten List.) For Suzuki to move from Yakuza thrillers to almost avant-garde dramas would be like Sam Fuller suddenly making films like Andrei Tarkovsky—a strange transition to say the least. Suzuki was still directing in 1997,

though he's far better known in Japan today as a television actor, the patriarchal figure in a popular television drama modeled after TV's "Dallas." His motto? "Life is already crazy, so why not be crazy ourselves?"

Takano, Koichi (b. 1935)

Special effects cameraman associated with the genre for more than 40 years. Takano was a classmate of Eiji Tsuburaya's son Noboru, and made his feature debut as an assistant cameraman on *Gigantis the Fire Monster* (1955), where Takano made the now-famous error which resulted in Godzilla and Angilus fighting one another in fast motion. (Tsuburaya liked the effect, however, and left much of it in the film.). He worked for a time shooting documentaries before rejoining the effects master when the latter formed his own production company. At Tsuburaya Productions Takano served as the head of special effects for nearly all of its classic television programs, including "Ultraman," "Ultra Seven" and more recently "Ultraman 80" and "Ultraman: Towards the Future." He now serves as Managing Director at Tsuburaya Productions, and recently served as supervisor on "Ultraman Tiga," Ultraman Dyna" and "Ultraman Zearth."

Takarada, Akira (b. 1935)

Tall, talented and still very handsome, Takarada starred in the very first *Godzilla* (1954), and four of its sequels: *Godzilla vs. the Thing* (1964), *Monster Zero* (1965),

Godzilla versus the Sea Monster (1966), and *Godzilla vs. Mothra* (1992). His other fantasy film credits include *Half Human* (1955), *The Three Treasures* (1959), *The Last War* (1961), *King Kong Escapes* (1967), and *Latitude Zero* (1969). One of Toho's biggest stars, Takarada also appeared in action films like *100 Shot, 100 Killed* (aka *Ironfinger*, 1965) and its sequel, *Booted Babe, Busted Boss* (aka *Goldeneye*, 1968), dramas like Yasujiro Ozu's *Early Autumn* (1961) and Mikio Naruse's *A Woman's Life* (1964), and comedies like *Wall-Eyed Nippon* (1964). The actor even played Rhett Butler in a stage adaptation of *Gone With the Wind* (the burning of Atlanta was staged by Eiji Tsuburaya). In recent years, Takarada became a member in director Juzo *(Tampopo)* Itami's stock company of actors, and gave a terrific performance as the hotel manager in Itami's *Minbo: Or the Gentle Art of Japanese Extortion* (1992).

Tsuburaya, Akira (b. 1944)

The last surviving son of Japan's special effects master, Akira Tsuburaya bears a striking resemblance to his famous father. A producer in his own right, the younger Tsuburaya has put the family stamp on several Tsuburaya series released to American television as ersatz features: *Time of the Apes* (1974), *Fugitive Alien,* and *Star Force: Fugitive Alien II* (both 1978). For his own company, Tsuburaya-Eizo, Akira Tsuburaya has produced *Ultra Q: The Movie* (1990), and the direct-to-video hit *Mikadroid* (1991). His other credits include

Tale of a Vampire (1992) and *Wizard of Darkness* (1995); almost none of his films have been released in the United States.

Tsuburaya, Kazuo (b. 1961)
A third-generation special effects producer, Kazuo Tsuburaya is the grandson of Eiji Tsuburaya and the son of producer Noboru Tsuburaya. Noboru was more the businessman than either of his brothers (Akira and the late Hajime Tsuburaya), though Noboru did have well-publicized ambitions as an actor-singer, and even released a CD (!). Noboru's son took over the company upon his father's untimely death in 1995.

Tsuchiya, Yoshio (b. 1927)
Wonderfully eccentric actor who made his film debut in Akira Kurosawa's masterpiece *Seven Samurai* (1954) as the tormented farmer Rikichi, whose wife has been kidnapped by bandits, and who fiercely wants to hire seven *samurai* to rid the bandits from his village forever. Tsuchiya would appear in all of Kurosawa's films through 1965, including major supporting roles in *Yojimbo* (1961), *Sanjuro* (1962) and *Red Beard* (1965). Concurrently, Tsuchiya was appearing in Japanese sci-fi films directed by Ishiro Honda, following appearances in two fantasy films directed by Motoyoshi Oda, *The Invisible Man* (1954) and *Gigantis the Fire Monster* (1955). For Honda Tsuchiya specialized playing weird aliens (in *The Mysterians* and *Monster Zero*), men possessed by aliens (*Battle*

in Outer Space, Destroy All Monsters) and men on the verge of madness *(Son of Godzilla)*. His best roles in the genre include a starring turn as *The Human Vapor* (1960), as the Japanese soldier-turned-corporate executive in *Godzilla vs. King Ghidrah* (1991), and especially as the wealthy Kasai, whose money does him little good in the superlative *Attack of the Mushroom People* (1963). Tsuchiya is odd, even by an actor's standard, but gregarious and enthusiastic. He speaks as passionately about UFOs (especially the one he has seen) as he does about playing aliens.

Ueki, Hitoshi (b. 1927)
Primary star of a jazz/novelty band/comedy team known as The Crazy Cats. The seven-man group all had successful solo careers, but Ueki and Hajime Hana became the biggest stars, with each starring not only in official team comedies, but also in their own popular film series. Ueki's *The Age of Irresponsibility in Japan* (1962) is probably his best solo film, and considered a classic in Japan. His other credits include *Las Vegas Free-for-All* (1967), *The Crazy Family* (1984), *Ran* (1985), and *Memories of You* (1988). The team reunited occasionally until Hana's death in 1993.

Yamamoto, Michio (b. 1935?)
Director, almost exclusively for television, who brought style to a trio of otherwise undistinguished vampire movies made in the wake of Hammer Films' long-running success with the genre. The first of these, *The*

Vampire Doll (1970), is the best of the three, though it's not been available in the U.S. since the early-1970s. Yamamoto's *Lake of Dracula* (1971) and *Evil of Dracula* (1974) are available, both on commercial television and home video, but these versions are badly dubbed, panned-and-scanned prints needlessly edited for violence. Yamamoto also has the distinction of working as an assistant director for both Ishiro Honda and Eiji Tsuburaya, as well as Akira Kurosawa.

Yamazaki, Gan (b. 1929)
Nikkatsu screenwriter who co-wrote, with Ryuzo Nakanishi, Nikkatsu's family-oriented *kaiju eiga, Monster from a Prehistoric Planet* (1967). Yamazaki also penned several films for cult director Seijun Suzuki. Often misbilled as Iwao Yamazaki.

Yuasa, Noriaki (b. 1933)
Gamera director, who helmed most of the big turtle's classic adventures, including *Gammera the Invincible* (aka *Gamera*, 1965), *Return of the Giant Monsters* (aka *Gamera vs. Gyaos*, 1967), *Destroy All Planets* (1968), *Attack of the Monsters* (aka *Gamera vs. Guiron*, 1969), *Gamera vs. Monster X* (1970), *Gamera vs. Zigra* (1971), and *Super Monster* (aka *Gamera Super Monster*, 1980). Yuasa also directed the special effects for all of these films, as well as the 1966 *War of the Monsters* (aka *Gamera vs. Barugon*), and several Daiei-made war movies. He made his feature debut with 1964's *Clap if You are Happy*, and today works primarily in television.

Kinji Fukasaku The United States had participated in the war but were not directly affected by warfare in the same way Japan had been. That is, life for most Americans wasn't as difficult as it was for the Japanese during and after the war.

Kihachi Okamoto Watching movies was my only escape. On December 8, 1941, the Pacific War started and I knew that once I turned 21 I would have to join the army, and that I'd probably be dead by the time I was 23. So from the time I was 17 until I was 21—arguably the most exciting period in a person's life—there was this war going on, a huge reminder that you're going to die someday, so I was always thinking, "When am I going to die?" and "How am I going to die?"

Shue Matsubayashi I was 25 at the time, with 150 men under me. It was February 1945, and I went to the South China Sea. American planes dropped bombs on us and I was directing the fleeing sailors. The boat capsized. One plane got so close I could see the face of the American flyer who was shooting at us. He was also about 25 years old. I still remember him—he waved his hand as he left. I had lost many men; on the deck I could see many bodies piled up. That was my first experience fighting with American soldiers.

Kihachi Okamoto Before the war I wanted to watch as many movies as possible, but after the war started I discovered I wanted to be more than an audience member—I wanted to make films while I could, so then I joined Toho as an assistant director in 1943. Then in 1945 I was drafted in the army. My film *Human Bullet* (1968) is based on my experiences. I had been the 4th AD for Mikio Naruse, and as the war intensified, the company decided that they really didn't need four assistant directors, and so I was drafted to the Nakajima Airplane Factory, and became their mechanic for fighter jets. During this time, 100 B-29 bombers targeted the factory. Since the factory was partially underground I fortunately survived, but a lot of women students who were working above ground died. Only half of my classmates survived the war, and none of my childhood friends survived—I was the only one who came back. I

Kinji Fukasaku

Kihachi Okamoto

Shue Matsubayashi

developed this attitude that all this wasn't so much a tragedy as a comedy. You know, everything was so fucked up, everything was so sad it was funny. But I felt so lucky to be alive that I became really ambitious and strived to be a film director.

Noriaki Yuasa When I was young, after Japan had lost the war, the adults I looked up to suddenly went from being very militaristic to anti-militaristic. Because of this hypocrisy I felt like I couldn't trust adults anymore. I hoped that when I grew up I would, in my way, still be like a child. I think this sentiment can be seen in my movies.

Kinji Fukasaku World War II ended in 1945; I was 15 years old then. In Tokyo we could still see the damage of WWII. It was not a good life; I was fresh out of the university and felt a great deal of frustration and uneasiness about political activism. Japanese people felt relieved after World War II, and I wondered how to reflect that feeling of Japanese society on film. I was interested in films from all over the world at that time, but Japan had a strong interest in films from Italy and France and Germany because they too were affected [by the war] in much the same manner as Japan—they were all poor. Everybody was looking for the next vision of the world. I had never seen Italian or American or French films up to that time because it had been prohibited. You weren't exposed to the enemy's culture—it was forbidden. Suddenly there were a lot of foreign films flooding Japan—old ones, new ones—whatever I watched was fun. American Westerns [*laughs*], French films. It was all fun for me, and with directing I feel the same way—it's all fun.

Teruyoshi Nakano

Yosuke Natsuki Of course, I didn't get to see any foreign movies during WWII, but after the war I watched all the imported French movies. Later, when I was a high school student, I watched about 300 American movies a year, including Westerns, pirate films, love stories, musicals and comedies. Mind you, I was just a movie fan.

Teruo Ishii I watched a lot of Western films—mainly French films. Everybody wanted to watch the French films back then. Then, I came to find how good American films were.

Teruyoshi Nakano I lived in Niihama [Shikoko Island] from 1945–48. I had discount tickets from the company my mother worked for. There were four theaters in Niihama, whose programs changed weekly, so I went four times a week. I saw every single movie that was shown in Japan, all the Japanese films and even the American ones. I especially like Westerns, the Tarzan films with Johnny Weismuller, and slapstick comedies.

Kinji Fukasaku From Italy, I was especially influenced by Vittorio De Sica and Roberto Rosselini; Rosselini's *Open City* in particular; I was so moved by that film. From France, Marcel Ophüls.

Shue Matsubayashi American films and French films effected my way of making films. John Ford, William Wyler, Julien Duvivier—they compelled me to be a director. I was effected by their humanism. Recent films seem devoid of humanism; they're all production values and special effects. I want to describe the human side, poetically if possible, what it is like to be alive in the postwar period. Pure heart in film is everything.

Akira Takarada At the time Japan had six film companies: Toho, Shintoho, Shochiku, Toei, Daiei, Nikkatsu. Toei had *chambara* [i.e., samurai/swordplay] movies, Shochiku had Kabuki dramas. Toho had Toshiro Mifune, Hisaya Morishige, Keiju Kobayashi, Hiroshi Koizumi. Brand new and modern films. Sophisticated.

Yuriko Hoshi Each of the studios–Toho, Shochiku, Toei, Daiei–had their own particular style and atmosphere. We don't have that kind of individuality with the studios anymore.

Jun Fukuda [*looking around the nearly empty studio commissary*] It wasn't like this. A lot of stars, a lot of people yelling, making noises, running around. The stages were full; so full, in fact, we had to rent other stages off the lot because we were so busy. Now see, it's not really active.

Akira Takarada They shot two films a day: one in the morning and one in the afternoon. I played a lot of roles. I felt a responsibility to the company and tried my best. It was a busy time. Sometimes I mixed up the names of the women I was supposed to be married to!

Yu Fujiki Toho was huge! That was the best time for film in Japan. It was very common to have double features which were sold as a package; usually an A-film and a B-film. Every week the program was changed; in one year Toho did something like 104 films. I was in 24 features in one year! That was the atmosphere.

Eiji Funakoshi One film came after another and I didn't have time to hone my craft. I've been at it now for 50 years! I wanted to quit because I was so ashamed of my work. It was really active. We shot early in the morning, and often shot all night! There sometimes would be a back-up in the morning with a new crew waiting impatiently to use the stage! We had huge audiences in those days, so the studio was making a lot of money, thanks to the efforts of the actors and the crew. But don't misunderstand, the company made money, not the actors.

Yu Fujiki We had only one year contracts. Toho would then renew the contract every year. We got paid after the shooting; if we didn't work we didn't get paid!

Akira Ifukube When [my first film, *Snow Trail*] came out I discovered that my name was put at the very end of the staff list, even after the set dresser and wardrobe mistress! Only recently has the name of the composer been listed on the film's poster and in other advertising.

Masaru Sato One year I wrote 18 complete scores; that's my record. Last year I did three. Recently, with the Japanese film industry the way it is, I've slowed down to just a few each year. No one could break that record now—that was during the Golden Period.

Yu Fujiki I played a colonel in *Admiral Yamamoto* (1968), while the bottom-half of the bill I played a major in a Kei Tani comedy. I didn't realize that I was going to be in two films on the same program, and a lot of people asked me why I had been demoted!

The explosion of production after the war was such that Japan's film studios began holding annual "New Face Contests" of one sort or another. Winners were then built

Yu Fujiki

up over several years, first in tiny walk-ons, then in supporting roles and then, if the public took a liking to them, in leading parts. All the while these would-be stars were vigorously trained.

Akira Takarada [Toho's New Face Contest] was a one year program. We were taught film theory, classic Japanese dancing. It was similar to Lee Stassberg's The Actor's Studio in Los Angeles. Toho supported that philosophy and picked only a very few selected people to be in the program. Working directors and actors came over, from nine to five, Monday through Saturday. There's a cinematic way to acting, and that's what we learned to do. It was very hard training. But that method taught us that emotion has to last from shot to shot.

Mie Hama

Momoko Kochi I felt like I was going back to school; just like a student! It was fun, very energetic and active. Toshiro Mifune was there—a lot of great stars.

Yosuke Natsuki Mr. Toshiro Mifune and Ms. Yoshiko Kuga were part of the first class. I was part of the tenth. Mr. Yoshio Kosugi, who was a famous supporting player, and Ms. Atsuko Ichinomiya, and sometimes a director and cameraman taught us how to play a role and other particulars for motion pictures.

Momoko Kochi I took the examination, and passed it.

Kumi Mizuno I bypassed the New Face Program. I was chosen as a main player in Shochiku's *Crazy Society* (1957). And after I graduated from acting school I joined Toho where I became a leading player. **Yuriko Hoshi** I was part of the Takarazuka theatrical

company, close to Kobe. They were looking for teenage girls for a production of "Cinderella," and 3,000 girls showed up for the audition. Nine girls became finalists, and from them, I was chosen for Cinderella. That was a real learning period–learning from the great Takarazuka actresses. Once we took the night train to Tokyo, and visited Toho Studios. While I was there, the producer Masumi Fujimoto asked, "Why don't you stay here and become a movie star?" At the time I was a 15-year-old girl. I replied, "I would rather see what's going on with Takarazuka." Later, I returned to Tokyo during my summer vacation, and made my debut at Toho playing the younger sister of the main character in a film made for release the following year.

Mie Hama I was working on the bus as a kind of conductor, and some colleagues of mine applied to the New Face Contest and entered my name without telling me about it. I didn't watch those kind of films at all. I had no great interest in working in films; I was more interested in politics. I thought I'd just make a visit to Toho, and when I got their offer, I refused. But even my boss at the bus company thought that it could be a really good experience for me—he said my conducting job was similar to acting in films in the sense that I would be trying to please people and make them happy. I finally said, "Okay, I'll do just one film." It took three months to make, and once it was over, I learned that Toho had been secretly negotiating with the bus company and at the end of shooting, my position there suddenly became unavailable! So I had no choice but to stay and be an actress.

Yuriko Hoshi I was just a kid. They were shooting a

lot of films for double feature packages. Even blockbusters ran only two weeks in those days. I was still training as an actress. I just ran from one stage to the next, and around this time I was offered the role of Yuzo Kayama's girlfriend in the "Young Guy" series. I probably did 24 films in a year.

Yu Fujiki In 1951 I was a fencing student at the university, an All-Japan champion. Toei in Kyoto offered me a job in films as a *chambara* actor. I didn't have any ambitions as an actor, so at first I refused it. After graduation, I consulted with my elder brother, Ichiro Sato, who was a producer at Toho. I just wanted to be an employee, and he suggested I join as an advertising or PR person. I applied, but they said, "Why don't you become an actor for us?" I had already been asked by Toei! Anyway, that was one of the only ways to get into the company, so I said, "What the hell?" and was accepted. I wanted to move away from acting, but somehow I ended up spending 42 years at it!

Momoko Kochi Yumi Shirakawa and Kenji Sahara [Kochi's co-stars in *The Mysterians*] were classmates of mine, in the New Face program. They were like brothers and sisters.

Kenji Sahara I went through six auditions as a Toho New Face, and after that I went to an actor's school at Toho, and then, after about one year, I signed a contract. At that time *Seven Samurai* and *Godzilla* (both 1954) were in production, and sometimes I joined the shooting as an extra, and after that *Rodan* (1956) came along, and it was my first starring role. I began working regularly with Mr. Ishiro Honda, and worked on something like 20 out of 24 Godzilla films.

Akira Takarada Everybody was so ambitious. Such dreams we had! They didn't know what kind of future they had. Everyone was in their twenties, and didn't have much experience in life. We didn't have much experience to draw tears—just dreams.

Up the Ladder

Kihachi Okamoto In Japan it was a tradition that you would be an assistant director for a long time before you became a director.

Teruyoshi Nakano If you wanted to study movie-making back then, there was only one place to go: Nippon University's film department, so that's where I went.

Ishiro Honda Well, the university had what it called a film department, but it was a film department in name only. It didn't have any facilities, any equipment, any books. I think I saw a camera twice my entire time there. But it was like that in other departments, too.

Teruyoshi Nakano The assistant director was always the rookie of the company, the gofer. I could bear with the job health-wise and physically, but I had no idea what I was doing, and that was the hardest part. People running around and yelling at each other—I had no idea what scene was being filmed, nothing. If I just stood around, I got yelled at. I was just passing the days under these circumstances, and one day Mr. Tsuburaya called on me.

Kenji Sahara

Michio Yamamoto The first job for an assistant director was like being a best boy, and there was a strict code of protocol. [On *Throne of Blood*] we'd scurry around the mountains with radios on our backs. I thought, "why did I ever bother to go to college?"

Kihachi Okamoto I did *Four Love Stories* (1947), which was an anthology with four different directors. I worked on the segment directed by Shiro Toyoda; his was called "First Love"; I worked on that. Then, because I was a good skier I was switched from Toyoda's team and did *Snow Trail* (1947), which was the debut picture of Toshiro Mifune, and directed by Senkichi Taniguchi. And after Taniguchi's picture I worked on two more Naruse pictures: *Repast* (1951) and *Floating Clouds* (1955). After that I worked with Masahiro Makino—nine pictures in two years. I feel very fortunate to be working with so many good directors at that time. Naruse [taught me the most]. Makino taught me the most about technique. His technique was very extravaganza-like. Very huge scale. But Naruse's method was very subtle, so it was interesting to compare their styles. [Japanese film scholar] Audie Bock studied my pictures and she told me that my biggest influence was probably Naruse. She says my vertical cutaways are directly from Naruse. Neither of us like to talk much to the actors or give them lot of direction.

Tsugnobu "Tom" Kotani I graduated from Tokyo University in 1960 and passed two Toho entrance exams and an interview. I then studied under [directors] Hiroshi Inagaki and Mikio Naruse, learning about the myriad of things a director must know. Continuity, staging and so forth.

Kinji Fukasaku As a first-time director, you were usually assigned a short, little film, usually about 50 minutes, so that the studio could evaluate your ability.

Tsugnobu "Tom" Kotani There was a seniority rule at Toho when I was an assistant director. There were 52 assistant directors at that time. I simply calculated if only two assistant directors were promoted to directors each year, I wouldn't become a director for 26 years! I was stunned. But I became a director nine years after that, so I was very lucky.

Ishiro Honda Believe it or not, we naïvely hoped that the end of Godzilla was going to coincide with the end of nuclear testing.

Yoshio Tsuchiya During the final phase of shooting *Seven Samurai* (1954), I heard the rumor about the name "Gojira," but no one knew what that was. Very few people, even the cast, knew what Gojira was or would be. As the name was derived from *kujira* [whale] and gorilla, I imagined some kind of giant aquatic gorilla. I wanted to work for Mr. Honda on this film but unfortunately I had to work on *Seven Samurai*.

Ishiro Honda A lot of people contributed ideas. Producer Tomoyuki Tanaka and his associate Shigeru Kayama, for example, did much of the planning, and Kayama came up with the general story outline. But the real inspiration was that nuclear incident.

Akira Takarada At the time we had the very controversial news story of the tuna boat that was exposed to radiation. That was a major social issue. The radiation—the sleeping Godzilla—is coming from the deep sea, Honda said. Those were the kind of discussions we had. Akihiko Hirata and I switched roles. Mr. Hirata had more of a scientist-like face— simple as that.

Ishiro Honda [It took] about two or three weeks [to write the screenplay]. What really took time was storyboarding the film because that was the only way we could express our intentions. Our crew didn't have a clue. Obviously, we knew he was going to be big and eventually we decided that our model would be the biggest creature to ever walk the earth—namely, a dinosaur. Once that was decided, we had to figure out how we were going to make him move.

怪獣 東京大攻撃

The Birth of Godzilla

Yoshio Tsuchiya

Akira Takarada

Momoko Kochi

Yoshio Tsuchiya *Godzilla* was unusual, because at the time special effect movies usually began with the production of the live action sequences and the effects were shot later.

Ishiro Honda At first, we considered using stop-motion like in *King Kong* (1933), but gave up because it would have taken forever. So we decided to use a man in a monster suit. Even after we started shooting, we were still working on the rubberized suit. Don't forget that this was the first time this kind of monster had appeared in a film here, so there was a lot of trial and error involved in trying to make him look right. And getting permission from the Maritime Safety Board to shoot at sea was a very time-consuming process.

Yu Fujiki I played a sailor in the first *Godzilla.* I had tons of water thrown on me! I didn't feel embarassed at all, partly because I didn't know who Godzilla was! Honda would direct me to act surprised that Godzilla was coming, but since I didn't know what Godzilla would look like, it was kind of weird. So I asked him what Godzilla would be like, and he said, "I don't know, but anyway, the monster is coming!" It was very fun like that, very interesting.

Ishiro Honda At the time there was a big–I mean huge–fellow working in Toho's publicity department. Employees would argue, "that guy is as big as a gorilla." "No, he's almost as big as a *kujira.*" Over time, the two mixed and he was nicknamed "Gojira." So when [co-writer Takeo] Murata and I were stuck for a name, Tanaka said, "Hey, you know that guy over in publicity...?"

Akira Takarada The drama section and Mr. Tsuburaya and the special effects department worked far apart. I only saw a rough sketch of Godzilla at first. We couldn't see the rushes to see how the reaction shots were working. We acted like horses in a race and Mr. Honda was the jockey telling us, "Don't rush now!" That was our relationship.

Ishiro Honda We had a tie-in with Morinaga Confectionary. which is why Godzilla didn't destroy the tower with Morinaga's name on it.

But the rumor that the monster spared the Toho-owned Nichigeki Theater simply isn't true, is it?

Ishiro Honda Oh, no! Godzilla smashed the Nichigeki and Toho, too! Kerplat!

Akira Takarada I went to the very first screening of *Godzilla* on the Toho lot. I shed tears. Godzilla was killed by the oxygen destroyer, but Godzilla himself wasn't evil and he didn't have to be destroyed. Why did they have to punish Godzilla? Why? He was a warning to mankind. I was mad at mankind and felt sympathy for Godzilla, even if he did destroy Tokyo. For ordinary audiences, they wanted to see the film to be scared. It was like the first scene in *Jaws*–very scary with the sound effects, the music, the opening titles. Spielberg himself says he watched *Godzilla* as a kid and his horror and suspense directing comes from the *Godzilla* style of filmmaking.

Momoko Kochi My experience wasn't as strong as Mr. Takarada's. I knew the film was related to the theme of nuclear weapons and all that. I had the opportunity to see the film again recently, and realized that it isn't a bad movie, that it is a good film.

Ishiro Honda [Japanese film critics] called it grotesque junk, and said it looked like something you'd spit up. I felt sorry for my crew because they'd worked so hard. But if you believe in freedom of expression, you've got to be prepared to be criticized.

Did you think Godzilla *was going to be such a big hit?*

Ishiro Honda No. You have to remember that at the time, the biggest earners for Toho were special effects films. So I think [Toho's] attitude was, "Why not? If *Godzilla* fails, we've still got lots of chances to make money with all these other special effects films we're going to release."

Kimi Honda I had never read the script. Mr. Honda was the only person who understood the entire picture and what it was going to be. Nobody had any idea what was going on during shooting, and relied on him for direction. After the film came out, I passed a theater showing the film, and there was a long line around the theater. I was so happy for him I cried. Who could have imagined it would have been so successful? Even the president of Toho called.

Momoko Kochi People would look at me and shout "Godzilla! Godzilla!" I was young, you know! [laughs] I hated it. People think I became a really big star because of *Godzilla*, but I really didn't want to be known as a monster actress. That's why I went back to acting school.

Ishiro Honda Some people were probably reminded of [the war], but there were also a lot of young people in the audience who didn't have any first-hand knowledge, or only dim memories, of the war. Plus, as strange as it may sound, I think the film probably succeeded because I didn't completely succeed as a director. The film represents only about 65% of what I wanted to achieve; maybe if we had a little more time, money, freedom, we could have gotten 100%. Since we fell short, however, audiences could see that it wasn't a real story, that it wasn't like the war. In any case, *Godzilla* is a very speculative film, you know, what if a monster were to attack our city—what would we do?

Akira Takarada *Godzilla* was an attempt to warn the world about nuclear energy, but it still goes on to this day. If Mr. Honda were alive, I think he'd ask somebody to let him shoot his film again. I starred with Momoko Kochi in other films for Mr. Honda, and they were very serious works. One was a monster movie, another was a love story, yet both were the same.

Kenji Sahara Mr. Honda was a very romantic person, and like Mr. Tsuburaya, he loved the relationship between nuclear experiments and monsters.

Teruyoshi Nakano They both believed that nature was the strongest force on Earth, and that nobody could resist nature's will.

Kenji Sahara People today are too passive about nuclear issues, but at that time when *Godzilla* was shot, everyone was really concerned. Now it's all been pushed under the table.

Momoko Kochi When I saw Mia Farrow on the Academy Awards she was asked what her favorite movie was, and she said "*Godzilla*!" I still wonder why. Part of it is greed, and that Godzilla is a kind of warning to mankind. Seeing it again I came to understand that; I wish audiences would. That's why *Godzilla* came to be embraced by people as something more than a monster film.

Akira Takarada When Godzilla destroyed the big clock [in the movie], it was a metaphor for an alarm telling us we are running out of time. 40 years have passed, but deep down the message is the same. Mankind woke Godzilla, and today we have similar issues: air pollution, the ozone layer. That is also Godzilla. They're the same in that they were all brought on by mankind.

Would you say ... Godzilla is your best film?

Ishiro Honda Probably. But let me add that I never said "well done" after making any of my films. Eiji Tsuburaya and I would get together after filming and our conversations would go: "Well, what do you give this one? A seventy?" "No, maybe a sixty." And we'd get harder on ourselves as time went one because we were supposed to know more about filmmaking. Always in the back of your mind there's the realization that a film is forever and its influence is going to outlive you. So you tend to be very strict when judging the final product.

THE OLD MAN & TOKUSATSU (Special Effects)

Kenji Sahara [Eiji Tsuburaya] wanted to turn everything into a special effect.

Henry G. Saperstein He was *the* master of special effects. Everything from rear-screen projection, front screen projection, to miniaturization, to articulated models–that was all Tsuburaya. I worshipped the man. I used to love to just sit and listen to him and look at what he was doing. Steven Spielberg and George Lucas have said it in print many times, their inspiration in special effects was all the work of Tsuburaya. There wouldn't be *Terminator 2* and all that if it hadn't been for Tsuburaya and the Godzilla films.

Michio Yamamoto I think Tsuburaya-san contributed a lot to the films. In fact, I think Tsuburaya-san was really the leader of the Honda-Tsuburaya team.

Kimi Honda Mr. Tsuburaya was much older. They had known each other since Honda was an assistant director on Kajiro Yamamoto's war movies, so they had a long history.

Minoru Nakano He was a God at Toho! To Mr. Tsuburaya, the film studio was a very sacred place.

Kenji Sahara When I was young and a New Face going to actor's school, I often visited the effects stage. In that same area, on my way to the school in fact, was the special effects building, and I saw there was a miniature airplane, and below the airplane there was a big sheet of glass, and on top of the glass they had put pieces of cotton. Below that I saw a miniature battleship and a lot of tiny white caps. I thought, "Is this some kind of joke?" It looked like a toy. Soon thereafter I took a plane from Tokyo to Kyushu and looked down at the ocean, and it looked exactly like what I had seen at the studio! I was really impressed.

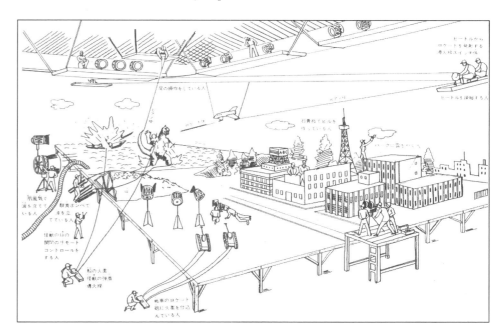

Teruyoshi Nakano In Japanese society, we tend to divide people into two categories. There are the scientific people, and ones who are more like poets, artistic types. I would describe Mr. Tsuburaya as someone who was both. He was scientific and artistic as well.

Yosuke Natsuki It took a very long time to make even one shot. Mr. Tsuburaya would sit in a director's chair for very long stretches, like a bronze statue. He was a great magician.

Koichi Takano Even if he needed just two seconds of footage, he'd shoot five or six angles just to make it more interesting, more exciting.

Eiji Tsuburaya on the set of "Ultra Seven," a television series produced by his production company

Michio Yamamoto One time, we were shooting a film that needed an avalanche. I was told to go see Mr. Tsuburaya, and he said, "There's one in the top drawer of my desk!" I looked, and indeed there was a roll of great avalanche footage. He would hide all of his best footage!

Minoru Nakano He was very shy, and also very enthusiastic about his profession. He put his life into his work.

Rhodes Reason He was the number one guy there. He was a heavy-set guy with glasses. Well, you know, they all have bad teeth and smoke too much.

Michio Yamamoto He was a genius! I learned a lot about editing from Tsuburaya, he was a mentor for me, as well as many others.

Kazuho "Pete" Mitsuta He taught me I could do anything, so long as I put all of my energy into it–a "just do it" kind of attitude. For example, if you are going to do a close-up, do it, but do it big. This philosophy isn't just for making films, but for life.

Teruyoshi Nakano Mr. Tsuburaya could have worn a t-shirt and shorts to work, but that wasn't intense enough for him. He wanted a certain tension, I think that's why he always wore suits. It was kind of like the vest worn by *samurai* in the old days. I once heard about an episode where Mr. Tsuburaya was on his way home and he ran into this woman who looked familiar. So he said, "Hello, it's been a long time." Do you know who that woman was? That was Mr. Tsuburaya's wife.

Noriaki Yuasa [Toho's] film *The War at Sea from Hawaii to Malaya* (1942), directed by Kajiro Yamamoto, was a shining golden tower in the Japanese special effects movie history, and no one has since made a film on that scale. It's impossible to guess how many miniatures there have been in the history of

Toho. [They] burned all the miniatures from the film to destroy any evidence and avoid being tried as war criminals. This movie is one of the great propaganda films of the war. Eiji Tsuburaya was the top man in the special effects department, and this organization was dissolved after the war, but I guess the people in the crews became the crew on *Godzilla*.

Minoru Nakano In December 1958, when I was 19-years-old and a freshman at Nippon University, I went, on my own, to his home directly because I knew where he lived. When I first went to the house his son Hajime was there, and he introduced me to his father. Mr. Tsuburaya brought me to Toho Studios and said, "If you help me, you can be my apprentice." At the university I was majoring in cinematography, but Mr. Tsuburaya insisted I quit school and be hired by Toho, but I refused. I was very excited with the prospect of working with Mr. Tsuburaya, but I wanted to understand the basic principals of cinematography first at the university. Another reason was because at Toho Tsuburaya was already a god, and all I'd be able to say there would be "Good morning, sir," and things like that. I wouldn't have been able to converse with Mr. Tsuburaya at Toho. You see, many of the older people in the industry looked down upon university students as being too smart for their own good. And besides, everyone that was coming out of the universities wanted to become directors or cinematographers— there wasn't anyone besides me wanting to be in the special effects field. At that time Mr. Tsuburaya possessed a kind of office and laboratory in his home. When he moved to Tokyo from Kyoto around the time of *Godzilla* he had a tiny laboratory to do his job. Afterwards, he had space at Toho but there were

certain effects and experimentation he just couldn't do within the Toho system.

Koichi Takano My father was a friend of Eiji Tsuburaya, so from time to time I would visit his house. Whenever I was in the house he would go off into another room, and often I'd hear him play the *shamisen* [Japanese guitar]. And I would spot all of the miniature props and sets ... a steam train I remember in particular.

Minoru Nakano At his home we were able to talk just like old friends, very equally. He respected my decision to stay in school, and whenever he had time off from the studio I'd quit studying and run over to his house and we'd talk about movies. In the laboratory, he had some nitrate film of *Mighty Joe Young* (1949) which he showed me frame-by-frame to study the masking and the movement of the people and the movement of the miniatures.

Koichi Takano He was all over: during the planning stages, during shooting, during postproduction. The think I learned most from him was cutting. Working with him at a Moviola. He was very involved with postproduction. For example, if he was shooting and accidentally caught something else that was totally unrelated but an interesting shot, he'd save it to use later on a different production. I was amazed by that.

Kazuo Tsuburaya I was in the 3rd Grade when he died, so my relationship was one of grandfather and grandson. When Eiji Tsuburaya was working he was really a tough kind of guy, but when I'd see him, say on a Sunday, he was very sweet and gentle. When I

Minoru Nakano

Koichi Takano

Kazuo Tsuburaya

would see him he would take 8mm films of us, or help me build model kits. One time I was making an airplane and I just couldn't make it and threw it away. He found out about this and got really mad. He did this because he had a special place in his heart for airplanes and afterwards he helped me build models. He was a really great grandfather.

Minoru Nakano He respected American films most–especially George Pal's *The War of the Worlds*–because Pal's films had no stars and the budgets went into the special effects. When I was working in Tsuburaya's home laboratory, he would be brought home by a chauffeur. Everyone knew the sound of the automobile and would say, "The Old Man is coming back." He was depressed when everyone wasn't working, so everyone always pretended to be busy shooting whenever we heard that car coming. Once he got home he would change from his suit to a *kimono* and relax, but he was very serious about his profession. Generally people collaborating in this way are very close within the studio, but once outside the various people may not be so friendly, even hostile. But the relationship between Mr. Honda and Mr. Tsuburaya was very exceptional. I never saw them quarrel, inside or outside the studio. They understood and respected one another, and could imagine how the other would interpret the script.

Akira Tsuburaya My general impression was that he was never at home, and I didn't have all that much of a direct relationship, but during my childhood I received special toys no other child had. These toys were, of course, miniature props taken from the set at Toho. Indirectly, I learned to create something from nothing. My brothers, Hajime and Noboru, were about 10 years older than I, so I didn't play with them because I was too young. I played by myself, and created things from scratch for my own amusement, such as model airplanes. When I was in junior high school, my father was working on *Godzilla* (1954). There was a big stage at Toho—Number 10— and my friends and I went to see the shooting of the special effects scenes. But for us there was another reason to go there: on the lot was a coffee shop, and my dad would buy me and my friends hamburgers, which was a big deal! Anyway, I remember seeing my father shoot the scenes of Godzilla in Tokyo harbor very vividly. I also remember a miniature train around this time that was actually powered by coal which he put in our backyard; I used to ride on it. When I was a kid you couldn't go to the store and buy a plastic model kit like you can now. I would carve it out of wood and bamboo. So, even when I was very small I lived in the atmosphere of special effects.

One of Eiji Tsuburaya's many and elaborate miniatures constructed for "Gorath" (1962)

KAIJU EIGA IN THE 1950s

Ishiro Honda Directors at that time weren't associated with series so much as with particular genres. So I wasn't really classified as a director of Godzilla films, but of special effects films. While I was off doing something else, [director] Motoyoshi Oda was handling the sequel [*Gigantis the Fire Monster*, 1955].

Yoshio Tsuchiya Because I was doing *Seven Samurai* I couldn't appear in the first Godzilla. That's why I insisted they put me in the sequel.

Koichi Takano The first film I worked on was *Gigantis the Fire Monster* (1955). At that time, there weren't a lot of experts in the field of special effects. We took people from various specialized areas–not so much film, really. The style and construction of the monster suits, for example, was based on the kind of costumes found in circuses, made of bamboo and paint and so forth. Originally we in the special effects unit had nothing to do with filmmaking. If you take a look at all the art department people, for instance, they were all highly specialized painters and what not from art school. I myself began working on these films part-time. At that time everything–all the miniatures–were hand-made. We didn't use any sophisticated machines or computers or anything. When we make miniature buildings today, for example, if we need a big sign we'd just cut it out of a magazine and use it. In those days we didn't have such things and everything was hand-

drawn and painted. So I'd have to say my main impression of the special effects unit was how everything was hand-made.

Minoru Nakano There was some experimentation [with stop-motion animation] on *Half Human* (1955) for a long shot of an automobile moving down a winding road, only it was done on an open set, which meant that the sun was moving across the horizon during the shot! At the screening they realized what happened, and because of this experience Toho decided that stop motion didn't fit the production system, which is one reason so little stop motion animation was done, and that's why he had his own laboratory at home—there he could do the experimental effects which Toho discouraged.

Angilas (Katsumi Tezuka) and Godzilla (Haruo Nakajima) tango in Osaka in "Gigantis the Fire Monster" (1955)

Teruyoshi Nakano At first, I hated what I was doing, but later on I realized that special effects are at the core of movie making. Movies are made from hard and soft elements, a combination medium. Special effects are all about techniques, and I thought by learning techniques, I could develop a vision of my own. So that's how I decided to get involved in *tokusatsu*.

怪獣 東京大攻撃

Koichi Takano The special effects technique is very Japanese—the look, the pace—it has become a characteristic of Japanese science fiction films. One of the reasons I like it is because we could see things happen during filming that we never could have expected. For instance, in *Rodan* (1956), there is a moment when the wires broke and Rodan caught fire; the effect is startling, but if we had been using a computer we never would have thought of such a movement.

Yoshio Tsuchiya [Honda] was quite open to other people's opinion. One example is the bilingual language of the Mysterians [in *The Mysterians*, 1957]. I'm not sure about the dubbed version, but in the original the aliens speak their own tongue which was then translated with the translation layered atop the Mysterians' language. That very strange approach was devised by me. I imagined this automatic translator, and thought that if it were possible that the voice out of the machine would be mechanical and colloquial: "I-am-a-Mys-ter-i-an," and so on. At the time I was very interested in the Space Race, and belonged to an organization which promoted a mission to the moon. I got all my fellow actors to join—Mifune, Shimura. Then I learned that this organization was crooked and really wanted to divide up the moon and sell it as real estate! I was so outraged that in the movie when the earth scientists balk at giving the Mysterians some land on Earth, I ad-libbed, "But you're trying to divide up the moon and sell it!"

Teruyoshi Nakano At first, I worked as an assistant director. One of my first assignments was *The Three Treasures* (1959). It was so hot on the set! Directors like Kurosawa liked to pan and pull focus, and the film we used back then wasn't as sensitive, so we used a lot of lights. In the summertime it was hot enough even without the lights, so when the temperature started to rise outside, it would become a living hell in the studio. The heat from the lights would burn the actor's wigs, so as assistant director, one of my most important jobs was to put wet towels over the wigs between takes ... it was just really hot. The thermostat on the ceiling would say 80 centigrade! And the special effects set was even hotter than that! We used stronger light, we used high speed photography, so there was a lot more lights than principal photography. I was basically an intermediary between the special effects teams and principal team on that film. My job was to schedule the actors. It was the height of Tsuburaya's career; he had 90 people on the special effects staff. It was a happening work environment, but it was a very hard job. They used the term "3-K" for the crappiest jobs. "3-K" stands for *kitsui*, a hard job, *kitanai*, a dirty job, and *kurushi*, a stinky job. But special effects work was more like a 7-K or 8-K job! The crew was covered in mud and sweat and they were just running around.

Michio Yamamoto [Tsuburaya] was asked to shoot special effects films, but he wanted to shoot dramas.

Shue Matsubayashi I think that Tsuburaya wanted to work with real live people and not just miniatures and monsters—with human beings. And so, even though it was kind of my domain, I said, "Please come and shoot some of the drama if you'd like." I saw the rushes and the actors didn't act like human beings, but like miniatures, almost like toys! It was very strange, I never told him; I didn't want my reaction to be a disappointment. I've never told this story before. I suppose it is the same with all special effects directors. However, he was a genius at shooting miniatures, and making inanimate objects come alive–I certainly don't have the talent to do that.

Ishiro Honda,
Kaiju Eiga Auteur

Tatsuo Matsumura He was a great person, a real gentleman. He had a warm heart, and paid delicate attention to people. I cannot understand why he was always shooting Godzilla movies.

Henry G. Saperstein A very nice man. Very quiet and shy. Totally efficient. He knew what he was doing.

Ishiro Honda When I was still in elementary school, I became really interested in the *benshi* silent film narrators–in fact, I was more interested in them than what was happening on the screen. I guess I was a little bit of a *benshi* myself. My father was a Buddhist priest and didn't go to the movies. I'd come back and, as kids do, I'd tell him the entire story of whatever I'd seen. He enjoyed my telling those stories so much that he overlooked that, technically speaking, it was illegal for a kid my age to go to a theater without an adult. But, as you know, the police didn't really care, so I was always sneaking in. I watched movie theaters being built and regular theaters being turned into movie theaters and eventually I realized that there could be a pretty well-paying future for me in the business. And by the time I was in high school, critics were writing about film as

something cultural, as an art form. So it all came together: I enjoyed telling stories and could find work in an industry that was financially successful to boot.

Kimi Honda He was very modest about his work. Whatever the budget, he tried to do his best. He put such effort into every film–it was painstaking work. Perhaps his films have remained popular because the audience feels his passion.

Akira Kubo I expect everyone gives the same answer [about Ishiro Honda]–very gentle and calm, serious, wonderful.

Momoko Kochi That fits into my picture of him, and he always wore a cap.

Ishiro Honda About the only special effects films I saw [when I was younger] were these *ninja* adventures where the *ninja* would disappear in a puff of smoke and be replaced by a frog. Pretty dull stuff. I've always been interested in the natural sciences, though, and that's why I've enjoyed doing the films I've done. My first film as a director was about a woman diver [*The Blue Pearl*, 1951], which gave me a chance to deal with the relationship between humans and nature. That's a subject I think I'll never tire of.

Teruyoshi Nakano Mr. Honda's first film was *The Blue Pearl*, a semi-documentary about the lives of pearl divers. Before then, he had worked on documentaries, which is why his films had such a strong connection with nature, and with people's daily lives. For example, do you remember the scene where a woman is taking a bath and she sees a monster through the window [in

Kimi Honda

Akira Kubo

Yuriko Hoshi (right), with Yu Fujiki and Akira Takarada in Honda's "Godzilla vs. the Thing" (1964)

Yuriko Hoshi in 1996

The Mysterians]? That illustrates his basic approach to making movies. Even if the movie was about something as unrealistic as monsters, he wanted to show how it would affect people's lives. Yet, in spite of the fact that Mr. Honda cared about nature and about daily life, he also tried to create the most exciting kind of scenes, the type that other directors are usually embarrassed to show. For instance, in the first *Godzilla*, there is a scene where a newscaster is broadcasting from a tower as the monster is approaching him. Godzilla destroys the tower, and the newscaster screams, "Now Godzilla is destroying the tower! What am I to do!" In real life, the newscaster would try to run away! Mr. Honda cared about reality, but he also wanted to make the movie fun.

Yuriko Hoshi I made my debut with a small role in his film *Inao—The Story of an Iron Arm* (1959), about a famous baseball pitcher. The location was on far-off Oita, in Kyushu, and because Honda was so busy with the film, we didn't get to my scene—which was no more than a few lines—and I was stranded there for a month. Several years later, when I made *Godzilla vs. the Thing* (1964), Honda apologized for making me wait so long in Kyushu! I was surprised he even remembered.

Kimi Honda I also worked at Toho [as a script girl], and we were all one big family. We used to have a much bigger house because of all the guests we constantly had over. Whether it was a guest of Honda's or a guest of our son, everyone was treated equally. Likewise, the children of people at the studio became our friends and so on. Mr. Honda liked entertaining people at home because he didn't like to go out and drink very much. He'd say, "Why don't you come over to my place?" a lot. He would sometimes bring 20 people at a time to the house. The actors always came by to visit, and they really loved him.

Yosuke Natsuki All of us, the actors and the crew, went to his house near the studio and drank beer or had barbecues with his family after work. He was a gentleman with a smile both at work and at home.

Yoshio Tsuchiya I wanted to work with Mr. Honda on a science fiction film, and eventually, I was commissioned to play the young hero who protects his girlfriend in *The Mysterians* (1957), but I didn't like that type of stereotyped character. I wanted to play only interesting, strong and/or twisted characters. I learned there was a role for the leader of the alien invaders and I said, "A role of the alien leader! Why didn't you tell me!?" They said, "Well, he has to be totally masked, so your face can never be seen." Initially, Mr. Honda said the same thing. He said, "You're a young star, and the company wants you to show your face to the audience." "That's all right," I said, "I just want to play the alien!" Mr. Honda was moved by my passion about this, and it was at that point that we became very deep friends.

Teruyoshi Nakano Honda used to say movies are the only art form that can utilize real nature and scenery as a background. In theatrical plays, you use a scenic backdrop, but it isn't real, it's just painted on. And if you are a novelist, you write about nature and scenery, but it's just writing. But, Mr. Honda also said, you can't pay too much attention to the background, because if you do it won't have the impact you intended. If you want to film the ocean, and you spend time trying to find the best angle to shoot it, it's like you're trying too hard, and killing the real look of the most beautiful ocean.

Mie Hama Honda was an actor's director.

Kenji Sahara He was an Art Major at Nippon University, and he was really good at instructing actors. He would sometimes read the actors lines for the actor and they would often say, "you can do this better than I can!" [1]

Akira Kubo I learned [from Honda] that the actor has to squarely tackle the theme and role, from his personality and character.

Rhodes Reason He knew how to make films for his audiences. He was always very introspective, very thoughtful. But to me, I hate to say, Honda-san was a hack. I've worked with hundreds of hack TV directors and he could fit beautifully over here doing a number of motion pictures and things. He knows his craft, but there was nothing special about Honda-san as a director. His direction was, a little bit, from outer space.

Yoshio Tsuchiya Off the set he was very generous, but during production he was very preoccupied, but he was quite open to other people's opinion. During the making of *Battle in Outer Space* (1959), I kept trying to tell everyone about the moon's low gravity, and that

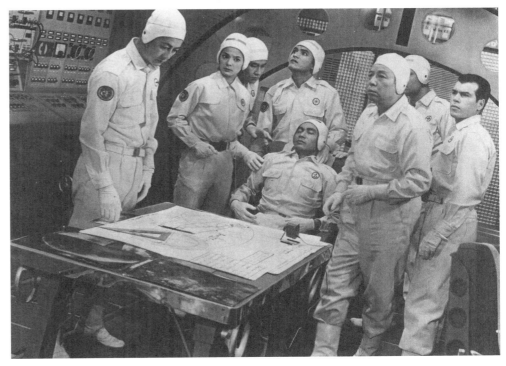

everyone should try to "float" and walk in slow motion. Everyone thought I was crazy, but Mr. Honda liked the idea, and that's what we did. Mr. Tsuburaya was very open to suggestions as well. When Godzilla does the little dance in *Monster Zero* (1965)—I suggested that.

Left to right: Ryo Ikebe, Kyoko Anzai, Nadao Kirino (looking up) and Koreya Senda flank the alien-possessed Yoshio Tsuchiya (seated) in "Battle in Outer Space" (1959). The actor between Anzai and Kirino appears to be Noboru Tsuburaya, son of effects master Eiji

----

1. Indeed, on-set photographs of Honda often show him "acting out" roles for his actors. His "performances" in these pictures uncannily match those in the finished films.

Tatsuo Matsumura I think he should have been making stuff like Ozu's work. He wanted to shoot about ordinary life in Japan. He never said he wanted to shoot film that way, but when Kurosawa invited me to dinner, Honda happened to be there. The three of us had dinner together and Honda talked about seeing an ordinary, daily life movie, and he talked about the end of the picture, when there was a quiet, ordinary street scene. He spoke very thoughtfully and elegantly about it, and it made a strong impression on me. I thought he should shoot a film about ordinary life in Japan.

PORKY & BLACKIE

Kimi Honda [Honda and Kurosawa] had shared 50 years together, and had become old gentlemen together. The joy of working together was everything. Some people have suggested they were brothers even before they were born. It was a very special relationship and very difficult to explain in words. Their feelings just came together; they respected each other's attributes and failings. They were on different tracks, but bound very deeply. They respected each other.

Mie Hama Mr. Honda was a really great director, totally different character from Kurosawa. Kurosawa is very active. Mr. Honda was very quiet and gentle. I really liked his way of directing film—very quiet direction.

Michio Yamamoto I wasn't afraid of Mr. Kurosawa; he was in his own world, rather than hard on his staff. In the middle of shooting *Throne of Blood* (1957), I was asked to prepare lunch for Kurosawa and I had a

chance to listen to him and learn about him as a human being. I came to know what film is. Then I came to work for Honda and learned how easy it is being in the film industry! Much different!

Yosuke Natsuki Mr. Honda was very gentle. I worked on several of his films, but I never saw him get angry. Mr. Kurosawa was a gentleman like Mr. Honda, but he had an atmosphere in which no one wanted to go near him. He was very kind, but once he was working, he'd sell his soul to the devil for a good shot. The stage [of *Yojimbo*] was filled with tension. No one talked about anything except the work at hand. It was very quiet. He was called *Tenno* ("Emperor") Kurosawa . What he did and said was always right. The word "compromise" didn't exist in his dictionary.

Kimi Honda Their way of expressing their great passion–film–is totally different. Kurosawa is like *ogatanakura* [mostly shouting]. Director Honda is like *toga* [elegant and urbane]–very patient.

Momoko Kochi Akira Kurosawa, [fellow Toho director] Senkichi Taniguchi and Ishiro Honda were very close. The three of them were all really tall and handsome. Honda was the most gentle of the three. Trustworthy. He was a wonderful director.

Yoshio Tsuchiya After *Seven Samurai* (1954) was completed, I was often not around during the shooting of the subsequent films Mr. Kurosawa was making. He was very anxious about how I was doing—I was out mountain climbing, escaping from the studio! But Mr. Kurosawa was worried, and invited me to his home and let me stay there about two years. During that

Akira Kurosawa on the set of "Kagemusha" (1980)

time, one director frequently came to Mr. Kurosawa's home. He was a very nice gentleman and a very close friend of Mr. Kurosawa going back to their days as assistant directors under Kajiro Yamamoto. Mr. Kurosawa was the first chief assistant director and this gentleman was the 2nd chief assistant director. That was Ishiro Honda and my first introduction to him. Mr. Kurosawa wouldn't allow me to appear in the films of second-rate directors or screenwriters, but he said that if Honda was making it, then it must be a good movie and allowed me to appear in those films.

Honda's friendship with Japan's greatest filmmaker ended only with Honda's death in 1993. The directors' affectionate nicknames for one other were the Japanese equivalents of Porky and Blacky.

Akira Kurosawa Porky is "Ino-san." The first Kanji character of his name means "Inoshishi" ["wild boar"]. "Kuro" of Kurosawa means black, so I was called" "Kuro-san." We used to board together in the heyday of movies, and worked very hard every night. His honesty and sincerity never changed. There was not enough wood for the open sets at that time. He always drew the grain of wood, so he was called the "protector of the grain of wood." He worked hard even with minor, trivial things. He was concerned with people's feelings, so he took care of all of the actors and crews. He calmly solved all problems. He was very quiet, and he always smiled. As a director, he was very patient, tolerant, and a hard worker. He never argued with the executives of the film companies, but I always have trouble with them. Sometimes it was hard for me to understand him—he had his own way of thinking.

Besides environmental/nuclear concerns, what themes run through Honda's best films?

Akira Kurosawa His war experience was hard, yet he had a warm heart for mankind. His mind was full of hope that no one would have as sad a war experience as his. His movies are full of his sincere humanity and his tender personality–films like *Godzilla*. I like it very much. His films have remained popular because they were shot honestly and sincerely–they're naturally good.

Honda is credited as "directorial advisor," or "associate director" on your recent films. What exactly did he do?

Akira Kurosawa He advised me about the special effects scenes, and shot the supplementary sequences as director of "B Group." He made an effort to communicate with the crews and teach acting. I was able to concentrate on other things without anxiety thanks to his good work. Ino-san helped me a lot for the special effects scenes in *Dreams*. I learned a lot from him and his movies. He was my mental support.

Kimi Honda They discussed what his title should be, but Honda said that there should be only one director, and so he chose Associate Director. "I don't need the title," he said. Everybody wondered why he was called that, journalists from all over the world asked him, but he said he couldn't explain why–it just was. But his modesty was never false; he hated that. He was never pretentious or competitive.

Yu Fujiki Kurosawa had a really great interest in shooting Godzilla type of movies. Kurosawa always made very expensive films, so if Toho had let him make a Godzilla movie, can you imagine what the budget would've been? So they wouldn't let him touch it, and tried to make sure he didn't have the opportunity to even talk about it!

Akira Kurosawa We were best friends for 50 years, yet we never argued. And that was because he was so very patient with me, not because I was so great. Both of us love movies. I have unlimited memories of him, the period when we were assistant directors, when we lived together, when he went off to war, when we worked together every day, and the five movies from *Kagemusha* (1980) to *Madadayo* (1993). I can't finish it. I'll be sad if I try to remember more.

Dubbing

Ishiro Honda I felt that if *Godzilla* was going to be shown overseas, then the American version was probably better, since it was so easy to understand.

Momoko Kochi We didn't have a lot of experience with dubbing at that time, so my impression was mostly surprise at how good the dubbing [of *Godzilla, King of the Monsters!*] was.

William Ross There is a bias against dubbing. In Japan, when they dub an English picture into Japanese, if it's a John Wayne picture they'll use an actor whose voice is close to his resonance, because everybody knows what John Wayne sounds like. But you tell me one Japanese actor whose voice is familiar internationally. The closest you could come is Ken

Takakura. If the dubbing is badly acted, that's a legitimate complaint, but that's not always the case. The fact is, it is a very difficult task because it's impossible to please the critics. There's a stigma attached to it. I was in Cannes once, and I was introduced to this producer as "somebody who does English dubbing in Japan." He said, "yeah, I've seen some of that shit." I asked him what he had seen, and he named a picture I'd never heard of. I said, "that wasn't my work," and he said, "yeah, sure." I got blamed for someone else's junk. There is very little English dubbing of Japanese films being done at present here in Japan. I have heard that some films are dubbed in Hong Kong because it's cheaper down there, but no sensible distributor would send their film there for dubbing. They go out into the street and pick up people. British, American, English speaking Europeans, and so on. A real mishmash of dialects. I am the only one doing English dubbing for the major Japanese film companies and at present, business is very slow.

Henry G. Saperstein I had to buy this Japanese James Bond film [*Kokusei himitsu keisatsu: kagi no kagi/International Secret Police: Key of Keys*] to preserve my relationship with Toho. They showed it to me in Tokyo and when it was over asked me what I thought. I said, "I thought we had agreed you weren't going to make any western world films without talking to me about it." "Well, we thought with James Bond being so big, we'd make one." "You've got a problem," I told them. "This is a very good production, but everyone's Japanese. Where is it going to play?" And then I made the all-time mistake, I said to myself I don't want to buy this but I can't turn them down—I'd lose face. I'll name a figure so ridiculously low that they can't take it, but at least by doing so I showed a willingness. I named this low figure—and they said, "Deal." So I get on a plane that night and fly back to Los Angeles. I'm sitting there thinking nobody in the theaters is going to like it. In fact, they're going to laugh at it. Wait a minute. What do you do when people are going to laugh at you? You beat 'em to the punch. You do a spoof!

Mie Hama I'm surprised the Japanese producers let them do it!

Henry G. Saperstein At first I wanted Lenny Bruce, but he objected when I insisted on an approval from the Catholic Legion of Decency. "I don't write hand-cuffed," he said. My major mistake was that I didn't put on a big reel of tape and let it run from the time Woody [Allen] and I walked into the studio until we walked out. Woody would look at the picture [now called *What's Up, Tiger Lily?*] and say, "He's going through a door! Gimme door jokes!" And then they would fire machine gun-style jokes, and you had 30 or 40 door jokes. The character onscreen would sit down, and Woody would say, "Gimme sit down jokes!" and there would be lots of sit-down jokes.

Rhodes Reason [*King Kong Escapes*] was redubbed when we got back, at Glen Glenn Sound. Since all of the Japanese parts had to redubbed in English, they had Paul Frees do all of the males voices, except mine, of course. And Julie Bennett did all of the female

voices, including Linda Miller, even though she spoke English. Her voice was rather squeaky and nondescript and, of course, Julie Bennett was almost cartoonish in her approach to the voice, so you go from one extreme to the other. I was there every day doing all the dubbing which was kinda fun because all I was doing was looping to my own voice. [Paul Frees' voices] all sound somewhat alike because he has the same rhythm. He used to live in San Francisco, and he used to phone in everything. He got the point where they were able to do everything telephonically. He's what you would call the failed actor, but he had a voice that'd work. As a visual actor, he was

terrible, but as a vocal actor he had a great feel for the sound of voices. He said, "I don't even know why you're here, I can do your voice. I can probably do you better than you can do you." [*laughs*] It took about four or five days.

THE FATE OF THE WORLD HANGS IN THE BALANCE AS KING KONG FIGHTS THE KING KONG ROBOT!

...Two King Kongs fight to the death!

ALL NEW!

KING KONG ESCAPES!

A TOHO CO., LTD. PICTURE in TECHNICOLOR*

STARRING RHODES REASON · LINDA MILLER · MIE HAMA · AKIRA TAKARADA
Screenplay by WILLIAM J. KEENAN · Producer/Director ARTHUR RANKIN, JR A UNIVERSAL RELEASE

William Ross In 1959, I was contracted by So Yamamura, a well-known Japanese actor, and asked if I would use my voice in dubbing a Japanese film into English. When I came to the sound studio, Aoi Sound Studio, there was a Japanese film director in the sound booth whom I knew from doing bit parts in films. As I was the only foreigner he knew, he asked me to sit with him in the booth. He would tell me the directions for the voice actors and I would translate and tell the actors. I soon found out that he had assigned parts by looking at the facial features of the foreigners, many of whom couldn't act their way out of a wet paper bag. He told me to do what I thought was best. I then proceeded to run an audition and choose voices for the major roles, the bit parts and the odd voices of extras and crowds. I was taking a big chance, as I had not seen the film, which was a pirate epic that had been sold to a Philippine distribution company and So Yamamura's office had contracted to dub it into English. We got through the first day of dubbing and when I came to the studio the next day, So Yamamura was there to tell me that the Japanese director had quit, claiming he just could not handle the job, which required so much English. Yamamura told me that I was now the director. The voice actors had already accepted me as the director, so we finished the film without any problems. That was how I became involved in dubbing films. Bingo! I was an instant director.

TOMOYUKI TANAKA

THE ONLY MAN WHOSE NAME APPEARS ON ALL 22 JAPANESE-MADE GODZILLA MOVIES, PRODUCER TOMOYUKI TANAKA REMAINS SOMETHING OF AN ENIGMA. WHILE THE CONTRIBUTIONS OF ISHIRO HONDA, EIJI TSUBURAYA, AND AKIRA IFUKUBE ARE OBVIOUS, TANAKA'S CREATIVE ROLE IN THE SERIES—AND IN VIRTUALLY ALL OF THE STUDIO'S FANTASY FILMS—REMAINS AMBIGUOUS. WHO WAS THIS MAN WHO INSISTED GIANT MONSTERS BE ADDED TO SOME FILMS THAT DIDN'T NECESSARILY WARRANT THEM (*THE MYSTERIANS*, *GORATH*), AND WHO GRADUALLY CHANGED GODZILLA'S IMAGE FROM CITY-SMASHING MONSTER TO SAVIOR OF THE EARTH?

Kimi Honda Everybody says things about him, but I think he and Mr. Honda got along pretty well. As the producer, he had to talk with the director on matters such as cutting the budget; even so, they didn't quarrel, and Tanaka thought very highly of Honda. He respected him.

Jun Fukuda Godzilla is a kid, the son of producer Tanaka. I'd say he's responsible for 80-90% of his changes.

Henry G. Saperstein He should be considered a legend in his time.

Kihachi Okamoto My debut film as a director was actually produced by [Sanezumi] Fujimoto, but the first person to take note of my scripts when I was an assistant director was Tanaka, long before I was a director. At Toho Fujimoto always did the subtler, drama films while Tanaka did most of the action movies. Those were their favorite genres and that's how they were divided.

Yuriko Hoshi At the time, the men's films were all done by Tanaka-san: action films, monster movies. Fujimoto-san was able to handle love stories and women's films. Tanaka was really good at hard-boiled kind of things; Fujimoto didn't like that kind of stuff.

Shue Matsubayashi Tanaka adored the Navy. No Army films, just Navy films. I think they are his favorite.

Kihachi Okamoto [Our relationship] was just like the cartoon "Tom and Jerry." He produced most of my movies, but he was also my harshest critic. For instance with *The Age of Assassins* (1967), he made the decision not to release the film, and put it in a warehouse. It was controversial and its release was held up for about eight months. [Tanaka] and everyone at the studio said it was ten years ahead of its time. I think he was influenced by the other producer, Fujimoto. Fujimoto regarded my films as "curve ball" pictures. Every time I make a picture I think I'm throwing a straight ball but I have this natural curve to it—the ball doesn't end up in the catcher's mitt. I think Tanaka was influenced by Fujimoto's views in the case of *The Age of Assassins*.

Teruyoshi Nakano Mr. Tanaka was hospitalized while we were filming *Godzilla vs. The Smog Monster*. He was much older and more restrained than Mr. Banno and I, so we were kind of happy to be able to make the movie freely. We decided to go for it. But after he returned from the hospital, Mr. Tanaka saw the movie

and he wasn't pleased. He told Mr. Banno, "you ruined the Godzilla series!" It was Mr. Banno's first and last movie as a director.

Teruo Ishii & Starman, Japan's Man of Steel

FROM THE STARTING GATE, TOHO STUDIOS DOMINATED THE FANTASY GENRE, BUT THAT DID NOT MEAN THE OTHER MAJORS WERE SITTING IDLE. IN 1956 DAIEI PRODUCED *MYSTERIOUS SATELLITE OVER TOKYO* (TELEVISION TITLE: *WARNING FROM SPACE*), JAPAN'S FIRST COLOR FANTASY FILM, WITH A SCREENPLAY BY HIDEO OGUNI (1904–1996) WHO CO-WROTE NOTHING LESS THAN KUROSAWA'S *IKIRU* (1952) AND *SEVEN SAMURAI* (1954). RIVAL SHINTOHO GOT INTO THE ACT THE FOLLOWING YEAR WITH A SERIES OF LOOPY FILMS KNOWN COLLECTIVELY IN THE U.S. AS "STARMAN," MOVIES THAT HELPED KICK OFF THE SUPERHERO GENRE IN JAPAN. ECCENTRIC, LOOKING LIKE AN ELDERLY, JAPANESE BEATLE WHOSE MANNERISMS SUGGEST SIR JOHN GIELGUD, TERUO ISHII TODAY IS ONE OF JAPAN'S TOP ACTION/THRILLER DIRECTORS. HE FREQUENTLY WORKS WITH KEN TAKAKURA, THE CLINT EASTWOOD OF JAPAN.[1] IT'S THEREFORE HARD TO IMAGINE THIS FAMOUS AUTEUR STARTED HIS CAREER WITH THOSE WONDERFULLY DIPPY, FURIOUSLY PACED AND FREQUENTLY CHARMING FILMS STARRING

1. Takakura, whose "Lark Cigarettes" billboards were all over Tokyo at the time of the interview, is one of the few Japanese film stars to appear in American movies. He starred opposite Robert Mitchum in the excellent *The Yakuza* (1975), and Michael Douglas in Ridley Scott's *Black Rain* (1989).

Teruo Ishii It was 37 years ago, so my memory is a little hazy.

Your films have a cult following in the United States.

Teruo Ishii I didn't know that. In fact, I wasn't even aware Americans even had an opportunity to see them. I joined Shintoho as part of the "Flag of Ten" strikes at Toho Studios. It began as a strike at Toho itself. It was during the period of Communism in Tokyo; some people broke away from the studio, and formed their own company. Then I joined Shintoho. We were all wandering around, wondering where we should go, and wound up on the second floor of a Chinese restaurant, at someone's house, and so forth. There was one really shabby technical institute that was owned by Toho, and we settled in there. At first, [Shintoho's] films were mainly entertainment pictures shot in a really short time—only ten days—and because the films were made in such a hurry, we were able to use the really big stars like Kazuo Hasegawa. [Producer] Kunio Watanabe was the anti-Communist leader of Shintoho. I was an assistant director on his first film at Shintoho—shot in ten days—and it was a really big hit. Gradually, the studio became more and more ambitious and began making bigger and more serious productions.

How did the Starman films come about?

Teruo Ishii

Teruo Ishii The producer was of my generation, and he was also a screenwriter. Suddenly, he stopped by and showed me the Starman story. I thought, "That's a kind of weird story, but it sounds interesting." Then I said, "Sure, why not?" There was no plan for a series. But, by chance, the first one was really successful, then one after another. Mind you, I wanted to make better quality ones! [*laughs*] I wanted to do a favor for my producer/screenwriter friend. We worked very, very quickly. After the second film of the series we spent maybe 25 days for each film, though some of the more elaborate ones were done over two months. Shintoho treated its new directors pretty well, even with the low budgets. Sometimes the art and set directors would sneak off to the backlot and on their own time work on the sets without letting the company know, in order to make them better and more elaborate. What they did was strip portions of the backlot and reuse the wood and whatever to build the Starman sets, and would then put it back when we were done! That's why they were so popular, and why the directors wanted to use them. It's something that could have been dreamed up by a kid. There was suspense, and they had the flavor of Rampo Edogawa's novels. Kids could enjoy that. [Ken Utsui]'s relatively active on television, and now he's really ashamed of having worn that suit! [*laughs*] He doesn't like to talk about it. I guess it's a quite a comedown for an actor. He flies in the sky, right? He was hanging by piano wires all day long; it was really difficult for him. To be honest, I had no concept of a man flying at all until I began making the films.

Did you ever have the opportunity to see the films with an audience?

Teruo Ishii I saw each one in Shinjuku, in Ginza, in Akasaka—in many different locations, and I saw a wide variety of audiences and audience reaction. It seems like they enjoyed it. After four films, I quit suddenly because a kid tried to imitate Ken Utsui. He made a cape out of a sheet, and jumped out of an apartment building. He was seriously injured, and that really scared me, and I lost my passion for it.

The Hardest-Working Men in Show Business

Rhodes Reason Of course, the Japanese actor who is most revered, with regard to [Japanese monster] movies, is the guy who jumps in the little suit with the zipper up the back and goes through all the antics. [Haruo Nakajima] came up to about my shoulder, which was kinda cute. But everyone revered him because [in *King Kong Escapes*] he was King Kong inside the suit.

Teruyoshi Nakano Mr. Nakajima was a very diligent man. He was always going to the zoo and studying the movement of the animals, thinking about how he was going to portray Godzilla in the next film. When we were shooting, Mr. Nakajima and I would get together and plan Godzilla's movements, but sometimes he would just demonstrate a movement, and we'd go with it. Inside the Godzilla suit, it was very dark, lonely and isolated. Usually the person who wears the suit becomes nervous and anxious. During summertime it's very hot, it can become hell in there. But Mr. Nakajima always persevered. He acted in the suit underwater, he was buried underground, he withstood

pyrotechnic explosions ... and through it all he was always Godzilla.

Noriaki Yuasa We tried to make Gamera stand up less on two legs, and more on all fours like an animal. It was much easier to shoot when Gamera he was crawling, but we did it on purpose. My principal is we'd never have made such a big hit if we had imitated something else.

Minoru Nakano [Nakajima]'s very active in his roles, even though he cannot expose his own face. He's very aggressive and ambitious. When he was playing Godzilla, he went to the zoo to study the movements of the animals. He's very proud of his work. The costume of the larva *Mothra* (1961) was 12 meters long, and he was in the head, and behind him were students from the university!

Noriaki Yuasa There were many who played Gamera. For the first one, the New Face actors played him, but

A sequence probably inspired by "The Beast from 20,000 Fathoms," from "Gammera the Invincible" (1965)

there was a limit physically, so strong young crew members supported them. From the second Gamera on, we had enough of a budget to pay someone specifically to play that role. At the time on TV there were people who regularly played monsters, and many

Above and opposite: the Shue Matsubayashi-Eiji Tsuburaya war epic "I Bombed Pearl Harbor" (1960)

of them became stars. We couldn't afford a star monster actor. We always had three different people.

Robert Dunham In *The Green Slime* it was mostly kids! The little babies were all school children and the big ones were adults. There was no mechanical stuff; there were just people in suits. As I recall, they weren't controlled by wires, it was done from inside. There was one scene, where we shoot this one as he's coming

down the ramp and [co-stars Robert] Horton, [Richard] Jaeckel and I are trying to get the net over him and then shoot him with a ray gun; this was one of the little ones, and there weren't any wires or anything like that. They were kinda funny. There were only one or two scenes where they looked a little spooky. When they caught the doctor in the hallway and burned him—that was a little gross. But my first impression of them was that they looked pretty ridiculous and not threatening at all.

Noriaki Yuasa When we were making *War of the Monsters* (1966), we weren't able to ask Mr. [Masao] Yagi to do the suits, so we asked [Ryusaku] Takayama. Mr. Yagi produced 80% of the monsters, including Godzilla and Gamera in Japan. I'm sure Mr. Masao Yagi, who was the president of the *kaiju* suit company X Productions, introduced Mr. Takayama to Daiei. Takayama's suits were the best, because he understood what we wanted. They was very easy to move about but, if I have to find fault with his work, it was that they were also very fragile and easily broken. It's natural they would break during shooting, but they were more fragile than the others that I remember.

Eiji Tsuburaya at War

THOUGH OBSCURE IN THE UNITED STATES, EIJI TSUBURAYA WAS NEARLY AS REVERED IN JAPAN FOR HIS SPECIAL EFFECTS-LADEN WAR MOVIES, WHICH WERE DONE ON A SCALE EVEN BIGGER THAN HIS *KAIJU EIGA*, AND CRAMMED WITH ALL-STAR CASTS. AND JUST AS TSUBURAYA WORKED HAND-IN-HAND WITH ISHIRO HONDA ON THE MONSTER PICS, THE EFFECTS DIRECTOR

WAS REGULARLY PAIRED WITH SHUE MATSUBAYASHI FOR A SERIES OF HIGHLY PROFITABLE WAR FILMS, INCLUDING *I BOMBED PEARL HARBOR* (AKA *STORM OVER THE PACIFIC,* 1960), WHICH WAS FINALLY RELEASED TO HOME VIDEO IN THE U.S. IN 1997.

Shue Matsubayashi [Eiji Tsuburaya]'s number one. After the Japanese defeat at the end of the war, our country did not have any aircraft—no warships, nothing—it was all at the bottom of the ocean. Everything was done with miniatures, and yet it doesn't look like miniatures in the film. Mr. Tsuburaya often told me that he most enjoyed his work in *I Bombed Pearl Harbor* and *The Last War* even over his Godzilla movies.

Teruyoshi Nakano My first real encounter with special effects was during the making of [Matsubayashi's] *Submarine E-57 Never Surrenders!* (1959). This was a black and white movie, but the special effects sequences were shot on color film, using the blue-screen traveling matte process. I was fascinated by this and wanted to find out how it worked. That's one of the reasons I got into special effects.

Shue Matsubayashi [The navy veterans] were very pleased [with the miniatures]. It was an important time in their lives. Especially those who had been on the *Yamato*; it was made ⅙th scale and an exact replica. All of the veterans came to see the miniature. It was filmed in the large special effects pool, and was something like 15 meters long. The aircraft were about one meter and very realistic also. My navy films were very popular but by the time I made *Attack Squadron!* (1963) I was concerned that the battle scenes were beginning to dominate the human story. I had been a part of that war, and for me to make money on films which showed only the action made me question what I was doing. I felt guilty about it. Was I making a trivial piece of entertainment out of such a serious and deadly part of history? And so, popular as they were, I walked away, rejecting all offers to do more.

Kihachi Okamoto For my war movies, art vs. entertainment is really all about theme. Depending on the theme of the picture, it could be either art or entertainment, so my preference is to break it down.

Teruyoshi Nakano I would say [Tsuburaya] probably preferred war movies. Myself, I have made a lot of movies including horror, disaster movies, war movies and *kaiju eiga*, but I prefer war movies over the other genres. I wanted to send a silent message through my war movies. At the end of *Imperial Navy* (1981), the *Yamato* battleship sank and exploded.[1] [*At this point, Nakano grabs a paper napkin and sketches an exploding battleship, with a huge fire rising from it in the shape of a flower.*] When the *Yamato* exploded, I wanted it to resemble a rose opening up. To express this, I layered six composite shots, one on top of the other, then I added the zero fighters flying around. The image of the planes was inspired by traditional Japanese black and white drawings which are sketched with a brush, called *fude.* I wanted to express the sadness of the *Yamato* sinking, and I wanted to give a rose to all the loved ones of the men who died. When there is victory in war, the victors celebrate, but I wanted to express the sadness of defeat, the mourning. Recently, many Americans have become interested in the Japanese art of Zen. I think those people would appreciate what I tried to express in that scene.

Shue Matsubayashi I am the only Imperial Navy officer to have become a director. Many of my colleagues died during the war; as a movie director, I wanted my five films to serve as a memorial to my comrades. All of them. They are all reflected in my work.

----

1. The *Yamato*, which saw action in the Battle of Midway, was sunk by allied planes in April 1945.

Monster Music

Masaru Sato [My fantasy film scores] were just for fun. They're not realistic; I enjoyed playing with the sound. Mr. Ifukube is the pioneer in that field. My work would have been meaningless if I had not tried to do something very different from him. I think in general the studio felt my tastes were ill-suited to fantasy films. Jun Fukuda asked me to write music for him which is how I became involved in most of those. I scored Honda's fantasy film *The H-Man* (1958). Somehow it was popular in the States, although it's not that great.

Akira Ifukube Mr. Honda was the best [director to work with]. Directors who we consider to be "masters" almost never claim to know music.

Masaru Sato I really just want a good director; he'll help inspire me and my work.

Kihachi Okamoto [Masaru Sato] is my favorite composer because he and I always agree about the placement of music–we always think exactly the same way. We don't even really have to talk about it–he instinctively knows how to write music for an Okamoto movie. My own direction to the composer doesn't involve creating the melody or anything, but I'll specify which instruments I want to hear; that's how I'll limit the composer's freedom. But with Sato we're always in agreement: when I say "guitar," Sato says "guitar," and so on.

Jun Fukuda Usually composers just write music with indifference toward the film itself. Not Masaru Sato. He knows how important music is to a film. He prefers working with the director, rather than just himself. Whatever the film, he tries to understand the directors intentions–that's why I liked working with him.

Akira Ifukube Kurosawa is a very great director, but unfortunately the script for the one I did [for *The Quiet Duel*, 1950] was not good—very illogical. However great Kurosawa may be the outcome of the affair was obvious. The story is about a doctor's [Toshiro Mifune] suspicion that he was contaminated with syphilis. He knew that there was a very quick and clear way to determine contamination—any doctor would have known that! But as a film director, I think Kurosawa is very great.

Masaru Sato To me the timing of the music is much more important that the content. That's the most important thing. Then the tone and the manner of the music come next. It depends on the director. Sometimes the director will point out if a film is being under- or over-scored and this is very helpful.

Akira Ifukube The equipment isn't as important as the sound of the studio space itself and the ear of the recording engineer–and the performance of the players, of course. Nowadays, recording is getting very sophisticated, yet there is a kind of de-evolution. Back in the 50s, I could adjust every instrument but now, with digital equipment, it has become much more difficult. Toho had the biggest recording stage, even though it is about half the size it was back in the 60s; however, much of the room has been taken up by equipment.

Akira Ifukube

Masaru Sato

Masaru Sato [Before *Yojimbo*,] *chambara* films had a very particular style of music. It was total nonsense to my ears–it had no sense of universality. Mr. Kurosawa said, "Write whatever you'd like, but please don't write *chambara* music!" So I started from scratch, with elements from Westerns, traditional Japanese instruments–I tried to reflect the barbarism of the period. Since then, *chambara* music has changed quite a bit. He didn't give me any direct advice. He would say, vaguely, "Could you please try something a little bit different?" He wanted to do a lot of improvisation, not realizing that with an orchestra that was very difficult, that someone has to write the notes! In that sense, he is the only demanding director in Japan.

Noriaki Yuasa Gamera was born on the 10th anniversary of the first Godzilla, and we swore we'd never imitate him— we had respect for Godzilla.

Gamera—
The Children's Monster

Noriaki Yuasa The president of Daiei, Masaichi Nagata—he was the producer of *Rashomon* (1950)—was flying home to Japan and saw the crowds on the small islands from his plane, and he imagined a turtle flying through the sky, and he proposed the idea.[1]

Eiji Funakoshi Nagata did all of Daiei's big budget movies; they were all under him. He was the studio

chief, and later he was a board member of Daiei. He introduced Japanese films to people all over the world. One of the great producers in the history of the Japanese film industry, but as a manager, well, maybe he should have done something else. [laughs]

Noriaki Yuasa [Screenwriter Nisan] Takahashi wrote a story called "Higuigame Tokyo o osou" ["Fire-breathing Turtle Attacks Tokyo"] which became *Daikaiju Gamera* ["Giant Monster Gamera"]. I don't know why Daiei let a young director like me make such a risky special effects movie. But I guess now older and bigger directors must have turned it down because it would have been too much work and not enough money. But thanks to that a big chance came my way. At that time, following Toho's *Godzilla*, every film company tried to compete with its special effects, but only our studio—Daiei—continued to make one film a year for seven years.

Eiji Funakoshi [Yuasa was a] really round guy! Cuddly. He was the son of the actor Hikaru Hoshi, who was an actor at Shochiku, then he moved to Nikkatsu and Daiei. Yuasa, therefore, came to Daiei with the support of his famous father. They spoke ill of Yuasa at the time. His father's name is Hoshi; *hoshi* means "star" and *hikari* means "shining" and we used to say Yuasa was beneath his father's shining star.

Noriaki Yuasa Daiei had made several science fiction movies, but the only *kaiju eiga* Daiei planned prior to Gamera was "Daigunju nezura" ("Swarm of Rats"),

Eiji Funakoshi

1. *Godzilla* was similarly conceived en route to Tokyo. Are all Japanese monsters conceived on flights to Japan?!

which had a large number of rats attacking Tokyo. It was never made. That's why Daiei was so worried about *Gamera*, and why the budget was so small. It went over budget a little bit, but they didn't blame me because the picture turned out to be a bigger hit than we had expected.

"It was giriminjo." Eiji Funakoshi fleeing from "Gammera the Invincible" (1965)

Eiji Funakoshi It was *giriminjo*. It means a kind of personal relationship, a duty to producer Masaichi Nagata and his son, Hidemasa. *Gamera* was really Hidemasa's first film as a producer. The president, Nagata, asked me, "Could you please help my son?" That's why I agreed to star in the film. And then it became a blockbuster hit. I starred in a couple more after that. Then I did it for laughs.

Noriaki Yuasa Mr. Takahashi seemed to have a secret aim when writing scenes such as when Gamera protected the child in the first movie. And I was the first one to agree with it. After the first film was released, we got a lot of information about the reaction of children to that film. The first and the second ones had children playing on the floor, or buying popcorn out in the lobby during the adult scenes, so from the fourth film we made them like a children's storybook.

Kon Omura I tried to imagine Gamera in my mind while I was acting. This is because my second son, who is now an assistant director in Hollywood, would greet me very excitedly each day as I arrived home asking questions like, "Did you see Gamera today?!" "Did you meet Gamera!?" "How big is he?" I tried very hard for his sake.

Noriaki Yuasa The first [*Gamera*] was a B-movie, but that turned out to be a big hit, so the second one [*War of the Monsters*] was promoted to an A-budget. I think Daiei thought I wouldn't be able to handle such an A-movie. It was the most expensive one; it cost ¥80,000,000 (about $225,000). *Return of the Giant Monsters* was about ¥60,000,000 ($167,000), the black and white *Gamera* was about ¥40,000,000 ($111,000). *Destroy All Planets* and *Attack of the Monsters* were about ¥24,000,000 ($67,000), and *Monster X* and *Zigra* about ¥35,000,000 ($97,000). Every company had a different way to prepare the budget, so I can't compare ours to the other studios but, in any case, the salaries and stage management, the advertising, and the developing fees weren't factored into the budget. I was shocked to hear that from the fourth film, *Destroy All Planets*, we had to make do with the budget of an ordinary film. I think that might have been a sign that Daiei was going bankrupt.

Kon Omura Yuasa was very free with his direction. He pretty much let me do whatever I wanted; he gave me a lot of freedom. During production, Mr. Yuasa would teach the child actors how to act not by memorizing their lines, but rather he would let them kind of act it out. He would tell them what was going on, and then he would "be" the monster. He would be Gamera or whatever. The young actors responded very well to that.

Noriaki Yuasa I guess if Daiei hadn't gone bankrupt, [the series] would have kept on going. Those seven years were a great honor for me. Our young and energetic crews got together and were crazy about making those movies.

ACTING WITH MONSTERS

Akira Kubo I had to act like Godzilla was right there in front of me, when, in fact, he wasn't there at all. That kind of thing was fun.

Mie Hama I didn't know what was going on. I was put in the palm of King Kong's hand [in *King Kong vs. Godzilla*, 1962], and in front of the blue screen running away; I had no idea what it was all going to look like. It was very impressive technically, thanks to Mr. Tsuburaya's special effects.

Kenji Sahara I had to be very careful about what I was reacting to in terms of my size compared to the monsters. Also, blue screen matting was in its infancy back then, and I had to be really careful about how I moved. If a giant monster were to suddenly show up, how would we react? Mr. Honda taught me to act and respond to monsters in a very natural, down to earth way.

Yuriko Hoshi At the time, I didn't know what the *kaiju eiga* were like, but I had a strong interest in it. Actually, I didn't have much opportunity to act with Godzilla! I was in front of the blue screen in composite shots. After the shooting, I came to know what it was all about and was impressed.

Barugon, left and not to be confused with Bar-a-gon from "Frankenstein Conquers the World," vs. Gamera in "War of the Monsters" (1966)

Robert Dunham Japanese directors—overacting, over-expressions—this is what the Japanese wanted.

Akira Takarada It's easy to overact, especially in *kaiju eiga*, but you really don't have to do it that much. If you overact too much, the very important balance is going to be lost.

Mie Hama (left) "I didn't know what was going on. I had no idea what it was all going to look like."

Seijun Suzuki All actors are crazy! In life they appear to be like everyone else, but when they play a role on film this craziness comes out through their performance. For instance, if a scene calls for an actor to get angry, he'll go over the top and break furniture, break glass, and basically go nuts! They're all egotistical and crazy! That's why I'm not an actor—I don't have the qualifications!

Robert Horton Japanese people have a tendency to run where ever they go. You know, not trying to break the speed limit but run. And [director] Mr. Fukasaku-san [sic] asked me if an American hero would run, and I said I don't think so, I think he would stride. He would walk positively, but I don't think he would take a little jog ...

Rhodes Reason You can tell from the other actors in [*King Kong Escapes*]; everybody's bigger than life, you know, with the mugging and it gets to the point where it's ridiculous. I had to work to underplay to bring the film some credibility. Even the make-up. I began to notice after a while there was too much mascara; it was almost like Kabuki. I had to work to make sure I didn't look too much like a Geisha girl.

Robert Dunham There were no problems in my scenes because [Honda and I] would talk and he'd ask me, "How would you do this scene performing it as a foreigner?" Of course my dialogue was in Japanese. He knew what he wanted for a particular a scene and was diplomatic about getting it.

Kumi Mizuno I enjoyed making the *kaiju eiga*, but I couldn't have turned it down even if I had wanted to because of my contract with Toho. During shooting, I'd find actors and actresses who didn't want to make *kaiju eiga*, but I was very positive about it and always tried to have fun.

Kihachi Okamoto The bit players were so-called *obeya yakushuya*, which means they're "stand by" actors. They were always hanging out in this big room—*obeya* means "big room." Probably the American equivalent is "bit player." It's above extra. Unlike big actors they didn't have their own make-up room or trailer or anything like that—they were just standing by in this huge room and I liked a couple of them so I always picked the same actors, which is why you always see the same faces from picture to picture.

Robert Horton It was funny. I can't say [making *The Green Slime*] was rewarding, but it began to become funny, because you didn't for a minute believe the monsters and that is the crux of the situation.

ACTORS

Akira Kubo [Toshiro Mifune] is *the* great actor. After World War II Kurosawa said, "Without Mifune, I can't make movies." When Mifune was young, he looked like a wolf! We did six or seven films together. Usually top stars look down upon the lesser-known, younger actors, but not Mifune.

Akira Takarada Toshiro Mifune and I were both from mainland China. I was from Manchuria. People like [Hisaya] Morishige and Mifune and myself could all speak Mandarin and understood each other very deeply. The atmosphere was very good because we could share that aspect of our lives.

Shue Matsubayashi I did two films with Mifune. He

was a really big and great actor. He's got a *samurai* mind at heart.

Akira Takarada I don't discriminate any kind of job. To work as an actor is the same in any film–getting pissed off, being sad, being in love. The *kaiju eiga* were real learning experiences for the actors. Every actor had to devote himself to the role ... it's no different than being a monk.

Shue Matsubayashi I worked with Takarada a lot. Akira Takarada was a really good postwar, modern-day kind of actor. He's really polite and gentlemanly, and a pleasure to work with.

Momoko Kochi [Takarada] was a classmate of mine; we spent six months together in the New Face Program, like brother and sister. He has a really Continental atmosphere about him—very cool.

Rhodes Reason Oh, [Eisei Amamoto] was perfectly cast [as the villain in *King Kong Escapes*], of course, because he looked like a skeleton.

Robert Dunham There was one guy on [*Dagora the Space Monster*] who works all the time. My god, he looked like he just stepped out of a coffin! As far as his facial expression he's perfect for the parts he gets because of this overacting type of thing. Sometimes directors would try to get me into that mode.

Kihachi Okamoto Everybody says Amamoto looks like me, and I don't know if that's the reason, but he's in almost all of my movies. He's really into Spanish culture, and for the Spanish duel in *The Age of*

Seijun Suzuki

Robert Dunham

Assassins he brought his own record and played that scene to it. That's my strongest memory of Mr. Amamoto. His most famous role was in the [superhero] TV series "Kamen Rider," in which he played Dr. Death. Once when I was shooting a movie

"My God, he looked like he just stepped out of a coffin!" Cult actor Eisei Amamoto menaces Mie Hama in "The Lost World of Sinbad" (1963)

with a small, second unit crew a couple of kids approached me and said, "You must be Dr. Death! You must Dr. Death!" "No I'm not," I said. "Go away!" But they didn't believe me, and finally I said, "All right, I am Dr. Death, now go home!" As time goes by, the more experienced actors became more expensive, and some developed an attitude like they were big stars and

some didn't. Once they started developing an attitude, that's when I stopped wanting to use them. At the time, there was always another *obeya* actor standing by who was good and cheap.

Yosuke Natsuki Mr. Tanaka wasn't just a producer of *kaiju* films, and didn't make me become a *kaiju* star. I worked on many *jidai-geki*, comedies, and action films produced by him. Monster movies are just a tiny percentage of all the movies I did. I guess he tried hard to make me a versatile star.

Yoriko Hoshi [Yosuke Natsuki] was very unique among the Toho actors. He was a real practical joker. He commuted back and forth to the studio on a motorcycle, and he used to give me rides.

Robert Dunham [Natsuki] was a neat guy to work with. Of course, we were together a lot in [*Dagora*], although except for a few phrases he didn't speak any English in the film itself, but offscreen he was fair.

Mie Hama Yes, it's true, Akiko Wakabayashi and I switched roles when we made *You Only Live Twice* (1967). I didn't have much confidence with my English at the time. It was a sudden offer. I was asked by Toho to do it, but I didn't think I could handle the role. I studied English for several months, but in the end we switched roles.

Robert Dunham I fell in love with [Wakabayashi]— of course! She was a hot item at the time, and from here she spun off and went into the James Bond picture. Not a really great actress, but she had a great body.

Yuriko Hoshi She became very big in foreign productions.

Yosuke Natsuki Ms. Wakabayashi was so charming she was picked to be a "Bond Girl" of 007's, but I didn't think she was passionate about her work. She was more feminine than Yuriko Hoshi. I still don't understand why she retired so suddenly.

Kumi Mizuno I didn't want to play women who were just beautiful and wholesome. I wanted to play real, strong women who had real problems. I enjoyed playing those kind of roles.

Akira Kubo Mizuno made her debut at Shochiku, but Toho's producers picked her up and we worked together on her first Toho film, *A Bridge for Us Alone*. It was a pure downtown Tokyo love story, about two factory workers. She had been in all the golf magazines, as a model. When she showed up on the first day of shooting, she had makeup on not like a factory worker, but like a model! I worked with her a lot. She got to be really gorgeous. However, once we were on location and, because of the shape of her nose and eyes, she was mistaken for a man in drag! [Offscreen she was] sexy. The actors at Toho were unpretentious—even Mifune only had one assistant. We were all very urban, very sophisticated. At Toei they had a very old system: someone of Mifune's stature would've been a tycoon with numerous assistants. Mizuno was similarly unpretentious.

Jun Fukuda Kumi Mizuno works very hard. She likes to create the characters she plays and make them her own. She likes to have long discussions about who her character is, on how the director views this character. She's talented in the sense that she has a keen understanding of what's expected of her and her character. Before appearing in films she did some theater—she knows what acting is all about.

Yosuke Natsuki I had a great time soon after *Dagora, the Space Monster* working with Yoko Fujiyama for a year on the hit TV series "Seishun towa nanda?" ["What Is Youth?"]. She was beautiful and looked like a traditional Japanese woman, but she was very active and drove a sports car. After she worked with me, she married a businessman who lived in Kobe and retired. I ran into her last November. She's still beautiful and happy. She had a shorter tongue, so she made a lot of NGs [bad takes] when she said long sentences.

Akira Kubo I was really sad when Akihiko Hirata passed away. I was acting in the theater when I heard the news and was so sad. Everybody was so nice at Toho. He was *the* great person at Toho among the actors. He died too young. When we worked together on the stage we hung out a lot together—every night. He's from Tokyo University. He went to the very best prep school, he was among the top elite in Japan. He looks like a square, and serious on screen, but in private he was very laid-back, easy to talk to. He liked chasing women [*laughs*].

Yoshio Tsuchiya He was a man of common sense, unlike me.

Jun Fukuda Very serious. Whatever the role was he researched it intensely. He was one of my favorite actors.

Exotic Akiko Wakabayashi threatened by assassins in "Ghidrah—the Three-Headed Monster" (1964)

Yosuke Natsuki After reading the script [of *Godzilla 1985*] I had no doubts about appearing in the new Godzilla movie. When I read the script it dawned on me that I was now old enough to play the older university professor part. I learned that Mr. Akihiko Hirata had cancer after we started. And I learned that he had been

Yosuke Natsuki (right) with Akihiko Hirata in "Ghidrah—The Three-Headed Monster" (1964)

looking forward to appearing in the film until he was hospitalized. The role would have been perfect for him. I also heard that he left the hospital so that he could see some of the shooting, but I didn't get to see him.

Akira Kubo Yoshio Tsuchiya's one of my best friends. He studies a lot about his roles, researches his characters. He likes to play aliens. [*laughs*]. He's really good at it.

Noriaki Yuasa [Kojiro Hongo] was a big Daiei star, and he did both *jidai-geki* and modern movies. He was one of the rare stars who did both successfully, and I still deeply appreciate him for agreeing to appear in the Gamera movies. If I were to describe him in one word, it would be "sincere."

Momoko Kochi Takashi Shimura played my father [in *Godzilla*]. He was really like a severe papa. His role in *Ikiru* (1952) is a really strong image of him for me.

Yoshio Tsuchiya Mr. Shimura was a very fine actor and just like my uncle. In fact, I always called Mr. Shimura "Uncle," and never called him Mr. Shimura. He was my primary image of an actor. He gave superb performances in *Seven Samurai* and *Ikiru* but, in my opinion his finest work on film was the Daiei production *The Life of a Horse-Trader*. Shimura's character was a type of a good bad guy. Deep down he is a good guy, but on the surface he is a bit of a bad guy—a very twisted characterization, and every time I saw Mr. Shimura I'd say, "Hey, Uncle! Act just like you did in *The Life of a Horse-Trader*!" He loved it every time I mentioned that film.

Jun Fukuda [Bibari Maeda] was not so easy to work with. She was kind of demanding. I think she really didn't understand what I wanted from her as an actress.

Yosuke Natsuki When Yuriko Hoshi was just starting her career we co-starred in many films together. She was an honest and hard worker. She was also stubborn.

Hitoshi Ueki Mie Hama was one of the great actresses to come out of the young generation in the Toho Company. We classify actresses into two basic groups: traditional Japanese and Western style. Hama can do both, which is very unusual. She's very sharp. That's also why she could be a Bond girl. And also a very charming lady. The company kept wanting to put her in comedies, but she didn't want to do to it too much. It was not an easy job to get her to do them, and when she did I showered her with attention. At the time, we had the "Young Guy" series with Yuzo Kayama. It might have been easier to get her to star in the "Young Guy" films instead of working with Hitoshi Ueki—she must have felt a lot of frustration!

Mie Hama When I was 17 I went to Rome and saw Marcello Mastroianni on stage there, and went every day for a week. Then, one day at the theater, a lady asked me if I was a fan of Mastroianni, and I said, "Yes, I am." And she said that it might be possible for me to meet him. The next day, right after the performance, I was introduced to him. At the time I had long hair, I wore jeans and a t-shirt, just like a student. He asked what I did for a living, and I said I was a young film actress in Japan, and I told him I wanted to quit. I said it was kind of boring for me. He said, "Can you see how much I'm sweating? Have you ever tried so hard to please an audience that you worked up a sweat?" That really surprised me, and I became more serious about acting. But even though I became a big star, I rarely had a chance to work up a sweat as an actress. Even though there were great actresses making great films, I was working with Hitoshi Ueki and Godzilla. Still, over time, I came to understand it and have fun with it.

Into the Sixties...

Henry G. Saperstein The Japanese crews were so efficient. We do an eight hour day and if we have three minutes of film [in the can] we've had a very good day. They do an eight hour day, with a half hour lunch, and you've got seven-and-a-half hours of hard time. When the director yells "Strike!" get outta the way 'cause you're gonna get knocked down by people in a hurry to take down the scenery.

Yosuke Natsuki I always went to theaters in Tokyo, Osaka, Kyoto, Nagoya, Hiroshima, Sapporo, and Fukuoka to greet the crowds and hold press conferences when my movies opened. Sometimes I'd even go to Hong Kong and South America. *Kaiju* movies usually opened during the two big holiday seasons, New Year's and during the summer. I remember long lines in front of the theaters.

Yu Fujiki In Japan we can do science fiction films less expensively.

Kumi Mizuno with Toshiro Mifune in "The Lost World of Sinbad" (1963)

Shue Matsubayashi Most films at that time cost ¥200,000,000 (about $400,000). The war movies and *The Last War* (1961) cost five times that.

Robert Dunham Even on [Honda's] monster pictures the budget wasn't too big and so the faster they worked the more money they made.

Henry G. Saperstein [For *Monster Zero*] you're looking at $800,000 to $900,000, but keep in mind that the yen was worth 360 to the dollar then; it's about 92 right now! So the budgets were really closer to $2 million in today's money. When I made the first film there [in 1965], my suite at the Imperial Hotel was $32. Today it's $600!

Teruo Ishii The president [of Shintoho], Mitsugi Okura, owned a movie theater, but it wasn't in a very good location. There was a strike, Toho meanwhile became a major power, and gradually Shintoho lost the battle. I had an offer from Toei, so I went there. Toei was like a dragon! They wanted two-thirds of the film market in Japan, and created a subsidiary, New Toei, for that purpose. But their mainstay was *jidai-geki* [period dramas],

The Peanuts, Emi and Yumi Ito—(or is that Yumi and Emi Ito?) in "Mothra" (1961)

which were shot at the studio in Kyoto. The studio in Tokyo was an addition. The Tokyo studio also had ambitions, wanting to compete with the Kyoto studio as well. Shigeru Okada, who was the director of Kyoto studio, was sent to Tokyo after my 10th film, and became the head of the studio here. I worked mainly in Tokyo. Okada did a really great job, but on the other hand, the Kyoto studios declined as a result, and Okada asked me to work in Kyoto. And so I became a POW in Kyoto for three years! [*laughs*] My first job at Toei was with Ken Takakura. At the time he wasn't a big-name star, but I thought he was a really nice guy. The film was a big hit, and we turned it into into a mobster series. He's very talented, and the type who hangs around the set even when he's not working— that's why everyone came to love him.

Ryuzo Nakanishi All of [Nikkatsu's] top talent were also pop stars, so for a time we were the most financially successful studio—we could tie the music and the films together, you see? All of the other studios tried to copy that, but none were really as successful as we were. Yujiro Ishihara, Akira Kobayashi ... they were all from Nikkatsu. Sometimes I couldn't even get into the door at a Nikkatsu theater. But as a business, Nikkatsu was not very well run.

Gan Yamazaki Toho was melodramas and monster movies and salaryman comedies. Shochiku was melodramas and love stories. Nikkatsu was an action film company.

Robert Dunham I think it was The Peanuts that carried [*Mothra*, 1961]. I don't know whether they wrote the script around the Peanuts or what. Twins in

Japan are very rare, and especially twins like them, with talent, so they were really a top commodity.

Shue Matsubayashi America and the Soviet Union were in the midst of the Cold War. The world was terrified about the possibility of World War III. It was a very dangerous time, and very tense at military bases. What would happen if a war was triggered accidentally? In *The Last War* (1961), we showed the world end: The White House, Red Square, all of the capitols of the world [are blown up]. Because of the scale, Eiji Tsuburaya built all of the buildings out of cake. When the bombs hit Tokyo, every living thing dies, and anything that has any shape changes and becomes something else. This is a kind of Japanese philosophy which we have inherited throughout our history—that everything changes and does not last forever. I wanted to say that.

Akira Takarada It reflected quite effectively the social issues of that time. It was also quite a good movie, too.

Yuriko Hoshi It was very frightening, the possibility of a worldwide holocaust. I was a young lover in the film, but the young lovers had to die. I also had a good family and they had to die, too. A very sad movie.

Yu Fujiki Tadao Takashima and I did B-salarymen movies. They were originally supposed to be smaller companions to these films—released separately, but of the same type. The theaters paid less for these films and the attendance was almost the same, so naturally the theaters began wanting to buy our movies instead. After probably ten of these films, the great producer Masumi [Sanezumi] Fujimoto said, "You're too young to be competing with great actors like Hisaya Morishige!" He said, "Why don't you make one last film with Takashima, then end your collaboration?" Well, it turned out to be *King Kong vs. Godzilla* (1962)!

Ishiro Honda I honestly can't recall the reason why we waited seven years [to do another Godzilla sequel]—production problems, conflicting schedules, I guess. As for changing Godzilla, that was due to a huge fall ... oops, maybe I shouldn't phrase it that way, since my critics might want some ammunition to use against me. But I suppose there's no other way to say it: there was a huge fall in the average age of Godzilla fans, so Toho decided it would be a good idea to make him more heroic and less scary. I didn't like the idea, but I couldn't really oppose it. We didn't have many rights then. Once you made a film, it became company property.

Yu Fujiki No one expected it to be that big of a hit. When I went to New York for my honeymoon, I had the opportunity to see *King Kong vs. Godzilla* on a marquee, and realized how popular Godzilla was in the States. RKO had the rights, and Toho leased the rights to the character, with

Tadao Takashima and Yu Fujiki in "King Kong vs. Godzilla" (1962)

怪獣 東京大攻撃

a guarantee of ¥80,000,000 [about $200,000]. At that time Takashima and I were only making about ¥500,000 per picture [about $1,300]. King Kong was a really expensive actor! We planned to shoot the film on location in Sri Lanka, but because of RKO 's guarantee, we couldn't afford to let Kong leave Japan! It was decided to shoot the island scenes on Oshima, an island just outside of Tokyo. King Kong took all the money!

Minoru Nakano In *King Kong vs. Godzilla,* I did stop motion animation during the sequence with the octopus when it grabs several natives. I also did a very brief stop motion shot of Godzilla's flying kick of King Kong. Around this same period Ray Harryhausen's films were being released in Japan, using the Dynamation technique, which was partly why we tried a little of this sort of thing in *King Kong vs. Godzilla*.

Teruyoshi Nakano I was a snobby movie buff back then, so when I read the script I wasn't impressed with it. The first *Godzilla* had such a social impact, because Godzilla was the aftermath of the bomb. I wasn't sure if it could be transformed into something that was entertaining and comical. But commercially, it was very successful, and after that the Godzilla series became one monster vs. monster movie after another. But it was totally opposite to what the

Up, Up and Away, King Kong (Shoichi "Solomon" Hirose) gets a free lift to Mt. Fuji in "King Kong vs. Godzilla" (1962)

first film was about. It was a little confusing to me. After that particular film, the flow of Godzilla movies and *kaiju eiga* completely changed. It had been hard, but after that, Godzilla movies became soft.

Tatsuo Matsumura [Comic actor Ichiro Arishima's] appearance in *King Kong vs. Godzilla* made the film much more interesting. I was in that playing an engineer or something like that. At the time I had to make a living!

Teruyoshi Nakano I believe that without any changes to Godzilla's character, the series would not have been able to continue. If Godzilla had remained a villain, probably only hardcore Godzilla fans would have watched the movies, and not the general audience. I think it was correct to change Godzilla's character; it was a reaction to the times and the changes in the audience. But myself, I basically like a scary Godzilla, rather than a good Godzilla.

Kumi Mizuno My strongest memory of Mr. Honda was when we went on location to Oshima—an island close to Tokyo—to film *Attack of the Mushroom People* (1963). We lived there for a month, and Mr. Honda was the only one who didn't change during that time.

Yoshio Tsuchiya Mr. Honda took the entire cast aside the first day of shooting and said, "This is a very grim story, and I want you all to take your roles very seriously." We did, and while I think the final film is very good, I was a bit surprised when we saw the actual mushroom creatures. [*In English:*] Too pretty!

Kumi Mizuno It's my favorite movie. I like it because the monsters aren't really the mushroom people; it wasn't an ordinary ghost story. And after the film was released an American film company asked me to be in a film with Jack Palance playing the prince of China. That film was canceled, so I didn't get a chance to do it.[1]

Akira Kubo It's all about man's subconscious desires. American soldiers tell me all the time, "Hey, I've seen you in *Attack of the Mushroom People*!"

Kumi Mizuno I didn't realize that it was so popular in the United States as well! It wasn't just monsters fighting monsters, it was about man against man. That is, I think, the most attractive part of that film.

Teruyoshi Nakano The assistant directors were classified as first, second, third and fourth rank; four assistant directors, and one director. Only when I became first assistant director [with 1964's *Godzilla vs. the Thing*], did I receive credit on the screen. Do you remember the scene where Godzilla was buried underground, and he raised himself up from beneath the Earth? It was my idea to have him shake the dirt off his body. That's why I think that was the best shot in the movie!

Yuriko Hoshi I was really impressed by The Peanuts' singing, and how they were made to appear so tiny!

Robert Dunham Production [on *Dagora, the Space Monster*] was about eight weeks, and about half of those were working days. The dubbing job was pretty bad. Whenever I show it to anybody, I always tell them, "Now remember, that's not my voice!"

1. Ms. Mizuno may be thinking of the Italian-French production *Il Mongoli* [U.S. title: *The Mongols*], which starred Palance as the son of Genghis Khan. However, that was made and released a full two years prior to *Attack of the Mushroom People's* release in Japan. Then again, we are talking about 30-odd years ago, so the actress's sometimes hazy memory is certainly understandable.

JUN FUKUDA

Yosuke Natsuki I had known Mr. [Jun] Fukuda since he was an assistant director, and I played a main character in his first movie. We'd talk to each other about anything and everything. I worked on almost all his films. He was nervous, jumpy at the studio. I think that is the difference between him and Mr. Honda. I was worried about him because he put so much of himself into his work.

Mie Hama Mr. Fukuda was easy to work with. At Toho, people were able to be very individualistic and pursue their own style. They could express their own character.

Akira Kubo Jun Fukuda and Honda were both more concerned with the visuals than the acting. The director had to take care of everything.

Teruyoshi Nakano Mr. Fukuda was a skilled craftsman, someone who could do many types of things very well. He was equally skilled at directing *kaiju eiga*, action films, comedies. I guess he didn't like *kaiju eiga* all that much. But I think sometimes the greatest movies we make are ones we don't necessarily like.

Jun Fukuda Godzilla was born of nuclear power, and in that social environment *Godzilla* appeared. Originally, Godzilla didn't have any emotions—he shouldn't have any emotions at all. But in [*Godzilla versus the Sea Monster* and *Son of Godzilla*] Godzilla had a human being's emotions, especially in *Son of Godzilla*, where Godzilla had a father/son-like

relationship. I don't think Godzilla should be like that. Godzilla should be more emotionless. When I saw *King Kong vs. Godzilla* (1962), I was really surprised in a similar way. I had seen the original *King Kong* (1933), and felt that no one could do any better than that. For the same reason, no other film can beat the original *Godzilla*. In the later films, we always had to come up with an monster opponent for Godzilla, and Godzilla always had to beat the other monster. With that premise it's pretty hard to make an interesting human story.

Kumi Mizuno I was very busy with a very tight schedule—I was making so many movies during this time, I have a hard time distinguishing one film from another. I remember *Godzilla versus the Sea Monster* very well because I played a South Seas native woman, and covered with body makeup for the role.

Akira Ifukube [For the music in those two films,] Toho was probably experimenting with change. Also, I realized that the focus was not on Godzilla, but on all the sub-plots. Also, I became principal of the Music school at the Tokyo College of Music. Well, can you imagine–the principal writing music for Godzilla movies!?

Jun Fukuda I was going for a lighter, leaner style. That's why I changed the composer to [Masaru] Sato. With the change of the composer the atmosphere—everything—changes.

Masaru Sato [For *Son of Godzilla*] my aim was to make Godzilla and his son like human beings, and to show the affection of the two toward one another. I

Jun Fukuda

tried to devise something unexpected for the audience. Godzilla can't act, right? Therefore I had to express his feelings through music. It was a little over the top, but it was necessary to express their affection. Mr. Ifukube cherished Godzilla, and treated Godzilla's story as a great tragedy, whereas I always treated Godzilla and the son as friends.

Jun Fukuda [We shot *Son of Godzilla*] in Guam. We really had fun. It was very hard for Japanese people to travel overseas back then, and also at the time there was only one hotel on Guam. The wife of the Chief Immigration Officer was Japanese, and her Japanese Wives organization really helped us be able to shoot there. The government backed them up, and so the Guam officials provided us cars, anything we needed during our stay for free. They were very helpful, as they were in America. In Japan they don't understand shooting films very much. Whenever I go outside of Japan, I get jealous about how film-conscious the rest of the world is. I had the experience of shooting a film in Spain, in the Canary Islands. The police stopped traffic for half a day—that would never happen in Japan.

Teruyoshi Nakano As I said, Mr. Tsuburaya was both a scientific and poetic type of person, but Mr. Arikawa [Special Effects Director of *Son of Godzilla* and *Destroy All Monsters*] possessed only the scientific side. Mr. Arikawa became a special effects director after being a cameraman. I believe a director should direct the entire movie, and should create the drama. In other words, the special effects sequences should be approached as part of the entire movie, not a separate part. But Mr. Arikawa was a cameraman.

So, Mr. Tsuburaya directed, and Mr. Arikawa shot. That's the best explanation I can give. It's difficult to explain further.

Minoru Nakano Tsuburaya was very excited about working in a new medium—television—and he knew that his programs could be sold in the foreign market as well.

Big Monsters

on the Small Screen

JUST AS JAPAN'S MAJOR STUDIOS WERE LOSING THEIR HOLD ON AUDIENCES TO TELEVISION, EIJI TSUBURAYA HIMSELF STRUCK GOLD ON THE SMALL SCREEN WITH EFFECTS-FILLED SCI-FI PROGRAMS LIKE "ULTRA Q" (A KIND OF JAPANESE "OUTER LIMITS") AND "ULTRAMAN," WHICH PROVED POPULAR IN THE UNITED STATES AS WELL, PAVING THE WAY FOR CURRENT FAVORITES LIKE "MIGHTY MORPHIN' POWER RANGERS."

Akira Tsuburaya After World War II and television broadcasting began, initially no one had television in their home—except for our house. All the neighbors came over to see TV and he also got a Denchikyu, the very first stereo system. He bought any kind of audio-visual technology that was new and trendy. He also bought one of the very first 8mm cameras.

**Top: Ultraman vs. a redressed Godzilla suit.
Middle: Banila, from Ultraman episode #19.
Bottom: Ultra Seven vs. Godola, from an episode directed by Kazuho "Pete" Mitsuta.**

Kazuho "Pete" Mitsuda

"Ultraman Leo"

Akira Tsuburaya

Minoru Nakano He was very open-minded towards any new technique, and he was very hungry to digest new technology.

Kazuo Tsuburaya He loved new technology, so whenever a new TV or appliance came out, he was always the first to rush out and buy it. My grandmother had a hard time with that! Since he liked everything new, if he were alive today, he probably would utilize all of the new technologies, and his style would be very different. He would've embraced computer animation. He was, obviously, very interested in monster suits and miniatures, so maybe he would've settled on a mixture with all the best elements of both.

Kazuho "Pete" Mitsuta Personally, he was a good grandfatherly type to everyone, but when it comes to work he's very tough, very *shacho* [company president] and a tough director. One episode I remember occurred during production of a show I was directing called "Kaiju Buska," and I went to his house for direction on some of the technical aspects of the next day's shooting. He gave me some advice, and the next day he stormed in and said, "Why are you shooting this! This is costing a lot of money!" I said, "Because that's what you told me to do!" He responded, "That's because you were speaking to Eiji Tsuburaya the man. However, as the president of this company, I don't like this idea, take it out!"

Koichi Takano It's difficult for me to explain. I would probably have used more machines and computers, but I still prefer the more conventional way. Both [hand-made miniatures and computer animation] have good aspects, but I think with monsters the hand-made approach is better. Hollywood today uses much more computer animation than here, where we still use wire works and men in suits and all that. Even when we have a plane flying we will use a model on a string; it's all still very much hand-made in Japan. I still prefer to use wires and hand-controlled effects, for example, when a plane is banking. When we're using monster suits, it makes more sense for us to use wire works because we have better control over the timing of all of the elements of the effects—it's more natural—and we can have more control to go with our "hunches" during filming than we could if we were using a computer.

Minoru Nakano For "Ultra Q" and "Ultra Man" Tsuburaya was credited as "Executive Producer," but he wasn't just loaning his name to the title—he was actually doing many of the effects and much of the editing. He was there to teach the new generation of effects artists to practice in the new medium of television. It was the foundation of Tsuburaya Productions. Originally, his company was called Tsuburaya Special Photographic Productions, focusing just on the special photographic effects, and he was spending a great deal of money and soon went way over budget. The company was great danger, and so he changed the name to Tsuburaya Productions.

Koichi Takano When Eiji Tsuburaya was about to launch Tsuburaya Productions, he saw one of my TV documentaries and said, "Why don't we hire him?" I did learn many things, however, while making documentaries, which I was able to use in programs like "Ultra Q." I learned about paying attention to detail, so that if, for example, I'm shooting an explosion, I watch closely for larger pieces that go flying so I can shoot inserts later. When Ultraman and the monster are fighting, I can closely watch and decide which areas to concentrate for close-ups and inserts.

Minoru Nakano At the time, the sensitivity of the color stock was quite low and the resultant color itself was different from reality. We had to do many test shots. For example, the matte painters had to paint in a slightly different color in order to get the hues we ultimately wanted on film. Also, the members of the Science Patrol [in "Ultraman"] wore bright orange-colored uniforms because of the character of the color stock. It was very painstaking but very enjoyable.

Koichi Takano No one had ever seen anything like it before. A television program with giant monsters was very fresh at the time, with a new surprise every week. And kids really like the idea of gigantic superheroes, especially an alien one—it allows kids to dream. I was having a really good time making those shows, and that was true with everyone on the special effects crew. We all thought the possibilities were endless, that we could do anything—and this dream, I felt, must be able to run off onto the kids as well. The system in Japan is such that normally I would have been an old man by the time I became a true cinematographer. The great thing about Eiji Tsuburaya was that he asked even young crew members to learn and take care of everything. The average age of the effects crew at the time was 24, so I think he was looking for new creativity. That's what I really appreciated.

Minoru Nakano Also at Tsuburaya's home, in the laboratory, was a very talented man named Tetsuo Kinjo, who created the "Ultraman" series and was a protegee of [screenwriter] Shinichi Sekizawa. Kinjo was a very good friend and the same age as me, and a good friend of Mr. Tsuburaya's son Hajime. Tsuburaya was very understanding and broad-minded toward me and Tetsuo Kinjo. Kinjo was Okinawan and had a very hard time in mainland Japan—it's just like England and Ireland—and this was reflected in several of his scripts for "Ultra 7" and others. Some of these scripts were very controversial, but Eiji Tsuburaya permitted them to be made, and it is this humanity I still respect.

Ishiro Honda I think anyone would rather see large-scale, rather than small-scale destruction. If Godzilla goes on a rampage in the middle of an uninhabited desert, there's nothing to hold the audience's attention. If he heads for an oasis where there are people and big, flammable buildings, then you've got a story to hold their interest. I think the city you destroy is less important than the size of the destruction.

怪獣 東京大攻撃

Tokusatsu Part II

Kinji Fukasaku In Japan, the special effects director is a really special kind of artist who is always thinking about better ways to shoot film.

King Kong Kidnapped! Colorful miniture from Eiji Tsuburaya's team for "King Kong Escapes" (1967)

Akira Tsuburaya When I saw *King Kong* (1933) I was really impressed by all the stop-motion animation. My father's response was *Godzilla* (1954), and it's very Japanese. Because of the Japanese film market, it was done with a very low budget compared to American films. The budget limitations forced us to be inventive

and imaginative to be effective, and I think that's really great. Japanese filmmakers can't afford to set real buildings on fire, to do everything full-scale, so Japanese special effects are as much a budget-conscious art as a creative one.

Henry G. Saperstein Felt like Paul Bunyon! Tsuburaya had a stage that was a block and a half long. And when you walked in there, there were—in miniature—cities, mountains, and highways, the traffic lights worked, the cars moved, the water flowed in the river. It was fascinating to see!

Kihachi Okamoto The Toho sci-fi special effects films were made very differently; the director would direct only the live action, and the effects crew would handle the rest. I wouldn't have liked that.

Teruyoshi Nakano In movies, actors are playing what the director wants them to play. It's as if the director is acting out his vision through everybody. But in special effects, the director can portray his ideas using visual images, without words. That's what attracted me. I don't have actors to express myself—I can express myself using special effects. I believe movies have to express something, even without words. The visual image itself has to say or address something.

Akira Tsuburaya My father told me he didn't want the audience to be able to tell which parts were special effects and which parts weren't. "If you could tell," he'd say, "that was no good." The idea was that there would be so many special effects cut into the drama it would become seamless for the audience. When I saw *Forrest Gump* (1994), the drama and the effects were blended very naturally, even though you knew when Tom Hanks was shaking hands with Kennedy it had to be some kind of effect. It melts into the story–this is very important. It's very natural.

Jun Fukuda [Tsuburaya and I] had many, many discussions about the continuity. I'd visit the effects stage and see what they were shooting and say, "Ah, that's how you're doing that sequence." We'd watch the dailies and discuss any problems.

Minoru Nakano Because he was an ex-cameraman, he knew everything about lenses and camera, and enjoyed any kind of optical work. For instance, when using rear-projection, the edges of the image come out somewhat darker, and audiences picked-up on the technique, which he didn't like. So he did it the same way, but moved the camera a step forward to eliminate the darker parts of the screen. Another thing he liked was also used by George Lucas in *Star Wars* (1977). For *Chushingura* (1962), there are very long corridors in the castle, and since the stage wasn't really big enough, Tsuburaya used forced-perspective, with very tall actors in the foreground, and short actors and set in the background. The director, Hiroshi Inagaki, liked the idea so much that he used it on most of his subsequent films.

Rhodes Reason You know, the helicopters to lift King Kong off the island and all that stuff, it was so interesting because to make a helicopter look farther away they made them smaller. They had this great perception for depth; you know—one would be half the size and it would look like it was half a mile away. The same thing with the submarines they used.

Teruyoshi Nakano Mr. Tsuburaya had a very strong sense of pride and professionalism. He always told me, "make movies as a professional–don't make something you have to apologize for." When we had planning meetings between the principal and special effects teams, the principal director would ask Mr. Tsuburaya, "Do you think this kind of effect is possible?" It would

be something totally new, and which even an expert photographer would have a hard time to film. But Mr. Tsuburaya would say, "Of course we can do it." When he said that, he had no idea how he was going to do it, so I asked him why he said that, and he answered, "Unless you say you can do it, you won't get any new

"Daiei wouldn't have a special effects director per se. I believe this was out of respect for Eiji Tsuburaya." "Gammera the Invincible" (1965)

ideas. You can think about how you'll do it later on, until your stomach starts hurting from nervousness." That's what he said!

Noriaki Yuasa The special effects shooting [on the Gamera pictures] usually took two months. The live action took about four weeks from start to finish. The most difficult part was after the script was finished, we spent one month on storyboards, and that was very, very hard. [Kazufumi Fujii] was always a special effects cinematographer; Daiei wouldn't have had a "special effects director" *per se*. I believe that this was out of respect to Eiji Tsuburaya—even though he was from a rival company, he was respected. Mr. Fujii didn't mind what his title was, he just worked very, very hard, and threw himself into making movies.

Minoru Nakano It was Toho's policy to build up a new generation of special effects experts. In Teruyoshi Nakano's case, he had already graduated from the university when he joined Toho. He had written screenplays in college and originally wanted to be a director.

Noriaki Yuasa I had been an assistant director [prior to *Gamera*], and I asked too much of [cinematographer Fujii] because of my inexperience; I didn't understand how a lot of it worked. But he accepted it, and even though I asked too much of him, he always searched for a way to do everything I asked of him, however difficult. After that, I worked quite a lot, but I never met anyone as sincere as him. He is a teacher now and he enjoys his life, and I still appreciate and respect him.

Hitoshi Ueki

Teruyoshi Nakano There are always all kinds of limitations in this field: not enough time, not enough budget, impossible projects that you have to do. Every time I have to face a situation like that, I remember what Mr. Tsuburaya used to say, "I'll try" or "I'll approach it as a professional."

Comedy Relief

WHILE TOHO STUDIOS WAS BEST-KNOWN ABROAD FOR KUROSAWA AND GODZILLA, THIS REPRESENTED JUST A TINY FRACTION OF THE STUDIO'S TOTAL OUTPUT. PROBABLY MORE THAN ANY OTHER GENRE, SALARYMAN COMEDIES, LIKE THE "CRAZY CATS" AND "SHACHO" ("COMPANY PRESIDENT") FILMS WERE TOHO'S BREAD AND BUTTER, WITH THE STUDIO CRANKING OUT DOZENS OF THESE MOVIES EVERY YEAR. MANY KAIJU EIGA REGULARS, BOTH IN FRONT OF AND BEHIND THE CAMERA, WORKED ON THESE FILMS, AND AS TIME WENT ON, THE STUDIO EVEN BEGAN INCORPORATING SCI-FI ELEMENTS AND TSUBURAYA-DIRECTED SPECIAL EFFECTS HOPING TO SELL THESE PICTURES ON THE INTERNATIONAL MARKET. SEVERAL OF THESE FILMS EVEN USED PROPS AND COSTUMES LEFTOVER FROM THE STUDIO'S GODZILLA PICTURES. THESE INCLUDE THE JAMES BONDIAN *BIG ADVENTURE* (AKA *DON'T CALL ME A CON MAN*, WITH SPFX BY EIJI TSUBURAYA, 1965), *IT'S CRAZY—I CAN'T EXPLAIN IT WAY OUT THERE* (1966), *MONSIEUR ZIVACO* (1968), *COMPUTER FREE-FOR ALL* (1969), AND *THE CRAZY'S BIG EXPLOSION* (FEATURING SPFX BY TERUYOSHI NAKANO, AND PROPS FROM *DESTROY ALL MONSTERS*, 1969). AS OF THIS WRITING NONE OF THEIR FILMS ARE AVAILABLE IN THE UNITED STATES.

Yu Fujiki Salaryman comedies were really Toho's main genre. That's where the studio made its money, which was then given to people like Kurosawa to make their movies.

Shue Matsubayashi After the war, Japan was in ruins; Tokyo had been thoroughly destroyed. I wanted to help cheer people up. The Japanese people worked very hard in the postwar period, from morning 'til night, and for very little money. Everybody worked for companies like the one in the [*Shacho*] series. And what I tried to do was to show the Japanese people what the company president was like, in a comic manner, and to present the joy company life could be. I shot up to four of those films every year. 23 *Shacho* films in ten years. One of the famous film critics said the series was "the engine of the white collar age." Many salarymen coming home from work would stop off at the cinema and watch these comedies. It was the Golden Period, and there was much competition, so the fact that the series made as much money as it did for Toho was a real feat.

Tatsuo Matsumura In the morning the salaryman went to work early, had a very hectic day at the office, with their boss looking over their shoulder, they went home late and exhausted. The films depicted a stability, a relaxed atmosphere the Japanese people so envied.

Mie Hama To be honest, I was not too crazy about making them. It's a story with a lot of contradictions. It was fun, but I often argued with director [Kengo] Furusawa about the characters I had to play, and wondered when I could quit.

Yu Fujiki It really wasn't until the comedies that I really became marketable. I could market myself as an actor thanks to the Crazy Cats.

Tatsuo Matsumura I think I always had a kind of fatherly, salaryman-type look. I always wanted to play intelligent mobsters, but it was difficult finding those types of roles. I was always playing teachers, professors. [*laughs*] Directors would take one look at me and say, "No way!"

Hitoshi Ueki Daily life is hectic for Japanese people. Audiences want to recover from that, and these films, I suppose, were a kind of catharsis.

Robert Dunham It was like having fun and getting paid for it. The cost of living at the time, the food, the women, the freedom.

Big Fishes in a Little Pond

WHETHER YOU WERE DIPLOMAT, TELEVISION EXECUTIVE, ATTORNEY, OR ALL-AMERICAN COVER GIRL, IF YOU NEEDED EXTRA MONEY AND WANTED TO GET INTO SHOW BUSINESS, *GAIJIN* (FOREIGNERS) LIVING IN TOKYO COULD ALWAYS CALL WHEELER AND DEALERS LIKE OSMAN "JOHNNY" *(THE STREETFIGHTER)* YUSEPH AND HIS KOKUSAI AGENCY, WHICH PLACED CAUCASIAN EXTRAS IN JAPANESE MOVIES BACK IN THE 1960S. THE PAY WASN'T GREAT, BUT IF YOU COULD SPEAK A LITTLE JAPANESE AND HIT YOUR MARK YOU COULD, AS IN THE CASES OF ROBERT DUNHAM AND WILLIAM ROSS, BECOME A FAMILIAR FACE TO MILLIONS OF NIPPONESE FILMGOERS.

William Ross After the Korean War, I went to Tokyo to study Japanese, with the idea of joining the state department. I was attending a language school in Tokyo in 1957 when one of the other students asked me if I wanted to be in a Japanese motion picture. I went with him, and a few other foreigners, to Shintoho Studio and became a Russian naval officer in a film about the Japanese-Russian War, in which the Japanese sunk the entire Russian Far East fleet [*The Emperor Meiji and the Great Russo-Japanese War*]. Me and these other guys were dressed up like sailors and we were supposed to stand on this deck, singing the

Russian National Anthem as the ship sunk. None of us knew this national anthem, and we had to sing it in Russian, but there were about three or four white Russians who were also in the picture. They tried to teach us the song, but we just couldn't memorize those crazy words. Finally they said, don't worry, we'll write it on a big piece of plywood and put it on the ceiling, so we could look up and read it while we were singing. We came back from lunch and we got ready to shoot the scene, and nobody bothered to look up to see this sign. The director said let's do this in one take, and the cameras started rolling and we looked up and realized the sign was hung upside down! We ended up just mouthing it, and they took the four Russians into the sound studio to record the song. After that, I became a regular extra and bit player in many Japanese films.

Robert Dunham Bill Ross was a nice guy to work with—I was with him maybe over 12 years—he got me a lot of parts, though most of the work I did with him was dubbing. Ross is still in Japan. That was one of my main incomes. I dubbed almost every weekend for six to eight years. We could dub a feature film in about three days. I did a lot of *samurai* cut-ups, one of the most famous being the "Zatoichi" series, where most of the dialog was grunting and yelling.

William Ross At the time, the Japanese film industry was producing over 600 films a year, and using foreigners to play the baddies. Back then, they paid you about ¥1,800 a day. Today, if you can find the work, you get about ¥30,000 a day [$300]. The Caucasians who are used as actors in Japanese movies generally have no acting training; that's why they're so pathetic most of the time. I always took pride in my work.

Robert Dunham in "Godzilla vs. Megalon" (1973)

Robert Dunham We're talking about a time when there were ¥360 to the dollar. [*Gaijin* actors living in Japan were paid] generally anywhere from $200 to $400/day—this was for acting parts. Extras would get about $30/day–at that time ¥10,000. For stuntwork, this varied greatly, but generally this was around $700/week retainer; that is they locked you into the film, because you had to be on call. Then, depending upon the danger factor, it might run anywhere from $500 and up per. That was generally negotiated right on the spot with the director, and of course, you never said no. For pay I'd put Toho at #1, Toei at #2, Nikkatsu at #3, and Daiei #4. Toho paid the best.

William Ross I was in a movie called *The Alaska Story* (1977), which featured a number of non-Japanese actors. When the movie was released in America, there was one reviewer who went on about how awful the other foreign actors in the picture were, but he liked my performance. I still have that review.

Robert Dunham [I was recognized] many times, especially after a certain picture came out. They'd try to practice their English with "Hey, are you actor?" You'd give them an autograph and chat with them a little in Japanese. That happened many times.

William Ross I hired Bob Dunham as a dubbing actor and he became one of my regular on-call actors. He worked a lot for me. [*At this point, Ross withdraws an envelope and produces several 1960s-era pictures of himself. One photo is of a cocktail party and shows Dunham in a suit with a young woman*]. He was screwing the hell out of that broad. Everybody knew it except her husband. He always had a few girls going

on ... I never did that, I was always straight business with the people I worked with, I never got involved with them. Bob Dunham is OK, but he tends to exaggerate. He was a bullshitter.

Robert Dunham [*The Time Traveller*] was a film I financed, I wrote it and directed it, and starred in it. The claim to fame was that this was Linda Purl's first movie. It was about aliens replacing people on Earth with an exact copy. The main character, me, was in Air Intelligence, and they wanted to replace me with one of the alien robots to get into the system. They started to replace both [his] daughter and the wife. It starts out as a bad dream, and then goes to reality, then goes to the bad dream again, and then back to reality again, as though this was really going to happen. The end of the picture was that this was really going to happen. I sold it once to educational TV.

Yosuke Natsuki I remember *Mothra* with Robert very well. I was not allowed to do any dangerous sports, like skiing, riding motorcycles, racing cars. Robert participated in the circuit with a Hino Coutessa. We met in Shimoda one summer and raced each other, me in my Porsche 356cc and Robert in his Coutessa on the toll road by the ocean, barreling at top speed.

William Ross *Terror Beneath the Sea* (1966) was a co-production that I handled with Toei. It was filmed at Toei's TV division in standard 35mm format. It was

Andrew Hughes, startled by fishmen, in "Terror Beneath the Sea" (1966)

filmed in English, using local people from various countries as actors, and we had to post-dub some of the voices because you could not understand their English.

Shinichi "Sonny" Chiba [*laughs*] There were many Americans performing in *Terror Beneath the Sea*. The

Rhodes Reason with Akira Takarada and Linda Miller in "King Kong Escapes" (1967)

director of both films, Hajime Sato, was a relative of director Junya Sato. Hajime-san is dead now, though....

William Ross When I began acting back in 1957, there were a whole bunch of Turkish people who were working as agents.

Robert Dunham Johnny Yuseph [spoke perfect Japanese] because he was born and educated in Japan. I liked Yuseph—he got me a lot of work and was very easy-going—he's Turkish.

Anonymous Gaijin Actress/Model Johnny Yuseph hired people for extra work in those pictures, but his real line was supplying *gaijin* women to Japanese businessmen! I managed to avoid that, thank God!

Robert Dunham I rarely had a screen test at Toho after I got started. The director would call for me–it was just "Are you busy? Would you like this part?" The same thing happened at Toei after I got started.

William Ross The more Japanese I learned, the better parts I would get. I did some very interesting things, too. I did what is called *sayaku*, which means acting in two parts–twin characters. I knew it could be done, but I had never seen it. It was very interesting–one was a good guy and one was a bad guy. I had to do one side one day and the other side the next day, and then play my voice so you could get the timing down and everything. I think the good guy was a detective and the bad one was a criminal. I was trying to stop him–I didn't want to kill him, but he got killed when we went to pick him up. One of the other detectives shot and killed him to save me the Japanese embarrassment of killing my own brother.

Familiar Faces

Dunham and Ross were but two transplanted Americans who frequented these movies. Distinguished Andrew Hughes was the sole Caucasian in *Destroy All Monsters* (1968). Amateur Harold S. Conway (*Mothra, King Kong vs. Godzilla*) was in countless pictures, while crusty George Furness had major roles in *The Mysterians* (1957) and *Gorath* (1962). Model Linda Miller starred opposite Rhodes Reason in *King Kong Escapes* (1968), while Edith Hanson appeared as the American mother in the Gamera picture *Attack of the Monsters* (1969). The whereabouts of most of these staples of internationally-flavored *kaiju eiga* is unknown.

Kon Omura I remember Edith Hanson. Even though she wasn't a professional actress, she did a very nice job. She was just like a mother for the young actors and actresses on location. I saw her recently at a party, and she talked very excitedly about making *Attack of the Monsters*. She lives in the Wakayama Prefecture near Osaka, where she's very close to nature.

William Ross Edith Hansen, yeah, I'd like to kick her in the snatch! That's a terrible woman. She thinks that her you-know-what doesn't stink! She's living up in the mountains outside of Osaka now. Every once in a while her name appears in the papers, and she's got a lot to say. She was also working with Amnesty International; she was in charge of that over here for a while. She's just one of these busy bodies. The only time I ever acted with her was in a television show. She had a small part, and I had a small part as her husband, and she wouldn't even talk to me. I'd say good morning and she'd give me this, "Who the hell are you, to be working with me?" kind of thing. She's just a jerk.

Rhodes Reason [Linda Miller] was like 18 years old, and one of the top models over there, and [U.S. producer Arthur Rankin] selected her to play the Fay Wray role [in *King Kong Escapes*]. She was a cover girl in all the magazines, and Arthur cast her because of the way she looked; she had no acting background. She was a cute little girl who said her dialogue and that was it. I probably spent most of my time coaching her. And, of course, that was the first and last thing she ever acted in.

Robert Dunham Linda Miller, the last I heard, she was singing in Vegas.

Rhodes Reason Oh, maybe 15 years ago [I ran across her]—she was about 200 pounds married to a Mexican somewhere in Southern California and she was doing someone like getting loans for people in Real Estate. She went from being this cute little thing to being this overweight blob. I guess she didn't have a happy life after that. Her mother got a divorce from her father; he was a major in the Air Force and a meteorologist. And her mother was what you would call one of those theatrical mothers. I have no idea where she is today; I just kind of ran across her.

Robert Dunham [Harold S.] Conway and [Andrew] Hughes were a little blown up about their supposed ability to act. George Furness was just a nice old guy [*laughs*], and a fairly good actor. He had done some acting in the States and was actually a prominent lawyer in Japan, but because of his age they had to cast him as judges and things like that. Both Hughes and Conway thought they were pretty snappy.

William Ross [Andrew Hughes] was Australian. He did a lot of commercials for medicine. [Furness] was the doyen of the actors over here, the chief, the wheel. He was from Connecticut and he spoke with the kind of Connecticut type of English accent, he sounded like the Queen's messenger, a royal courier. He carried papers around in his pockets, and when he went to parties and stuff, he had little skits he would read for people. People loved that man, he was very well liked. He was awarded by the Foreign Women's Association the Best Dressed Foreign Male—he was really elegant. He was an attorney in the army during the war, and he came over here to work in the war crime trials. He was the defense lawyer for one Japanese general, and he got him off because of George's defense. This general became very powerful politically, and he fixed it so that George Furness became a member of the Japanese bar. That allowed him to act as a lawyer here, and also to appear in court. He opened a law office and he had a lot of Japanese lawyers and paralegals working for him. He never appeared in court, because his Japanese wasn't good enough. He could have though, if he had wanted to. He had an old, old, classic car that he used to drive, with wood interior, and he would show up at the different studios in his car, and they treated him royally. He's been dead for many years now; I'm not sure when he died.

Robert Dunham In the mid-1960s, I brought *Dagora, the Space Monster* to Hollywood. They rented a whole

George Furness

Harold S. Conway

theater and they ran the picture. I went to the Screen Actor's Guild to get a card and brought my scrapbooks and so forth but they said they couldn't give me a card unless I had a contract somewhere. No one could give me a card unless I had one, so it was a closed shop. I never met the producer, Tomoyuki Tanaka. I think the guy I met was somebody named Sid Saperstein. Typical mover and shaker with foreign films with a big cigar in his mouth.

Henry G. Saperstein My salesmen came to me and said, "We gotta have action films, preferably science fiction, monsters, something like that. Stations are dying to buy." I asked the librarian at The Academy of Motion Picture Arts and Sciences, "Who makes the best monster/sci-fi films?" The reply was Hammer Films in England and Toho in Japan. Well, Hammer was impossible to deal with, so I decided to look into Toho. I went to see *Gojira* at the Toho La Brea Theater. I sat and looked at the picture and looked at the audience. Godzilla was portrayed as the villain. In fact, the word *Gojira* means "devil-monster" [sic]. And the audience was applauding him like he was the hero! 'Cause why? He was chasing down guys who were stupid enough to set off atom bombs! I decided I had to meet Toho, but do it the right way. So I took a night course at UCLA in Japanese culture, traditions, history, what have you, to learn how to deal with the Japanese.

Robert Dunham At that time, Saperstein was casting *Frankenstein Conquers the World*, and the comment was that yeah, I did okay, but I wasn't a name, so they cast Nick Adams instead. So in the end, all the film and television work I did in Japan didn't amount to a hill of beans in Hollywood.

Henry G. Saperstein I told Toho they could have a world wide marketplace, particularly a North American one, if they would just slightly change their point of view in these films. I said I'd put my money where my mouth was–I would put up half the budget for territorial rights and we would consult with them on the script. They would shoot the film in Japanese, we would throw some Caucasian actors in it [with English dialogue] and we would dub the Japanese actors into English and vice versa. They thought the idea was so far-fetched they decided to do it.

Invasion!

IN 1965, GAIJIN TALENT FACED NEW COMPETITION— FROM HOLLYWOOD ITSELF. JAPANESE MONSTER MOVIES WERE POPULAR ENOUGH IN THE U.S. TO WARRANT FULL-FLEDGED CO-PRODUCTIONS BETWEEN AMERICAN COMPANIES AND THE JAPANESE MAJORS. AND SO, FILM AND TELEVISION TALENT, GENERALLY ON THE DOWNSIDE OF THEIR CAREERS, FLEW TO TOKYO UNAWARE OF THE CULTURE SHOCK THAT WAS AWAITING THEM ….

Robert Horton My agent called me one day and said there was a movie being made in Tokyo. I read the script, and I told him it really wasn't very good. And he said, "Yeah, but by the time this film is made you'll have two or three others in the can." So I did it. We made that film in September-October 67, and it was fun being there. My wife and I spent three really nice months in Tokyo. She came home with knowledge about *ikabana* and Japanese cooking and what not.

Patricia Medina Jo[seph Cotten] and I had never been to Japan. We didn't think it was a great script but we loved traveling, and we got to work together.

Rhodes Reason I had seen the first one, with Perry Mason. I knew the film was very bad before we made it. But I couldn't turn down the trip to Japan, because of the cultural experience. And the opportunity to work in the Japanese film industry, to see how their country actually made motion pictures compared to ours. I'm glad I did it, because I learned a great deal from the Japanese, other than shooting motion pictures, of course.

I was treated like an emperor from another country, though. I had a huge dressing room that took up half the floor in the administration building, I had drivers, I had handlers. All the wardrobe, including my shoes, were hand-made. There was nothing off the rack at Toho. I'd spend days looking through miles of cloth, and they'd ask me to pick the fabric for my uniform, knowing full well they would pick the fabric. I felt very privileged from that stand point. I couldn't ask for anything more. There was no pressure at Toho compared to Hollywood. They had the luxury of time.

Nick Adams (center) in "Frankenstein Conquers the World" (1965), the first of the Japanese-American kaiju productions

99

Nick Adams

By far the most popular American actor to work in Japanese monster movies, Nick Adams had become something of pariah in Hollywood. During the 1950s, Adams had good roles in

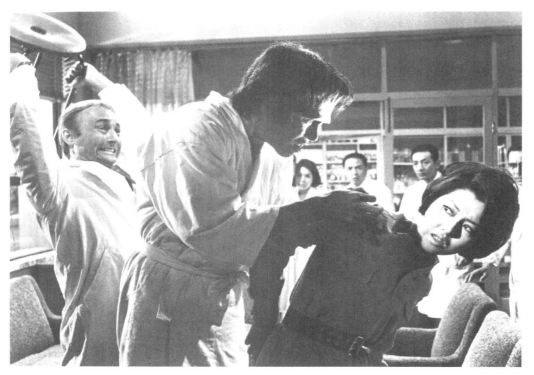

Kumi Mizuno terrorized by the Frankenstein Monster (Koji Furuhata) as Nick Adams lends a hand in "Frankenstein Conquers the World" (1965)

major pictures like *Rebel Without a Cause* and *Mister Roberts* (both 1955), but as he grew older he alienated much of Hollywood. He criticized "runaway productions," vowing "never to make a picture abroad." And his shameless Oscar campaign for 1962's *Twilight of Honor* only made the actor look foolish.

That he was nominated at all was surprising (adding to the irony, one critic said his performance "ranged in every expression from upset stomach to Godzilla") and, on Oscar night, he arrived early to practice his run down the aisle when he won. Only he didn't win, and by 1965 Adams was in Japan making *Frankenstein Conquers the World* and *(Godzilla vs.) Monster Zero*, humbled, apparently, by the experience.

Henry G. Saperstein People like Adams were not just for marquee names, but mainly for "tv Guide" listings.

Yoshio Tsuchiya There are many different types of personalities, in America as in Japan. Mr. Nick Adams was very outgoing and very cheerful, just as we imagined Americans would be.

Henry G. Saperstein Nick [Adams] was a pleasure, and a consummate pro. Russ Tamblyn was a royal pain in the ass. I guess he thought he was Clark Gable or something.

Kumi Mizuno Nick Adams immersed himself in Japanese culture and the Japanese film industry—he tried to understand Japan and its people. I sometimes invited him over for dinner to my house. Russ came to Japan with his wife and he didn't seem to like Japan or Japanese culture so I couldn't really talk to him. Nick was more popular than Russ. He was always joking around.

Henry G. Saperstein When we all came back, Nick stayed there for quite a while because he ended up having a love affair with that Japanese woman during the making of *Monster Zero*, which resulted in his divorce in the States.

Kumi Mizuno He would sometimes call me at night but I couldn't understand English so I would sit there on the phone, holding a dictionary, and try to guess what he was saying, and answer him. It's a very wonderful memory. He even proposed to me! I already had a fiancé so I had to refuse.

Yoshio Tsuchiya Mr. Adams had a very enjoyable personality—we were always doing mischief and telling bad jokes. I played many practical jokes on him. He asked me how to say "Good morning," and I taught him, in Japanese, "I'm starving!" He really was hungry because he was on a strict diet at the time, and once nearly fainted during shooting. Another time he asked me what to say when he met ladies, and I told him a *konsai* greeting, which is very comical for someone in Tokyo, comparable to having me speak in English like a Texan or an African-American. I used to tease him during his scenes, calling him an Actors Studio-type of Hollywood performer. He would get mad about this, and while I was playing the Controller of Planet X [in *Monster Zero*], he would say, in Japanese, "You're overacting!"

Akira Kubo We were able to understand roughly what the other said so it wasn't really too much of a problem, though it may have been more difficult for Adams.

Kumi Mizuno My script was translated into Japanese, so it was no problem. When I saw their faces, I didn't need a translator, I could tell what was being said.

Yoshio Tsuchiya For me once shooting began there was no language barrier. The nature of the actors is that they can sense the beginning or the end of the line. Mr. Nick Adams knew that after shooting, for the Japanese version, his voice would be dubbed into Japanese, and vice versa in the United States. I told him that for the American version "you must get Henry Fonda for me and, if you do, I'll get Toshiro Mifune to do yours!" He was badly introverted, but he cared about the other actors, and was a good friend. When he left Japan after shooting had ended, he asked me for an autographed photo. I asked him, "Why do you want a photograph of me?" And Mr. Adams replied, "I want to put it in a frame and put it in my room." At the time I thought he was just flattering me, just diplomatic conversation as he was leaving Japan. However, producer [Tomoyuki] Tanaka later visited Adams' home and found that my picture was really on his wall—it was true.

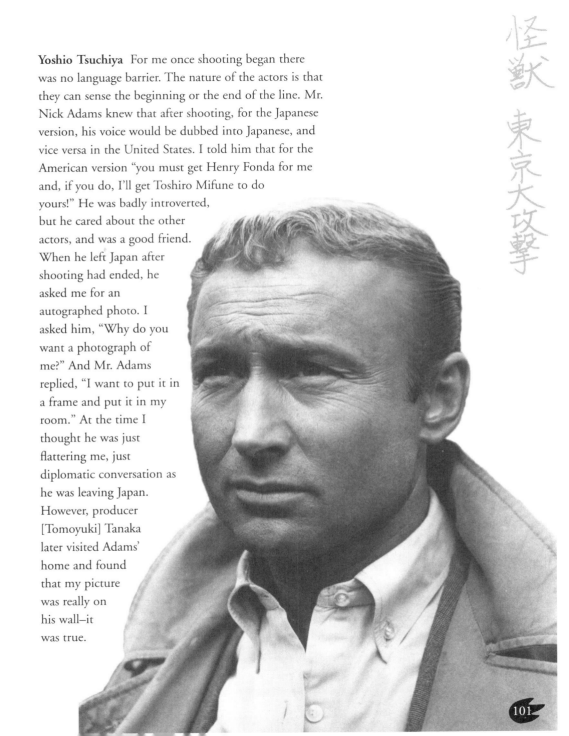

Henry G. Saperstein

The Case of the Missing
Devil-Fish

"FRANKENSTEIN VS. THE GIANT DEVIL-FISH," AS *FRANKENSTEIN CONQUERS THE WORLD* WAS FIRST CALLED, WAS THE FIRST OF THE SAPERSTEIN/ADAMS CO-PRODUCTIONS, ONLY BY THE TIME THE PICTURE MADE IT TO THE STATES, THE DEVIL-FISH WAS LONG GONE.

Henry G. Saperstein [In the United States] audiences

The Frankenstein Monster and the long-elusive "devil-fish" in a scene shot but not used in "Frankenstein Conquers the World" (1965)

do not have the patience. Every Japanese monster film starts with a conference. Either the press or government officials or scientists, and they lay the foundation for the story and the characters and the

threat and a plan of what they're going to do about it. This goes on for five minutes, by which time every American viewer tunes it out, particularly on television. We would edit the films and make such additions or deletions as we felt would make for a better progression. We felt the Frankenstein boy-monster character should have been the focal point and putting in another monster was a dilution. And [the devil-fish] wasn't that good, so we cut it out. We edited almost every film we distributed here so it would play better. This is a monster movie. They're saying "Where's the monster?" You can't bring him in ten minutes into the film.

Teruyoshi Nakano Do you know about the extra scene we shot at the end of *Frankenstein,* with the giant octopus? Well, not many people know this, but there was another special effects scene we shot at the request of the American distributor. Do you know the scene where Frankenstein goes to see his "girlfriend" [played by Kumi Mizuno] at her apartment? The American buyer asked us to add that scene too, because when we finished the film it was about three minutes too short. From what I understand, American audiences didn't like short films, all films were supposed to be a certain length or the people felt like they're getting cheated.

Rhodes Reason It was like Hollywood in the 1930s. For instance, instead of shooting a master shot, and then shoot over the shoulder for dialogue, they'd shoot one line, move the camera in the other direction for the next line, and over and over–talk about primitive. And then you'd go from primitive filmmaking to very high tech stuff we did with the front projection. We did a lot of interiors [at first], and then it was the Emperor's birthday and we had a whole week off. We then went to the island of Oshima for the scenes where we looked for King Kong and all that baloney. At first, we were on the island about two weeks doing nothing in lavish surroundings, just waiting for the weather to clear, so we spent all the time in the hotel eating and drinking and running around having dinners in everyone else's apartments—they just went on for hours and hours where you'd drink, and you'd smoke, and you'd eat, and then you'd drink, and then you'd smoke, and then you'd eat some more. We shot the last scene in Yokohama Harbor; we were on that PT boat—that was a lot of fun, jazzin' around in that thing.

Akira Takarada We had lines in both English and Japanese. During pre-production we hung out a lot together and drank a lot. We became friends before shooting and talked about the chick last night or whatever!

Rhodes Reason Akira Takarada spoke some English, but haltingly. He and I were very close during the whole shooting; he was a lovely guy and we got along beautifully. We used to go to dinner together, in fact we used to take baths together. We went to dinners with his beautiful wife—he was married to one of the Miss Japans; he was a sweetheart. He was, at the time, considered the Clark Gable of Japan. He didn't know what I was talking about half the time, and vice versa. The only person there was my translator, Henry Okawa, and Linda Miller, of course. Henry and I became fast friends, and he was a darling person. He and I used to eat in the commissary every day and slurp up noodles. We became part of the whole community at Toho Studios. He was fascinated with American

toilet paper, and so after I returned to California, I sent Henry a huge thing of toilet paper, and apparently he was terribly excited to have received it.

Mie Hama I didn't campaign for the role. I've never done any acting that I really wanted to do. Producer [Sanezumi] Fujimoto thought the role [in *King Kong Escapes*] fit me, and arranged it.

Rhodes Reason She used to call me "Bond-san." She had done the 007 picture earlier that year. We were a little more distant, albeit affectionately; we worked very well together. I had a few scenes with her where I subjected her to some of my Marlon Brando-isms

Eisei Amamoto (wearing cape) in his most famous role, Dr. Who, in "King Kong Escapes" (1967). Left to right: Naoya Kusakawa, Mie Hama, Kazuo Suzuki, Yoshifumi Tajima, Toru Ibuki, Sachio Sakai, Nadao Kirino, Amamoto, Rhodes Reason, Linda Miller and Akira Takarada

where I threw something at her to get a kind of unexpected, spontaneity to the scene. She was very structured as an actress, so I used a little cinematic brutality.

Mie Hama A few years later I left films and tried television drama, then I went to New York for a long time, and I became a news writer and got married. I wrote a book and for magazines and now I have my own interview program. I changed my career.

Rhodes Reason And the dialog! They had dialog [in the English-language script] like, "Sir, the water-sucking valve is dismantled!" Holy Christ, I thought! What's this all about? And I said, "Well, I think that's gotta be changed." That's rather pornographic to begin with. There are no unions over there, so when something has to be moved, everybody moves it. For example, when we had that hovercraft—it would have to be turned around—everybody within earshot would get in there and turn it. The way that was shot was we had railroad tracks and had a cable tied to the bottom of it. They just pulled it along with huge fans nearby. When they first showed me the submarine interiors I looked down and in the corner of my eye there was this lovely flower arrangement. Well, you know, this is not what

Full Rubber Jacket—"The Green Slime" (1968) as Vietnam parable

we'd have on a nuclear submarine! [*laughs*]. It was the same thing in the captain's quarters, at the table where all the maps and T-Squares were and all that. Instead of having just what was needed, they had like ten times more than that so it was like a garage sale. The whole table was just packed with triangles and calipers and a million maps. I said, "I'm sorry, but I won't need all these things here." It's like Spielberg. You know how he over populates the toy rooms of children in his pictures? He must have got that from the Japanese. To them it's poetic license, but it doesn't mean anything. American audiences laugh at it, but they love all the nonsense with King Kong and the lurid musical themes, the corny clichés, very childish and so on. It's all very simplistic, but it's what the Japanese love. [Honda and I] had our differences, but we were shooting a picture for two audiences. He would direct me in strange and exotic ways that only the Japanese would appreciate. Everything was exaggerated; everything was so stylized there was no reality to it. Henry Okawa would say things to me like, "Honda-san wants you to run through the door." And I would say, "Why should I run to the door when I'm just walking down the hall? Tell Honda-san I will *walk* through the door." And I would say, "Thank Honda-san for me. I just think it would be more appropriate." And this went on with every scene we did. It's not within the air of reality. [But] I have such great respect for the people over there, the whole experience was very wonderful, just incredibly enlightening.

William Ross *The Green Slime* was done as a co-production with Toei by RAM films, and was bought by MGM. The original title was "Battle Beyond the Stars," but MGM changed it. *Message from Space* was a Toei film, and I was in it because Kinji Fukasaku, the director, asked for me. But the part was so small, if you blinked your eyes, you would never see me. I became very friendly with him when we were doing *The Green Slime*.

Kinji Fukasaku *The Green Slime* was about three times the average Japanese budget, I guess. It wasn't really a big budget for an American film, however. The producer wanted to make the film in Japan. Instead of Japanese actors we used three foreign stars. And then amateurs from the military base. It was fun but as a director it was really tough.

Robert Horton I remember one morning we met at the studio–and I'd been under contract to MGM and Warner Bros. in my lifetime–and the Japanese have a thing where they sing a sort of company anthem for the studio. In other words, it's like [*singing*] "Hail, Universal! Universal's greatest film!"

Kinji Fukasaku [*In English*] *The Green Slime*—what does slime mean? [*After hearing the translation Fukasaku laughs.*] That was during the time of the Vietnam War. Japan was a base for America. What I wanted to do for *The Green Slime* was to pick up on this American stereotyped notion of Communism. I wanted to show America struggling with something it doesn't really understand and can't control, as was later reflected in American films like *The Deer Hunter* and *Full Metal Jacket*. *Alien*, too was also the same. After the Vietnam War, you began to understand it, but during the war you did not. I could do that kind of stuff in science fiction films. I wanted to show the base about to be overrun by this germ. I had a lot of discussions with the American producer, but in the

end I wasn't really allowed to make the picture I wanted. Still, I believe my concept was better than the producer's idea—human beings and monsters fight each other—I don't understand that. Science fiction was a venue to do this kind of thing.

Gorgeous Luciana Paluzzi flanked by stars Richard Jaeckel and Robert Horton in "The Green Slime" (1968). Linda Miller is behind Jaeckel, Robert Dunham behind Paluzzi

Robert Dunham Fukusaku was under a lot of pressure to get it done under budget and he was very quick and efficient, 'cause there were a lot of scenes with elaborate sets, with the rocketship and the monsters and all that. Plus it was a co-production and the American producers were around watching the dollars.

Robert Horton At a certain time I felt we should quit and that caused a little trouble because they were perfectly willing to go on until midnight and I wasn't. I wasn't used to that. I didn't see any reason why we had to work after six because my experience in the business was that most actors with any clout didn't.

Need a giant, winged lion? "Child's Play!" declares Cesar Romero as Patricia Medina looks on in "Latitude Zero" (1969)

Kinji Fukasaku Richard Jaeckel is a really nice, pleasant guy. I saw him in several American films—he did a really great job I think—he's a very good actor. Robert Horton injured his back prior to shooting; I was really worried about that.

Robert Horton I couldn't believe it. We filmed in a studio base floor that was like gravel, and these men—the grips and so forth—were lifting these huge brute lamps in bare feet on this gravel. I was particularly impressed by that.

Robert Dunham The whole production was about six or seven weeks, less than two months. As I remember, the American side supplied the actors and took up all their expenses and pay and so forth, and the Japanese studio contributed with the director and the grips and lights and set construction and all of that kind of stuff. I don't think any money exchanged hands. This was not unusual on a co-production.

William Ross Actually, I was assistant director on that picture, too, because the guy who was supposed to be it quit, went off to Taiwan or someplace. Fukasaku is very loud, but he is like a puppy dog, he barks but doesn't bite. [Incidentally,] we had some Iraelis in it as extras, they were students over here, and they got called back for [The Six Day War], but before they could leave, the war was over. So, they were all upset when they came to work every day, because they wanted to fight.

Robert Horton We came home to New York City, and the film was released there around November 1968. One day my wife came into my study with a copy of *Variety* and says "I think this is the movie you made in Japan, but I think they've changed the name to 'The Green Slimm-ee.'" And I looked at the picture and I said, "Honey, this is *The Green Slime*." She said, "I don't think I've ever saw the word 'slime' written down before." So the film began to be exploited, so if you were in mid-town Manhattan every time you came up to the curb there was a logo on the street that said *The Green Slime*, and I think that was from about 34th Street to where we lived at 74th & Park. And it was getting to be embarrassing. So then we learned that the movie had been released and we went down to somewhere on 34th Street, on the East Side, to see it. And when I realized that the movie was about to be over, I said "Let's get out of here. I don't want anybody to recognize me." And that's the whole enchilada.

Robert Dunham It was the era, and there was a certain cult involved. I think it was *The Green Slime* that somebody named as one of the worst films ever made! Despite the fact that many of them were pretty Howdy-Doody and you could see the wires and all that, it didn't make any difference.

Patricia Medina Oh, [the language barrier] was awful! Poor [Cesar] Romero had an awful time because there was one fellow—I don't know what he spoke but when he looked at me and when he spoke I started to laugh and got the giggles. Tears were going down my face, and Romero was saying, "Patricia, stop it! Stop it!" but soon he was laughing himself.

The last of the big U.S./Japanese co-productions, Latitude Zero *left a bad taste in Toho's mouth when the American financing fell apart just as its American stars arrived in Tokyo. Even today the picture's tangled legal web has curtailed a home video release of the picture, both here and in Japan.*

Patricia Medina I remember when Romero arrived, and I told him that the production manager was

coming down but don't mention money. And he said, "What do you mean don't mention money?! That's the first thing I want to discuss!" Romero went and called his business manager, who happened to be the same as Jo's, and they said that Jo's last three checks bounced. We phoned the interpreter—who was a horrible woman—and she said that three of Toho's executives wanted to come up and see Jo. They were terribly upset with the Americans! They said, "The producers weren't trustworthy. We would like to take the picture over, and we'd start you right away on expenses, and then we will pay you six months after the picture is over." So Jo said, "Hold it right there. When we do a picture and untrustworthy producers don't pay us we go home, and when the checks start coming we go to work. Call us in six months and if we're available we'll come back!" Well, one [of the executives] talked for about a week and then it was translated that he had gone over and had

Joseph Cotton (bottom left) looking for his paycheck in "Latitude Zero" (1969)

107

talked to [American producer] Don Sharp and was therefore responsible for making a deal with a crook. And, having made the deal, he was responsible and being responsible meant that he had to deal with it himself, and he knew what he had to do. And Jo said, "Just a minute," and we went to window. He said to Romero, "I want you in on this. I know Patricia's answer will be the same as mine, but I want to know how you feel. We'll trust them and finish the film." Romero said, "Let's do it and show them we're not all ugly Americans. If we don't do it you know what'll happen." And so Jo went back and told them we'd finish the film. Well, this man burst into floods of tears, I gave him an enormous Scotch and he fell flat on the floor—I thought I'd killed him.[1] Anyway, they carried him out, our expenses went retroactive and we all rushed to the phone to order room service.

Patricia Medina and Cesar Romero

Yoshio Tsuchiya I understand Joseph Cotten ... [was] very calm and reserved, and of a very dark nature, quite unlike the outgoing, happy-go-lucky image of the American people.

Patricia Medina Jo had a lot longer part, the hero of the picture. One morning, close to the end of Jo's part, I could hear groans from the bed next to me and thought "dear God!" The doctor came over and said, "I'm afraid your husband is very ill. If he were 21 he couldn't work." Jo said "I want to get out of here. I want to finish it. If they can prop me up and do close-ups and use another actor for the long shots I think, in a day, I can give them the picture. I want you

to suggest it to the director," who was a nice man. I did and the director accepted it. It was dreadful.

Akira Takarada No matter how many takes, [Cotten] never complained. His acting was like water, very smooth, very clear.

Patricia Medina We were supposed to leave the next day. We were on JAL and Jo said, "I want you to go downstairs and get us on an earlier flight." I called the studio and got the interpreter who said, "Oh yes, he's here pretending to be ill." When Jo came [back to the hotel] he just flopped on the bed. I called the man we saved from having to commit *harakiri* and phoned him and said "I have to get my husband out of here—he really is very ill—and I haven't got a car and I don't know how to do it." And he said "I will help you." We got Jo to a taxi, I got him on the plane and I went off to thank this man. Meanwhile Jo's screaming "Where's my wife! Where has she gone?!" And the stewardess said, "She talking with your friend," and he said, "What do you mean, we don't have any friends here!" But we did—whatever his name was. It was an experience. But six months to the day we got our money from the honorable Japanese gentleman!"

---

1. Medina is likely referring to producer Tomoyuki Tanaka, though when I mentioned his name it didn't ring a bell.

Gan Yamazaki It was kind of a mishmash of Godzilla, Gamera, and the rest! [laughs]

Ryuzo Nakanishi Garuda was the symbol of the Indonesian Airlines. Perhaps a bit of that was put into Gappa, too.

The Tale of Gappa

NIKKATSU'S ONLY *KAIJU EIGA* WAS A PICTURE CALLED *MONSTER FROM A PREHISTORIC PLANET* (AKA *GAPPA, THE TRIPHIBIAN MONSTER*, 1967), WRITTEN BY GAN YAMAZAKI AND RYUZO NAKANISHI, A MUTT AND JEFF-LIKE PAIR WHO GENEROUSLY AGREED TO SIT AND DISCUSS THEIR INTERNATIONAL CLAIM TO FAME: A 29-YEAR-OLD MONSTER MOVIE. THE WELL-GROOMED NAKANISHI WAS IMMACULATELY DRESSED AND SUGGESTED AN IMPORTANT CORPORATE EXECUTIVE, WHILE YAMAZAKI, WITH HIS STYLISH BUT BOHEMIAN WARDROBE AND GAUNT FEATURES, SUGGESTED A SCARECROW.

Ryuzo Nakanishi Let me explain first. We were contract screenwriters at Nikkatsu Studios. Each of us was asked to write a treatment. I wrote *Gappa* as a kind of halibut/flatfish monster. But it would have cost too much. At the time, Yamazaki was a very busy scriptwriter—he was writing 20 films a year. By 1967, however, he was only doing about six per year, and so he took over the task of turning the treatment into a workable script.

Gan Yamazaki Nikkatsu was one of the major studios, but had never done a *kaiju eiga*. Godzilla had become a very successful series, and so Nikkatsu became interested. If the film could be successful overseas in the international market and thus get hard currency, Nikkatsu could get financing from the Japanese government as part of its protection program. And so

"It was funny that we were asked to write a big budget monster movie to get government financing!" Gan Yamazaki and Ryuzo Nakanishi

Tamio Kawaji (right) and Yoko Yamamoto stumble upon Baby Gappa in "Monster from a Prehistoric Planet" (1967)

the film was financed in this manner. It was funny that we were asked to write a big budget monster movie to get government financing! The budget was ¥500,000,000 (about $1.4 million)—ten times the average cost of a Nikkatsu film. The governement paid for all of it! Of course, we had to pay it back, but the studio owned real estate—hotels, golf courses, and so on. Nikkatsu was in the red at the time, and they used all the money to pay back its debts instead of on the film! Suddenly, we had to make due with much less money, and this really pissed me off! [laughs]

Ryuzo Nakanishi Eisei Koi was the producer of the film. He was classmates with politicians in the Diet and used his political power to get the money.

Gan Yamazaki The director, Haruyasu Noguchi, tried to stick to the original script as much as possible.

Ryuzo Nakanishi He was famous for shooting films very quickly—in 17 days, usually, though *Gappa* took about 40 days. The special effects were probably done by the staff from Tsuburaya Productions, the same staff as *Godzilla*. We didn't have a department like that at Nikkatsu.

Gan Yamazaki The story was really big, but during this process it began shrinking. They cut corners everywhere. They shot all of the cave scenes in the studio, shots of the ships were done with plastic models. That kind of thing. The only kind of movie we could export internationally was something like *Godzilla*. It's not very interesting just to have a big monster destroy things, so that's why we created this story of affection between the parents and baby monster. That was the unique aspect of this story, and probably triggered the audience interest in the film. We also felt that kids could relate to the kid monster and the drama of him being separated from his parents and put on display in a carnival.

Was your film influenced at all by the British film Gorgo *(1961)? And do you think that your film in turn helped inspire* Son of Godzilla *(1967)?*

Gan Yamazaki No. We've never seen *Gorgo*.

Ryuzo Nakanishi I'm not sure about *Son of Godzilla*. Which came out first?

Gappa *was released in April 1967.* Son of Godzilla *was released that December.*

Ryuzo Nakanishi I don't know. We really didn't care about the other studios. The first *Godzilla* was very well done, but the later ones weren't so good. Godzilla and the other monsters became comics. Our film and *Son of Godzilla* were made during the decline of the Japanese film industry. Nikkatsu eventually began making soft-core porno films, and we walked away. Nikkatsu finally went bankrupt a few years ago.

"When He Died, I Didn't Know How to Live"

Teruyoshi Nakano In the fall of 1969, Mr. Tsuburaya's [physical] condition worsened and he was in and out of the hospital. That's when *Godzilla's Revenge* was in development. Mr. Tsuburaya's doctor ordered him to stop working, so Mr. Honda directed the special effects. I was first assistant director of special effects. Director Honda told me he wasn't sure of the details of the special effects, so he would look to me. I drew the story boards, and I added the flavor of fantasy to it. Come to think of it, maybe it was *Godzilla's Revenge* that Mr. Tsuburaya would have most wanted to be involved with, because he loved children. Because of that, this movie was one of my most memorable projects. I got along with Mr. Honda, however I didn't expect Mr. Tsuburaya to pass on like that. It came so fast, too soon. Mr. Tsuburaya died in January 1970. He had seemed very tired of late. I think the most difficult time for him was during production of *Battle of the Japan Sea* (1969). Mr. Tsuburaya was going back and forth between Toho and Tsuburaya Productions. He was so busy. He was also handling a big special exhibit for Mitsubishi at Expo 1970 in Osaka. In the middle of everything, he passed on.

Minoru Nakano Eiji Tsuburaya was a romanticist; he never showed extreme bloodshed in his movies. He hated bloodshed, even for the death of the monsters, unlike Gamera. One thing I respected about Mr. Tsuburaya was that he never criticized a movie, no matter how terrible it may be, and he tried to find its most beautiful moments. I respected him so deeply. My world was Eiji Tsuburaya. He was that important. When he died, I didn't know how to live. At the funeral, I cried violently on his coffin. Several days later Hajime Tsuburaya came to me saying "How dare you do what we sons could not do!"

Henry G. Saperstein I felt that after the death of Tsuburaya there was no progress. They were still doing the same kinds of effects they were doing in the 60s.

Akira Tsuburaya Special effects are his legacy. They haven't gotten much more complicated since his death–computers and so forth–but the foundation is pretty much the same. For example, to show an erupting volcano, five or six years ago we still filmed colored liquid being injected into water and filmed it upside down, which is then optically inserted into the footage to get the desired effect. It's very conventional, but is looked as good to audiences five years ago as it did 30 years ago. But in the last five years–thanks largely to computers–that has changed dramatically.

Collapse and the 1970s

Akira Kubo [The studios] realized [by the 1970s] that the films were going to be shown on TV and the budgets became low, and actors and actresses became very poor, and fewer people joined the acting trade.

Yu Fujiki The way of producing films had changed, the film industry was in decline, and the new president preferred to buy films and release them

Eiji Tsuburaya, at the end of his career, examines one of the elaborate miniatures from "Latitude Zero" (1969)

rather than produce them himself. Toho has a very strong business sense.

Teruyoshi Nakano I was a "poor director," because I had to continue making the [Godzilla] films during this difficult time. I hated [relying on stock footage], but there was no choice. Of course it hurt me when I had to re-use those scenes, but there was no other way — we did not have the time or the money. So, I tried to confront this situation as a challenge: how could I creatively edit the footage to create a completely new scene? I tried my best, but of course if you watch the movie you will recognize that these are scenes from previous films. When we edited the footage, we tried to make the old film look new, and the new film look old, so it would match and flow together smoothly.

Michio Yamamoto

Tsugunobu "Tom" Kotani My aim is simply to produce commercial entertainment, but I was influenced by men of art, people like Fellini, Godard, and Kubrick, as well as Truffaut and Hitchcock. This may be inconsistent with what I just said.

Kihachi Okamoto During the 70s Toho became more like Hollywood, and took away a lot of the directors' freedom. And so I thought that was a good time to quit the company. After that I had to work with less money, fewer resources, but it was much freer psychologically, and I was able to

Tsugunobu "Tom" Kotani

express more of my point-of-view. I think I quit at the right time, becoming independent at the same time when UCLA-influenced, anti-Hollywood films were being made by American filmmakers.

Jun Fukuda It's really sad that movies are so much a business venture. I switched over to making documentaries, mostly for television, partly because as the time constraints became tighter and tighter, the budgets became smaller and smaller. Because of the weather we were having to rewrite screenplays. I began to dislike being involved with that kind of filmmaking.

Michio Yamamoto At a wrap party, I started talking with someone and told them I'd like to make a film that would really make audiences scream. The producer was listening to that conversation, and three days later I was given the assignment. He sent me horror novels and comics. At first I refused; I wanted to shoot shockers, not horror movies *per se*. I wanted to make stuff like Hitchcock's *The Birds* (1963). The producer, Fumio Tanaka, misunderstood; he thought I wanted to make monster movies. He liked Dracula a lot. I told him that it's not a good idea to bring Dracula to Japan—you just can't beat Terence Fisher. But I had a passion for it and thought well, what can we do? What about all the crosses, the garlic, the castles? I finally found the answer by introducing a father/vampire-daughter complex. She died because of her father's affections. Then we made the film and it was a bit hit in Japan. Alas, I was asked to make another by Tanaka-san. He still wanted to shoot a film about Dracula. Shin Kishida was a good friend of mine, and his face always reminded me of Dracula! [laughs] He was pretty short and wore lifts in the film.

In fact, he got so used to them he wore them all the time. Anyway, he played Dracula in *Lake of Dracula* the following year.

Teruyoshi Nakano When we made [*Godzilla vs. the Smog Monster*, 1971], pollution had become a major issue, although the Japanese people didn't seem to be seriously concerned about it. Factories were polluting the rivers and the sea—we were killing ourselves with man-made pollution. "Please, let's be careful about what we are doing"—that was the message of this movie. The monster Hedorah reminded me of the original Godzilla, and in a sense, this film was similar to *Godzilla*—we were trying to shift the Godzilla movies in a new direction, but we were also thinking about the origins. When *Godzilla* was released back in the 1950s, the world was faced with the problem of nuclear weapons. Now, in the 1970s, it was the issue of polluted cities. Around that time, kids were watching *kaiju* TV programs, and *Godzilla vs. the Smog Monster* was to be released as part of the Toho Champion Matsuri Festival, which was a program of kids' movies and cartoons. A movie about social problems wouldn't appeal to children. [Director Yoshimitsu] Banno wanted to make an entertaining film for children, but I wanted to make something like the first film, that reflected social problems. That was the main conflict between us. Back then I was thinking, if we can't make it during these difficult times, Godzilla movies won't last, and they'll be gone from Toho. I always tried to have the Tsuburaya spirit—"we can do it, we *will* do it." We made Godzilla fly in that movie — that was outrageous, we probably shouldn't have done that. But Mr. Banno was looking for something extraordinary, and even though there was no flying sequence in the

script, we added it. Looking back, the movie seems kind of crude and heavy-handed. I was trying to show the serious threat of pollution with scenes of Godzilla's eyes being burned and people dying. I guess I became uncomfortable with it, even while we were filming, that's why we added the comical scenes. Hedorah had four stages—underwater stage, landing stage, flying stage and adult stage, and I think this was a unique concept. Hedorah came from the Japanese word *hedoro,* which means sludge. It's a chunk of junk, but if we just used a chunk of junk, it wouldn't be appealing visually, so we put eyes and a nose on it. Mr. Banno and I were still young back then, so we just went all out. Looking back now, I kind of feel sorry about what we did. Movies are entertainment, and Godzilla movies are mostly watched by children. We shouldn't offend the feelings and sensitivities of children. Mr. Tsuburaya

Hedorah ravages Japan in "Godzilla vs. the Smog Monster" (1971)

watches our movies. It could be families, it could be people from three different generations. We shouldn't make a movie that contradicts the lessons that are taught in families, such as, you shouldn't hurt people's feelings, you shouldn't steal, things like that. I went overboard and tried too hard, thinking "I'm going to tell the world about pollution." I started to feel embarrassed as I filmed the movie. It was kind of like an apology to the Godzilla fans who were children. I heard that an American critic chose *Godzilla vs. the Smog Monster* as one of the ten worst films of all time. Tell me, why would he say that about my best work? [*laughs*]

Noriaki Yuasa Right after *Gamera vs. Zigra*, I went on location to film a picture called *Maturity* (1971). Before I left for location, I proposed that Gamera's next enemy should be a two-headed monster. After I came back from location, Daiei went bankrupt and I got a dismissal notice. It is difficult to express the regret I felt. I will never, ever forget about the bankruptcy. After New Daiei came about, one person came to me to asked [me to direct *Super Monster*, 1980] and I was reluctant to accept because it was hard to see the old friends, many of whom had been having trouble, and I'm sure

The strongest in the universe! Gamera returns again! Entertaining! Spectacular! A fantasy of space!

SUPER MONSTER

PRODUCED by DAIEI FILM DISTRIBUTION CO., LTD.
Directed by NORIAKI YUASA
Screenplay by NIISAN TAKAHASHI

A DAIEI FILM
World Sales: SHOCHIKU CO., LTD.

SCREENING (English subtitled print)
May 12
May 16
May 20

SHOCHIKU CO., LTD.

Trade ad for "Super Monster" (1980)

Mr. [Nisan] Takahashi felt the same way. And the budget was very low. New Daiei didn't think of it as a new film and just wanted to cut the old footage together. I grieved for my son Gamera—it was a very strange fate.

Jun Fukuda Godzilla became an idol right before I started directing the series. At first children would come to the set and were too frightened to have have their picture taken with Godzilla. Now *everybody* wants to have their picture taken with him. I feel partly responsible that Godzilla's character was changed from being frightening to being an idol.

Teruyoshi Nakano The main idea behind *Godzilla On Monster Island* (1972) was to create a monster that was completely different from the previous film. Hedorah was a liquidy monster, so we wanted to make something solid, harder. We decided to work on the new monster in every detail, such as the size of the hands, and we wanted to add a mechanical feel to it. That's how we invented Gigan, whose hand was a sickle and stomach was a big knife. It was very new and different design, but its hands were so heavy because they were like big logs. I think the actor inside the costume, Kengo Nakayama [known later as Kenpachiro Satsuma], must have had a very difficult time. Gigan's mouth, back and chest are colorful — there is no other monster like it. We used eight different colors on its chest. We got the idea from *Junihitoe*, which was a type of colorful woven *kimono* worn by old women during the Heian Era [794–1185] in Japan. *Godzilla vs. the Smog Monster* didn't have much color in it, so I paid special attention to color in *Godzilla On Monster Island*. Since Godzilla is gray, I thought about how we could contrast from it. I also thought about the color of backgrounds, and the color of the sky—I used a completely different color for the sky from the previous Godzilla films. If I want to explain this movie with one word, I would say, color-conscious movie. But as the production proceeded, the Gigan costume got dirty and the color faded, so it was a pain for the art department to keep repainting the costume. Godzilla was an innocent at first, but by now he had become something of a "tainted hero." Tainted heroes, or heroes with weaknesses, were "in" at the beginning of the 1970s, so maybe Godzilla was influenced by that. Still, we had to make Godzilla the hero—we had stopped thinking about returning to the original theme. The hero has to be incredibly strong, but his enemy must be incredibly strong also. The bottom line, Godzilla has to win in the end. I didn't know what to do, because I had to create an enemy that was stronger than Godzilla, but something Godzilla can defeat—it was so contradictory, and it was such a headache. I had many meetings with the screenwriters … it might have been fun if we had made a movie where Godzilla did lose. I was involved with writing the script also, because the system at Toho was like that—the special effects team had the right to present its opinions during development and screenwriting. Since Godzilla movies were showing at the Toho Champion Festival, we had to make them fairly easy to understand for kids. Kids complained if there was some slow human drama or confusing scene, and they started to eat candy bars or run around in the theater. But once a special effects scene came up, they sat quietly and concentrated on the screen. So we had to show Godzilla every few minutes. But we couldn't just throw Godzilla in without any reason, so we had

to make the mystery linger throughout the movie to keep the kids at the edge of their seats.

Akira Tsuburaya We had the oil shock, and our economy was kind of down. If you look at the Ultraman shows from the 1970s, like "Ultraman Leo," and look at the later episodes, numbers 48, 49, you can definitely see we were spending much less money for the special effects, or used some alternate way to shoot the effects. Speaking of "Ultraman Leo," we started using miniatures in place of men-in-suits, and so forth. In other words, we were challenged to find less expensive ways to create decent special effects. We actually had fun trying to find creative ways to cut the budget.

Teruyoshi Nakano I remember *Godzilla vs. Megalon* (1973) was a very short shoot, probably about three weeks. That movie seemed to take forever to develop, then it went into production without enough preparation. There was no time to ask Mr. [Shinichi] Sekizawa to write the script, so he kind of thought up the general story and director Fukuda wrote the screenplay, which was completed right before crank-in. But it was not unusual; during the "Golden Era," when the studio was was putting out two features every week, everything was rushed. In this movie, there was a new character called Jet Jaguar, and we couldn't help but focus on that new character, so Godzilla was kind of like a sidekick in the end. We couldn't deny feeling a faded enthusiasm toward Godzilla in this movie — it wasn't that Godzilla was in fewer scenes, it was the way Godzilla was portrayed in the movie, I think.

GIANT AGAINST GIANT... the ultimate battle

GODZILLA VS MEGALON

ALL NEW NEVER BEFORE SEEN!

PRODUCED BY TOHO EIZO CO., LTD. DISTRIBUTED BY CINEMA SHARES INTERNATIONAL DISTRIBUTION CORP. IN COLOR

Jun Fukuda I did something like five Godzilla films. The monsters became the stars, and the human characters were put into the background. The human story was cut down. The original one is director Honda's. The original is the only one that's successful, that's really good. I give all of my Godzilla films a minus score.

Scene from Kinji Fukasaku's grand and gaudy "Message from Space" (1978). Left to right: Shinichi "Sonny" Chiba (wearing horns), Vic Morrow, Makoto Sato and Junkichi Orimoto

Teruyoshi Nakano [*Godzilla vs. the Cosmic Monster,* 1975] was called the 20th anniversary Godzilla movie, but I really didn't think about the 20th anniversary. All I tried was not to be stale. In the movies before it, Godzilla's opponents looked like just a costume, so I wanted to make something more unique. There was this robot called Mechani-Kong in *King Kong Escapes,*

so I was wondering if I could make something like that in a Godzilla movie. Actually producer Tanaka thought about it. Mechagodzilla reminded people of the bad Godzilla of the 1960s. We couldn't have made Godzilla the bad guy, because children wouldn't have liked it, so we created Mechagodzilla and acted out our feelings through it — we transposed our feelings of going back to the origins of the Godzilla series onto Mechagodzilla. The only way to bring Godzilla back to the original point was to have Mechagodzilla act as the greatest evil.

Jun Fukuda The budgets were cut in half. For *Godzilla vs. the Cosmic Monster* I felt that Mechagodzilla was the real star star, and wanted this cyborg Godzilla to beat Godzilla up. I felt that was the only creature that could beat Godzilla.

Teruyoshi Nakano I had a great time making [*Terror of Mechagodzilla*] because Mr. Honda insisted that making a movie should be fun, and that is how he approached his work. He also insisted that the entire crew have fun and enjoy what they are doing. It was his philosophy.

Ishiro Honda I [was worried] about the effect [making it] would have on my health. It had gotten to the point that I was losing about [10 pounds] on every film I directed. I just didn't know if I was going to have the energy to get through it ....[Then] Toho stopped bringing me any new projects. You see, I generally didn't develop projects myself, so when the film was finished, that was it for me.

Jun Fukuda The average age of the audience was getting younger and younger, and so we stopped making the films for a while, then the series was resumed in the 1980s.

Kinji Fukasaku *Message from Space* was heavily influenced by *Star Wars*. Eight people made up the story. If you saw the original treatment, which was loosely based on the 300-year-old *Satomi hakkenden* story, you might think it would have compared well with *Star Wars*. Unfortunately, the budget wasn't really sufficient, so I wasn't too happy about it. As a movie, it did well.

Tsugunobu "Tom" Kotani I had had the experience of being co-director on *Marco* (1973), a picture made by Toho and Rankin/Bass, which is how I got the job to direct *The Last Dinosaur* (1977). I also directed *The Bermuda Depths* (1978) and *The Ivory Ape* (1980) for them. I had a great experience. Arthur Rankin worked on the script and shooting, while Jules Bass worked on the music and general postproduction. Everything was shot in Kamikochi, in the national park in Nagano. Both of them understood my skills as a director even if I didn't speak English very well, and they gave me a lot of freedom. [Star Richard Boone] was such a heavy drinker that sometimes we just had to stop shooting. But he was charming, and I think he was well-suited for his character.

Kinji Fukasaku The Cuban Missile Crisis had threatened the whole world—it was a really dangerous period, not only for Japan. I wanted to reflect that feeling all over the world [in *Virus*]. Though the Soviet Union's Socialist system has collapsed, in France and China they are still testing nuclear weapons. It's very difficult for ordinary people to understand. Shooting it

was difficult. We couldn't get a nuclear submarine; it was very difficult to get a submarine to the South Pole! That was a most unsatisfying point! It was impossible to direct the actors unless they understood their words meticulously; I could only pull out their talents if they understood what they were saying. The actor who played the President in *Virus*, Glenn Ford, he couldn't remember lines. [*laughs*] He'd look for places to put cue cards!

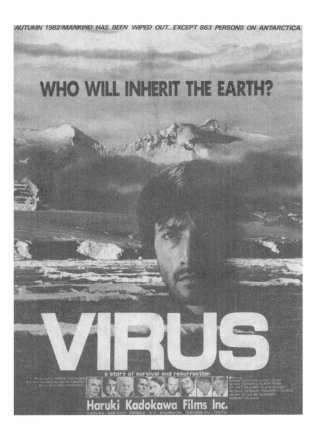

Tatsuo Mastumura

AUTUMN 1982:MANKIND HAS BEEN WIPED OUT...EXCEPT 863 PERSONS ON ANTARCTICA.

WHO WILL INHERIT THE EARTH?

VIRUS

a story of survival and resurrection

Haruki Kadokawa Films Inc.

Trade ad for Kinji Fukasaku's underrated "Virus" (1980)

LEGACY

Kihachi Okamoto I don't have very many good things to say about filmmaking in Japan today, but back in the 1960's, even in Hollywood, there was more freedom to try different things. Audiences and critics knew what good movies were. Film critics weren't afraid to criticize popular films, but not anymore.

Minoru Nakano A major difference is that American film producers care about their film heritage, but Japanese film producers only care about the film's opening–after that, who cares? During the Golden Age, there was a good combination of the younger generation and their new ideas and the older generation with their experience and know-how and understanding of the production system. Nowadays there is no inter-relation.

Masaru Sato In the Golden Period, we had a whole range of movies, big movies, little movies, then the average budget became smaller. We'd never be able to do a computer effects film like *Forrest Gump* with the cost. Godzilla movies are something of an exception. But today's Japanese movies are too much for kids. Directors like Kurosawa devoted themselves to the story and worked very hard on the script. Audiences today aren't patient enough.

Jun Fukuda Movies are 100 years old, and I have been in the film industry for half of that time, and as I look back I wonder what I've done. I guess I don't speak very confidently.

Eiji Funakoshi We were like a family, a very Japanese family. Our personal relationships were very strong, which is why you would have this sense of obligation, to do pictures when asked. We were like a brood.

Yu Fujiki It was a fun 42 years. It flew like an arrow.

Henry G. Saperstein [Toho and I] had a 30-year love-hate relationship. No matter how much money I deliver for them, I'm still an outsider, and that'll never change. Kipling was right: East is east and West is west, and the 'twain ain't never gonna meet.

Kimi Honda It's very strange–only after [my husband] passed away did I realize the impact of his work. Many people came to his funeral, people from foreign countries, and reporters from all over the world reported his death. *Godzilla* was the first Japanese film to earn a lot of money overseas; he never mentioned that kind of stuff to me. And I was his manager; I did his contracts and everything. I learned this from other people. He never bragged about his accomplishments. He simply devoted himself to making movies. He didn't like negotiating his contract when it came up for renewal. He didn't like marketing himself. He was the son of a monk at the temple; he was very old-style Japanese.

Henry G. Saperstein It's a morality play. It's the classic story of good vs. evil, white hat vs. black hat. Godzilla is knocked all around until the tenth round, then comes out swinging.

Akira Takarada At the time, 40 years ago, 10 million people came to see *Godzilla*. A kid that was 10 years old at the time is now in his 50s! Now these middle-aged men are all Godzilla collectors!

Henry G. Saperstein For ten years I pressured Toho to make [a Godzilla movie] in America. Finally they agreed, and now a $40 million dollar movie is underway. I guess my crowning glory will be when TriStar's movie is released.

Ishiro Honda My nightmares are almost always about war–wandering the streets, searching for something that's lost forever. But it's possible for me to will myself to have pleasant dreams. For me, the most wonderful fragrance in the world is new film. You open the canister for the first time and breathe deeply. That night, the same wonderful fragrance fills your dreams. It's grand.

Akira Takarada Godzilla is retiring from Japanese films and now the story is going to the States. To me, my New Face class had several great actors: Akihiko Hirata, Momoko Kochi—and Godzilla. As a leading actor in an American film, he's becoming the biggest star of us all.

Or, as Paul Harvey would say, the rest of the story: the men and women, the directors, the actors, the screenwriters, the guys in the rubber suits who made these amazing creations of modern cinema.

Who's Who

Adams, Nick (1931–1968)
American actor who starred in three filmed-in-Japan co-productions: *Frankenstein Conquers the World*, *Monster Zero* (both 1965) and *The Killing Bottle* (1967), all co-starring cult actress Kumi Mizuno, with whom he had an alleged affair.

Amamoto, Eisei (b. 1926)
Skeletal actor who played "that international Judas," Dr. Who in *King Kong Escapes* (1967) and the kindly inventor in *Godzilla's Revenge* (1969). He's also in *The Secret of the Telegian* (1960), *Gorath* (as a drunk, 1962), *Attack of the Mushroom People* (as a wayward mushroom man, 1963), *The Lost World of Sinbad* (as Granny the Witch, 1963), *Atragon* (as the High Priest of Mu, 1963), *Dagora the Space Monster* (as a neatly-dressed safecracker, 1964), *Ghidrah—The*

Three-Headed Monster (as the princess' aide, 1964), *What's Up Tiger Lily?* (as the character who talks like Peter Lorre, 1966), *Godzilla versus the Sea Monster* (1966), *Mighty Jack* (1968) and *Message from Space* (1978). Still active in films, and a favorite of director Kihachi Okamoto. He also played the husband in the classic *Twenty-Four Eyes* (1954).

Arikawa, Teisho "Sadamasa" (b. 1925)
Special effects cameraman for Eiji Tsuburaya who was promoted to special effects director for *Son of Godzilla* (1967), *Destroy All Monsters* (1968), and *Yog, Monster from Space* (1970). He also directed, uncredited, many of the effects scenes for *Godzilla versus the Sea Monster* (1966).

Arishima, Ichiro (1916–1987)
Character comedian who played Mr. Tako, the harried company man determined to bring Kong to Japan in *King Kong vs. Godzilla* (1962). Also played a lusty wizard in *The Lost World of Sinbad* (1963). Best known in Japan as Yuzo Kayama's father in the "Young Guy" film series.

Banno, Yoshimitsu (b. 1931)
Director of *Godzilla vs. the Smog Monster* (1971). His work was not appreciated by producer Tomoyuki Tanaka, and he never directed another monster movie.

Burr, Raymond (1917–1993)
The star of the American version of *Gojira* (1954), renamed *Godzilla, King of the Monsters!* (1956), Burr played reporter Steve Martin (!). He reprised the role for the awful American version of that film's quasi-remake/sequel, *Godzilla 1985* (1984). His other fantasy credits include *The Whip Hand* (1951), *The Magic Carpet* (with Patricia Medina, 1951), *Bride of the Gorilla* (also 1951), and the 3-D *Gorilla at Large* (1954). He was memorable as the heavy in Hitchcock's *Rear Window* (1954). In later years, Burr reprised his other big role, TV's Perry Mason, including a TV-movie filmed just one month before his death. He died of metastatic cancer of the liver.

Chiaki, Minoru (b. 1917)
The good-natured, self-sacrificing pilot in *Gigantis the Fire Monster* (1955). Best known for his outstanding work for Akira Kurosawa, including his role as the woodcutter *samurai* in *Seven Samurai* (1954) and as the peasant paired with Kamatari Fujiwara in *The Hidden Fortress* (1958); Chiaki's character was the basis for C-3PO in *Star Wars* (1977). Chiaki is the father of actor Katsuhiko Sasaki (q.v.)

Conway, Harold S. (1910?–1980?)
Familiar but amateur actor in Japanese productions, usually as some kind of government official. His sci-fi credits include *The Mysterians* (1957), *The Last Death of the Devil, Battle in Outer Space* (both 1959), *Mothra* (as the Rolisican official, 1961), *The Last War* (also 1961), *King Kong vs. Godzilla* (trapped in a sub, 1962), *Godzilla vs. the Thing* (1964), *Goke—Bodysnatcher from Hell* (in flashback stills only) and *Genocide* (both 1968). In the Crazy Cats comedy *Las Vegas Free-for-All* (1967), Conway plays H. Conway, manager of the Riviera Casino.

Cotten, Joseph (1905–1993)
Played Captain Craig McKenzie, commander of the Alpha, in *Latitude Zero* (1969). Married to his co-star, Patricia Medina. One of the screen's most underrated actors, he appeared in such classics as *The Magnificent Ambersons* (1942), *Shadow of a Doubt* (1943), *The Third Man* (1949) ....and he's also the only actor in this book to appear in both *Citizen Kane* (1941) and a Japanese sci-fi picture.

Daimon, Masaaki (b. 1949)
Dark, rather bland leading player in *Godzilla vs. the Cosmic Monster* (1974). He returned to the series, briefly, for a cameo at the beginning of *Terror of Mechagodzilla* (1975).

Daning, Mike (b. 1922?)
Portly amateur actor in Japanese genre films, he was memorable as Dr. Stein in *The X from Outer Space* (1967). He also appeared in *Rodan* (1956), *Terror Beneath the Sea* (1966), *Monster from a Prehistoric Planet* (1967), and *Genocide* (1968), making him perhaps the only actor to do monster movies for Toho, Toei, Shochiku and Nikkatsu.

Dekker, Albert (1904–1968)
Distinguished Hollywood character actor who played the Secretary of Defense in *Gammera the Invincible* (1965). Dekker also essayed—memorably—the title role of *Doctor Cyclops* (1940), and lent able support in films like *Kiss Me Deadly* (1955) and *The Wild Bunch* (1969), the latter released after Dekker's notorious accident/suicide.

Donlevy, Brian (1899–1972)
Gammera the Invincible's other American star was, like Albert Dekker, a longtime supporting player in Hollywood, usually cast as a tough baddie (as in *Destry Rides Again*, 1939), or as a surly antihero (*The Great McGinty*, 1940). The two actors even worked together prior to battling the giant turtle, in *Beau Geste* (1939). His genre credits include fine performances in the first two Quatermass movies, *The Creeping Unknown* (1956) and *Enemy from Space* (1957).

Fujita, Susumu (1912–1991) Beefy actor who almost always led the fight against some big monster. Played military leaders in *The Mysterians* (1957), *Atragon* (1963), *Godzilla vs. the Thing, Dagora the Space Monster* (both 1964), and *Frankenstein Conquers the World* (1965). Not to be confused with Jun Tazaki (q.v.), who played similar roles during this period. Fujita also played the lead in Kurosawa's first film as director, *Sanshiro Sugata* (1943), and its sequel, and in memorable character roles thereafter, such as the cowardly-but-wise *samurai* in *Yojimbo* (1961).

Fujiyama, Yoko (b. 1941) Beautiful innocent in the Yuriko Hoshi mode, Fujiyama played the ingenue in *Atragon* (1963) and *Dagora, the Space Monster* (1964).

Furness, George (1898–1994?) An American-born attorney who defended Foreign Minister Mamoru Shigemitsu in the International Military Tribunal for the Far East, Furness spent his later years appearing in films like *The Mysterians* (1957) and *Gorath* (1962). Unlike, Harold S. Conway and Andrew Hughes, Furness was actually a pretty good actor, and had substantial roles in

American movies filmed in Japan, especially in the disaster epic *The Last Voyage* (1960).

Hamilton, Kipp (1928?–1981) Former starlet at 20th Century-Fox, Hamilton was the "Special Guest Star" who warbled through "Feel in My Heart" (aka "The Words Get Stuck in My Throat") in *War of the Gargantuas* (1966).

Haynes, Linda (b. 1947) Sexy starlet in Star Trek-esque get-ups in *Latitude Zero* (1969). Her other credits include *Coffy* (1973) and *Rolling Thunder* (1975).

Healey, Myron (b. 1922) Minor actor who dominates—frustratingly—the Americanized *Varan the Unbelievable* (1958; the Healey version being released in 1962). His other genre credits include Abbott and Costello's *The Time of Their Lives* (1946), *The Unearthly* (1957) and *The Incredible Melting Man* (1977).

Hidari, Bokuzen (1894–1971) The eternal sad-faced old peasant in Japanese films like *Ikiru* (1952), *Seven Samurai* (1954) and *The Lower Depths* (1957); he played Kaoru Yachigusa's guardian in *The Human Vapor* (1960).

Hirata, Akihiko (1927–1984) One of *kaiju eiga*'s most important and recognizable character actors. Born to a wealthy family and educated at the prestigious Tokyo University's School of Interior Design, Hirata moved into still photography before joining Shintoho as an assistant director under elder brother Yoshiki Onoda. Hirata joined Toho in 1953, where his long face and intense features led to his casting as Dr. Daisuke Serizawa, the tormented scientist and inventor of the oxygen destroyer in *Godzilla, King of the Monsters!* (1954). Playing everything from snarling villains to easy-going government officials, Hirata became a genre star with a genuine cult following, though the unprecedented success of the first Godzilla film also typecast him. His association with the genre continued right up until his death; he helped announce the production of *Godzilla 1985*, but was too ill to appear in the film and his role was ultimately played by Yosuke Natsuki. Hirata's other sci-fi credits include *Rodan* (1956), *The Mysterians* (as a scientist duped by evil aliens, 1957), *The H-Man, Varan the Unbelievable* (both 1958), *The Three Treasures* (1959), *The Secret of the Telegian* (1960), *Mothra* (1961), *Gorath, King Kong vs. Godzilla* (1962), *Atragon* (1963), *Ghidrah—The Three-Headed Monster* (as a detective, 1964), *Godzilla versus the Sea Monster* (wearing an eye patch again, 1966),

Son of Godzilla, The Killing Bottle (1967), *Latitude Zero* (speaking English, 1969), *Prophecies of Nostradamus, Godzilla vs. the Cosmic Monster* (both 1974), *Terror of Mechagodzilla* (as the tragic Dr. Mafune, 1975), *The War in Space* (1977), *Fugitive Alien* [made for TV] (1978), and *Sayonara Jupiter* (1984). His non-genre credits include *Samurai I & II* (1954–5), *Chushingura* and *Sanjuro* (both 1962).

Hirose, Shoichi "Solomon" (b. 1918)
Monster suit actor who played King Kong in *King Kong vs. Godzilla* (1962), and Ghidrah in *Ghidrah—The Three-Headed Monster* (1964) and *Monster Zero* (1965).

Holcombe, Harry (1907–1987)
American character actor who interrupts the proceedings throughout the Americanized *King Kong vs. Godzilla* (1962). Though Holcombe appeared in numerous films and television programs (*Birdman of Alcatraz* [1962], *The Silencers* [1965], *Empire of the Ants* [1977], TV's "Batman"), he is probably best remembered as the grandfatherly fixture of Country Time Lemonade commercials.

Hongo, Kojiro (b. 1938)
Handsome leading man at Daiei Studios; he starred in several Gamera movies—*War of the Monsters* (1966), *The Return of the Giant*

Monsters (1967), and *Destroy All Planets* (1968)—as well as several other Daiei-produced films with fantasy elements, including *Buddha* (as Siddartha, 1961), *The Whale God* (1962), *The Return of the Giant Majin* (1966), *Kaidan botandoro* (1968), *Along with Ghosts* and *The Haunted Castle* (both 1969). He has a brief cameo at the beginning of *Gamera—The Guardian of the Universe* (1995).

Hughes, Andrew (1908?–1985?)
Western actor in Japanese films, most famously as Dr. Stevenson in the all-star monster epic *Destroy All Monsters* (1968). His other sci-fi credits include *The Golden Bat, Terror Beneath the Sea* (both 1966), *King Kong Escapes* (as a reporter, 1967), and *Submersion of Japan/Tidal Wave* (as an Australian ambassador).

Ibuki, Toru (b. 1940)
Tall Toho supporting player, best remembered as the long-lost brother in *Godzilla versus the Sea Monster* (1966). Ibuki's other credits include *Ghidrah—The Three-Headed Monster* (as an assassin, 1964) *Monster Zero* (as an X-ite, 1965), *King Kong Escapes* (as a Who henchman, 1967), and *Terror of Mechagodzilla* (as an alien, 1975).

Ikebe, Ryo (b. 1918)
Stoic star of numerous 50s romantic melodramas, Ikebe toplined three sci-fi pictures: *Battle in Outer Space* (1959), *Gorath*

(1962), and *The War in Space* (1977). He also stars in such classics as *Early Spring* (1956) and *Snow Country* (1957), and appears in *Mishima—A Life in Four Chapters* (1985) and numerous Toho war movies.

Iketani, Saburo (b. 1922?)
The eternal radio and television announcer in Toho monster movies, warning the populace to turn on their lights, turn up their radios as high as they'll go, etc. His credits include *Godzilla, King of the Monsters!* (1954), *Rodan* (1956), *Battle in Outer Space* (1959), *Mothra* and *The Last War* (both 1961), *Gorath* (1962), *Monster Zero* (1965), and *Destroy All Monsters* (1968).

Inagaki, Hiroshi (1905–1980)
Best known in the West for his epic period films, among the best received in the United States during the 1950s and early-60s. His credits include the "Samurai" trilogy: *Samurai I: Musashi Miyamoto* (1954), *Samurai II: Duel at Ichijoji Temple* (1955), and *Samurai III: Duel on Ganryu Island* (1956). Also *The Rickshaw Man* (1958), *The Three Treasures* (1959), *Daredevil in the Castle* (1961), *Chushingura* (1962), *Whirlwind* (1964), and *Kojiro* (1967). *The Three Treasures, Daredevil in the Castle* and *Whirlwind* (that is, a big tornado) feature elaborate special effects by Eiji Tsuburaya.

Ito, Emi and Yumi [see **Peanuts, The**]

Ito, Hisaya (b. 1938)

Tall, thin, and tight-lipped supporting player, best remembered as the Malmess the Assassin in *Ghidrah—The Three-Headed Monster* (1964), a role intended for Yoshio Tsuchiya. He's also in *The Mysterians* (1957), *The H-Man* (as the first victim), *Varan the Unbelievable* (both 1958), *Battle in Outer Space* (1959), *The Human Vapor* (1960), *Atragon* (as the kidnapping victim), *Frankenstein Conquers the World* (1965), *War of the Gargantuas* (as a detective, 1966), *Godzilla versus the Sea Monster* (as a scientist who threatens to blow up the island, 1966), and *Destroy All Monsters* (1968).

Ito, Jerry (b. 1927)

Eurasian actor in Japanese films, sometimes mis-billed as "Jelly Ito" (!). He was especially memorable as shameless showman Clark Nelson in *Mothra* (1961). He also appears in *The Manster* (as a detective) *The Last War* (both 1961), *Wall-Eyed Nippon* (a comedy with Akira Takarada and Yumi Shirakawa, 1964), and in the featurized *Mighty Jack* (a villain again, 1968).

Iwanaga, Frank (1915?–1963)

Played Security Officer Tomo Iwanaga in the filmed-in-Hollywood portions of *Godzilla, King of the Monsters!* with Raymond Burr.

Jaeckel, Richard (1926–1997)

American actor in films from the 1940s, Jaeckel went to Japan to star in *The Green Slime* (1968) and back again for *Latitude Zero* (1969). Best known, however, for his roles in American war movies like *Sands of Iwo Jima* (1949) and *The Dirty Dozen* (1967), and the occasional juicy supporting role, notably opposite Paul Newman in *Sometimes a Great Notion* (1971).

Kagawa, Kyoko (b. 1931)

Important actress in dozens of Japanese film classics, including *Tokyo Story* (1953), *Sansho the Bailiff*, *The Story of Chikamatsu* (both 1954), *The Lower Depths* (1957), *The Bad Sleep Well* (1960), *High and Low* (1963), and *Red Beard* (1965). More recently she appeared opposite the late Herb Edelman and the late Kiyoshi Atsumi in *Tora-san's Dream of Spring* (1979), and in Kurosawa's last film to date, *Madadayo* (1993). She played the news photographer in *Mothra* (1961), opposite the late Frankie Sakai.

Kato, Haruya (b. 1928)

Baby-faced actor, actually much older than he appears, who essayed various bit roles in Japanese films. His sci-fi credits include *The Mysterians* (as a doomed firefighter, 1957), *The H-Man* (as a doomed sailor, 1958), *Mothra* (as a rescued sailor, 1961), *King Kong vs. Godzilla* (1962), *Dagora the Space Monster* (as Sabu, an inept thief), *Ghidrah—The Three-Headed Monster* (as the reporter who asks the princess about her origins, both 1964), *Frankenstein Conquers the World* (1965). If you want to see what Kato looks like these days, he's among the group of elderly people praying (along with with Sachio Sakai) near the end of Kurosawa's *Rhapsody in August* (1991).

Kawakita, Koichi (b. 1942)

Special effects director at Toho since the late-1980s (he joined the studio in 1962), following Eiji Tsuburaya and Teruyoshi Nakano. His early work in films like *Sayonara Jupiter* (1984) and *Godzilla vs. Biollante* (1989) helped revitalize the genre, but he fell into a creative rut and mechanical sameness by the mid-1990s. His credits include *Nineteen* (1987), *Gunhed* (1989), *Godzilla vs. King Ghidorah* (1991), *Godzilla vs. Mothra* (1992), *Monster Planet Godzilla* [3-D short], *Godzilla vs. Mechagodzilla* (1993), *Yamato Takeru, Godzilla vs. Space Godzilla* (1994), *Godzilla vs. Destroyer* (1995), *Mothra* (1996).

Kawazu, Seizaburo (1908–1983)

A matinee idol during the 1930s, in middle age this former Shochiku star switched to character roles with great success, playing everything from underworld kingpins to UN delegates. He was the gang leader in *Dagora, the Space Monster* (1964) and lead the military in *Mothra* (1961). He also appears in *The Last War* (also 1961). His other credits include several early Ozu films.

Kayama, Shigeru (1906–1975)

Sci-fi novelist who wrote the story for the first Godzilla (1954), as well as *Gigantis the Fire Monster* and *Half Human* (both 1955).

Kayama, Yuzo (b. 1937)

One of Japan's biggest stars of the 1960s, Kayama starred in Toho's "Young Guy" film series as an all-Japanese college student. His trademark, touching his right index finger to the side of his nose, was copied by Godzilla in *Godzilla versus the Sea Monster* (1966). He starred with Toshiro Mifune in Kurosawa's *Sanjuro* (1962) and *Red Beard* (as the young doctor, 1965), and was featured prominently in Hiroshi Inagaki's *Chushingura* (as Asano, 1962) and Kihachi Okamoto's *The Sword of Doom* (1966). His sole sci-fi credit is Jun Fukuda's *ESPY* (1974).

Keane, Ed (b. 1911?)

Western actor in Japanese fantasy films of the late-1950s/early-60s. He was the mayor of Newkirk City in *Mothra* (1961), and figures prominently in Shue Matsubayashi's *The Last War* (also 1961). His other sci-fi credits include *Battle in Outer Space* (1959) and *Gorath* (1962).

Kimura, Isao "Ko" (1923–1981)

The youngest of the *Seven Samurai*, Kimura starred opposite drag queen Akihiro Maruyama in Kinji Fukasaku's *Black Lizard* (1968).

Kimura, Takeshi (1911–1988)

Toho screenwriter behind that studio's most ambitious sci-fi features, including *Gorath* (1962), *Attack of the Mushroom People* (1963), *The Human Vapor* (1960) and *The Last War* (1961). From 1964 he wrote under the pseudonym Kaoru Mabuchi. His other genre credits include *Rodan* (1956), *The Mysterians* (1957), *The H-Man* (1958), *The Lost World of Sinbad* (co-written with Shinichi Sekizawa, 1963), *Whirlwind* (1964), *Frankenstein Conquers the World* (1965), *War of the Gargantuas* (1966), *King Kong Escapes* (1967), *Destroy All Monsters* (1968) and *Godzilla vs. The Smog Monster* (1971).

Kirino, Nadao (b. 1937)

Western-looking Japanese actor—he always seems to be wincing—who was in a plethora of Toho monster movies during the 50s and 60, usually cast as a second-in-command military type. He played Kumi Mizuno's doomed husband in *Gorath* (1962); his other credits include *The H-Man* (as a waiter), *Varan the Unbelievable* (both 1958), *The Secret of the Telegian* (1960), *The Last War* (1961), *King Kong vs. Godzilla* (1962), *The Lost World of Sinbad*, *Atragon* (both 1963), *Dagora, the Space Monster* (1964), *Monster Zero* (1965), *War of the Gargantuas* (1966), *King Kong Escapes* (1967), and *Destroy All Monsters* (1968). Sometimes mis-billed as "Hiroo Kirino."

Kishida, Shin (1939–1982)

Sometimes mis-billed as "Mori" Kishida, this cult actor of the 1970s was a kind of subdued Eisei Amamoto (q.v.). He played the Interpol agent in *Godzilla vs. the Cosmic Monster* (1974), and the Dracula character in both *Lake of Dracula* (1971), and *Evil of Dracula* (1975). Kishida was also a sci-fi television writer and appears in *Shogun Assassin* (1972). He died of lung cancer.

Kobayashi, Keiju (b. 1923)

One of the stars of the long-running "Shacho" comedy film series of the 1960s, Kobayashi played the Prime Minister in both *Submersion of Japan/Tidal Wave* (1973) and *Godzilla 1985* (1984). He's also the *samurai* in the closet in *Sanjuro* (1962) and Nobuko Miyamoto's boss in *A Taxing Woman* (1987).

Kobayashi, Yukiko (b. 1946) Exotic-looking heroine of *Destroy All Monsters* (1968), Kobayashi also played an island native in *Yog—Monster from Space* and the title role of *The Vampire Doll* (both 1970).

Kodo, Kokuten (1887–1969?) A.k.a Kuninori Kodo, this elderly, toothless actor played the island chief in *Godzilla, King of the Monsters!* (1954) and virtually the same role in Kurosawa's *Seven Samurai* (also 1954).

Koizumi, Hiroshi (b. 1926) Somewhat bland but very popular leading player of the 1950s who starred as the handsome pilot in *Gigantis the Fire Monster* (1955), and played scientists in *Mothra* (1961), *Atragon* (1963), *Godzilla vs. the Thing, Dagora, the Space Monster, Ghidrah—The Three-Headed Monster* (all 1964), *Prophecies of Nostradamus, Godzilla vs. the Cosmic Monster* (both 1974) and *Godzilla 1985* (1984). He also played a sailor in the eerie *Attack of the Mushroom People* (1963).

Kosugi, Yoshio (1903–1968) The perennial South Seas native chief of Toho monster movies, the coarse-faced actor could always be counted upon to look fierce and menacing. His fantasy film credits include *Half Human* (1955), *The Mysterians* (1957), *The Three Treasures* (1959), *The Human Vapor* (1960), *Mothra* (1961), *King Kong vs. Godzilla* (1962), *The Lost World of Sinbad* (1963), *Godzilla vs. the Thing, Ghidrah—The Three-Headed Monster* (1964), and *Frankenstein Conquers the World* (1965). Kosugi also appeared in numerous Kurosawa and Inagaki films.

Kurobe, Susumu (b. 1939) Actor who won lasting fame as Ultraman's alter ego, Hayata, Kurobe also appeared in several Toho fantasies, including *Ghidrah—The Three-Headed Monster* (as an assassin, 1964), *King Kong Escapes* (as one of Who's henchmen), *Son of Godzilla* (1967), *Destroy All Monsters* (1968), and *Latitude Zero* (1969). He also played the villain in Woody Allen's *What's Up Tiger Lily?* (1966), and is one of the soldiers in the Frank Sinatra war movie *None But the Brave* (1965).

Kurosawa, Toshio (b. 1944) Star of several 70s sci-fi epics, including *Submersion of Japan/Tidal Wave* (1973), *Prophecies of Nostradamus* (1974), and *Evil of Dracula* (1975). No relation to Akira.

Mabuchi, Kaoru [see **Kimura, Takeshi**]

Maruyama, Akihiro (b. 1935) Campy drag star of *Black Lizard* (1968) and *Black Rose* (1969). Known today as Akihiro Miwa.

Matsukata, Hiroki (b. 1942) Huge Toei star—and still very popular today—who starred in Toei's only giant monster movie of the 1960s, *The Magic Serpent* (1966).

Mifune, Toshiro (1920–1997) Japan's greatest film actor, Mifune had a raw screen presence so electric he transcended all language and cultural barriers—you can't help but watch him. He is, of course, best remembered as Akira Kurosawa's leading player from the late-1940s to the mid-1960s, but the actor appeared in a wide range of films, including several features with fantasy elements, including

The Three Treasures (1959), *The Lost World of Sinbad* (1963), and *Princess of the Moon* (1987). However, his best work lay in such must-see masterpieces as *Rashomon* (1950), *Seven Samurai* (1954), *The Hidden Fortress* (1958), *The Bad Sleep Well* (1960), *Yojimbo* (1961), *Sanjuro* (1962), and *High and Low* (1963). He was also memorable as Musashi Miyamoto in Hiroshi Inagaki's *Samurai* trilogy (1954–56) and as *The Rickshaw Man* (1958). The actor also appeared in numerous Western productions, notably the Mexican-made *The Important Man* (1961), *Grand Prix* (1966), *Hell in the Pacific* (1966), *1941* (with Mifune, Christopher Lee and Slim Pickens all in one scene—amazing!, 1979), *Shogun* (1980), *The Challenge* (1982), *Journey of Honor* and *Shadow of the Wolf* (both 1990). When asked to speak English he was almost always dubbed. Sadly, failing health denied him that one last great role.

Mihashi, Tatsuya (b. 1923)
Toho star of the late-1950s through late-1960s, Mihashi was a kind of second-string Toshiro Mifune. He starred in *The Human Vapor* (1960), though was far more memorable in two of Kurosawa's best films: *The Bad Sleep Well* (1960) and *High and Low* (1963), playing the brother-in-law and assistant of Toshiro Mifune's characters, respectively. Married to *Battle in Outer Space* heroine Kyoko Anzai.

Miller, Linda (b. 1949?)
Cute model living in Japan who played the ingenue in *King Kong Escapes* (1967), a role for which she was dubbed in both the Japanese and American versions. She also appears in what amounts to an extra role in *The Green Slime* (1968). Where are you, Linda Miller?

Misumi, Kenji (1921–1975)
Daiei director who helmed *The Return of the Giant Majin* (1966). He also directed Japan's first 70mm production, *Buddha* (1961), and numerous "Zatoichi" and "Lone Wolf and Cub" films.

Mori, Kazuo (1911–1989)
Another Daiei director who directed a Majin movie and lots of "Zatoichis." Mori's Majin (wouldn't that make a great name for an antique store?) was the third, *Majin Strikes Again* (1966). Nobody seems to known for sure, but Mori's first name might be Issei, not Kazuo—at least it can be read that way, too.

Moritani, Shiro (1931–1984)
A longtime assistant director under Kurosawa, Moritani directed the most popular Japanese fantasy film of the 1970s, *Submersion of Japan* (1973).

Murakami, Fuyuki (b. 1911)
The scientist who turns Yoshio Tsuchiya into *The Human Vapor* (1960). His other credits, usually as scientists, include *Godzilla, King of the Monsters!* (1954), *Gigantis the Fire Monster* (1955), *Rodan* (1956), *The Mysterians* (1957), *Varan the Unbelievable* (1958), *Battle in Outer Space* (as the detective, 1959), and *Monster Zero* (1965).

Miyauchi, Kunio (b. 1932)
Jazz-influenced composer who scored *The Human Vapor* (1960) and *Godzilla's Revenge* (1969). Best known for his music for the Tsuburaya-produced series "Ultraman."

Nagata, Masaichi (1906–1985)
Daiei producer-executive who brought Japanese cinema to worldwide attention with the release of Kurosawa's *Rashomon* (1950) and Kenji Mizoguchi's *Ugetsu* (1953), among others. Nagata also executive produced and helped create the "Gamera" and "Majin" film series, as well as the occasional miscellaneous Daiei fantasy film. His son, **Hidemasa Nagata** (b. 1925) was the official producer of the Gamera films.

Nakajima, Haruo (b. 1929)
Actor-stuntman and the man inside the Godzilla costume from 1954–1972. He also played giant monsters in other Toho *kaiju*

eiga, notably Rodan in *Rodan* (1956), Mogera, the mole-like robot in *The Mysterians* (1957), Varan in *Varan the Unbelievable* (1958), Mothra in *Mothra* (1961), Magma the Walrus in *Gorath* (1962), Baragon in *Frankenstein Conquers the World* (1965), Gairah, the Green Gargantua, in *War of the Gargantuas* (1966), King Kong in *King Kong Escapes* (1967), a winged lion in *Latitude Zero* (1969) and Gezora the Giant Cuttlefish in *Yog—Monster from Space* (1970). Nakajima also played human characters—he was, for instance, one of the marauding bandits in *Seven Samurai* (1954), and the balding actor appears as a military advisor in *Destroy All Monsters* (1968). Today Nakajima is close friends with fellow Godzilla actor Kenpachiro Satsuma (q.v.) and is justly proud of his not-insignificant legacy.

Nakamaru, Tadao (b. 1933)
Not-quite leading player at Toho, mostly in crime and action films for Jun Fukuda and Kihachi Okamoto, Nakamaru played the teleporting villain in *The Secret of the Telegian* (1960). His other credits include minor appearances in *The Mysterians* (1957), *The H-Man* (1958) and in films as late as *Terror of Mechagodzilla* (1975).

Nakamura, Nobuo (1908–1990)
Thin, bespectacled old professor type in *Half Human* (1955), *Dagora the Space Monster* (1964) and *War of the Gargantuas* (1966) More significantly, Nakamura was a regular in

Yasujiro Ozu's films from at least the early-1950s, and made memorable appearances in Kurosawa's films also.

Nakamura, Satoshi "Tetsu" (1908–1992)
Japanese-Canadian actor, often in bilingual roles, he was the mad scientist who creates *The Manster* (1961). He also played Clark Nelson's chief henchman in *Mothra* (1961), one of the scientists who wears a protective cape in *The Mysterians* (1957), a kidnapped scientist in *Latitude Zero* (1969), a south seas island chief in *Yog—Monster from Space* (1970), and yet another scientist, eaten by *The Last Dinosaur* (1977). His other genre roles include *The Lost World of Sinbad* (1963), *Atragon* (1963), *The Killing Bottle* (1967) and *Marco* (1973).

Neal, Peggy (b. 1947)
Starlet featured in *Terror Beneath the Sea* (1966) opposite Shinichi "Sonny" Chiba, and *The X from Outer Space* (1967). She also played the femme fatal in the Crazy Cats comedy *Las Vegas Free-for-All,* made that same year. Where are you, Peggy Neal?

Negishi, Akemi (b. 1934)
The eternal exotic native girl, and a kind of 50s Kumi Mizuno, Negishi strutted her way through everything from Josef von Sternberg's *Anatahan* (as a native girl, 1953) to *Half Human* (another native girl, 1955), from

Kurosawa's *Record of a Living Being* (1955) and *The Lower Depths* (1957) to *King Kong vs. Godzilla* (once again..., 1962).

Nihonmatsu, Kazui (b. 1922)
Director of *The X from Outer Space*, Nihonmatsu made just four features before turning to documentary filmmaking and other pursuits. His other credits: *Oh, Lovers!* (1964), *Atta Guy! The Genius of Mischief* (1965), and the little-seen sci-fi/horror film *Genocide* (aka *The War of the Insects*, 1968), all made for Shochiku.

Nomura, Kozo (b. 1931)
Supporting player who essayed the leading role (in the Japanese version anyway) in *Varan the Unbelievable* (1958). His other credits include *Battle in Outer Space* (1959), *The Human Vapor* (1960), *Gorath* (1962), *Godzilla vs. the Thing* (1964), *Ghidrah—The Three-Headed Monster* (as a geologist, also 1964) and *Frankenstein Conquers the World* (as a reporter, 1965).

Oda, Motoyoshi (1910–1973)
The director of *Gigantis the Fire Monster* (1955) and *The Invisible Man* (1954) Oda primarily helmed programmers for Toho. His output was impressive, but his films, as near as can be determined, unexceptional.

Odaka, Megumi (b. 1972)
The most popular *kaiju eiga* actress since Kumi Mizuno, Okada made her genre debut, as psychic Miki Saegusa, at age 17 in *Godzilla vs. Biollante* (1989). She has reprised that role in *Godzilla vs. King Ghidorah* (1991), *Godzilla vs. Mothra* (1992), *Godzilla vs. Mechagodzilla* (1993), *Godzilla vs. Space Godzilla* (1994) and *Godzilla vs. Destroyer* (1995), making her by far the only actor to play the same [human] role in so many Japanese monster movies.

Okada, Eiji (1920–1995)
The project leader of *The X from Outer Space* (1967) is best remembered in the West as the star of two highly acclaimed films: *Hiroshima mon amour* (1959) and *Woman in the Dunes* (1964), among others. Shortly before his death he made a memorable appearance in the released-here *Traffic Jam* (1991). One film he's not in is *Ghidrah—The Three-Headed Monster* (1964), although he is often credited as such.

Okada, Masumi (b. 1936)
Danish-Japanese actor who accompanies Akira Takarada and Richard Jaeckel to *Latitude Zero* (1969). Okada also appears in *Living Skeleton* (1968) and *Sayonara Jupiter* (1984). He also had a major supporting role in the miniseries "Shogun" (1980).

Okawara, Takao (b. 1949)
Director of *Godzilla vs. Mothra* (1992), *Godzilla vs. Mechagodzilla* (1993), *Yamato Takeru* (1994), and *Godzilla vs. Destroyer* (1995), and one of the more promising directors of his generation.

Omori, Kazuki (b. 1952)
The writer-director of *Godzilla vs. Biollante* (1989) and *Godzilla vs. King Ghidorah* (1991), and the screenwriter of *Godzilla vs. Mothra* (1992) and *Godzilla vs. Destroyer* (1995), despite Omori's open dislike of *kaiju eiga*. A quirky talent whose work is sometimes interesting when it isn't derivative of Hollywood megahits.

Omura, Senkichi (b. 1923)
Broad bit player in Toho fantasy films, specializing in working-class go-getters and minor thugs. He was the man who offers to retrieve the hat in *Ghidrah—The Three-Headed Monster* (1964), and the translator in *King Kong vs. Godzilla* (1962). His other fantasy film credits include *Half Human* (1955), *Gigantis the Fire Monster* (as an escaping convict, 1955), *The Mysterians* (as a would-be fire-fighter, 1957), *Varan the Unbelievable* (1958), *The Secret of the Telegian* (as a fisherman, 1960),

Mothra (1961), *The Lost World of Sinbad* (1963), *Godzilla vs. the Thing* (as an egg-watching fisherman, 1964), and *Frankenstein Conquers the World* (1965). Active in films as late as Kurosawa's *Kagemusha* (1980). He also played one of the bandits in *Seven Samurai* (1954), and the man who hands the kidnapper the note in *High and Low* (1963).

Otaki, Shuji (b. 1925)
Much respected, longtime character actor, recognizable for his balding pate and dour demeanor, and as a regular in Juzo Itami's comedies (as the surviving brother in *The Funeral*, the choking man in *Tampopo*, the hotel owner in *Minbo*, etc.). His fantasy film work has been minor compared to the body of his work: *Lake of Dracula* (1971), *The War in Space* (1977), and *Deathquake* (1980). Memorable as the Takeda clan general Yamagata in *Kagemusha* (1980). Often mis-billed as Hideji Otaka.

Otowa, Nobuko (1925–1995)
One of Japan's best actresses—and the wife of director Kaneto Shindo—who gave several impressive fantasy film performances. She was the seriously ill mother in *The Last War* (1961), a ghost in *Kuroneko* (1968), and, perhaps most memorably, the possessive mother in Shindo's *Onibaba* (1964). Her other fantasy-laced output includes *The Three Treasures* (1959), *The Youth and His Amulet* (1961), and *The Strange Tale of Oyuki* (1992).

Ozawa, Eitaro (1909–1988)

Yet another longtime character actor, not especially known for his sci-fi work, nonetheless impressive as the lead detective in *The H-Man* (1958), as the Minister of Justice in *Gorath* (1962), and as the finance minister in *Godzilla 1985* (1984). He is far better known, however, as a reliable character actor in films spanning Mizoguchi, Naruse, and Itami. Billed as "Sakae Ozawa" in some pictures.

Paluzzi, Lucianna (b. 1931)

Sexy Italian actress who battled *The Green Slime* (1968). Probably best known as James Bond nemesis Fiona in *Thunderball* (1965). Her other fantasy film work includes *Hercules* (1957), *Captain Nemo and the Underwater City* (1969), and numerous TV appearances ("Thriller," "The Man from Uncle," etc.).

Peanuts, The [Emi and Yumi Ito] (b. 1941)

Twin pop stars from 1959 who gained immortality in the West as Mothra's priestesses in *Mothra* (1961), *Godzilla vs. the Thing* and *Ghidrah—The Three-Headed Monster* (both 1964). Since then their roles have been played by other actresses. The Peanuts were regulars on The Crazy Cats' TV show (the Crazy Cats, like the Peanuts, were managed by Watanabe Production [sic], and frequently made cameos in their movies, including *Big Adventure, Las Vegas Free-for-All*, etc.). They also starred in *Me and Me* (opposite Akira Takarada and Ichiro Arishima, 1962) and *Double Trouble* (aka *Young Comrades*, 1963). Emi Ito is divorced from actor-singer Kenji Sawada.

Romero, Cesar (1907–1994)

Exquisitely handsome actor, first a star in Fox musicals and costume adventures, then on television and films (notably as The Joker on "Batman" and in Disney comedies). He made one Japanese fantasy film, *Latitude Zero* (1969), as the wildly theatrical arch-villain Dr. Malic.

Ryu, Chishu (1906–1993)

Character actor whose career spanned at least six decades of Japanese cinema. Best known for his work with Yasujiro Ozu (he was in all but two of his films) and later as the priest in Yoji Yamada's "Tora-san" series and Itami's *The Funeral* (1984), Ryu played the teacher in *The Last War* (1961) and the 103-year-old man in *Akira Kurosawa's Dreams* (1990).

Sada, Yutaka (b. 1911)

Supporting player, mostly in small roles, who gave a moving performance as the chauffeur whose son is inadvertently kidnapped in Kurosawa's *High and Low* (1963). His numerous fantasy film credits include *The Invisible Man* (1954), *The Mysterians* (1957), *The Secret of the Telegian* (1960), *The Last War* (1961), *Godzilla vs. the Thing* (1964), *Frankenstein Conquers the World* (as the hospital manager, 1965), *Godzilla versus the Sea Monster* (1966), *Destroy All Monsters* (as a rural policeman, 1968), and *Godzilla's Revenge* (as Kenji Sahara's co-worker, 1969).

Sakai, Frankie (1929–1996)

Much-loved comedy star, also adept at drama, and best known in Japan for several film series made during the 1950s through the 1970s, among them the "Shacho" ("Company President") and "Train Station" series. He also starred as the tough reporter in *Mothra* (1961) and, that same year, gave a heart-breaking performance as a doomed patriarch in *The Last War*. Sakai also made numerous light-hearted ghost comedies, including a cameo appearance in the anthology *Uneasy Encounters* (1994). He won the Japanese Academy Award for Best Actor in 1996 but, sadly, he died soon after of a heart attack.

Sakai, Sachio (b. 1929)
Hulking, big-eared fellow (suggesting a Japanese Shemp Howard) who played the role of a reporter in the original *Gojira* (1954), a role that was largely replaced by Raymond Burr for the American version, *Godzilla, King of the Monsters!* (1956). Sakai remained a favorite of director Ishiro Honda, and appeared in numerous supporting roles for the director as late as *Rhapsody in August* (as a praying old man, 1991). He was one of Ichiro Arishima's lackeys in *King Kong vs. Godzilla* (1962), and a bumbling bank robber in *Godzilla's Revenge* (1969). His other genre work includes *Half Human* (1955), *Secret of the Telegian* (1960), *Gorath* (as a physician, 1962), *The Killing Bottle* (1967), *King Kong Escapes* (as one of Who's henchmen), *Yog—Monster from Space* (as a magazine editor, 1970), and *The Vampire Doll* (as a driver, 1970).

Sanada, Hiroyuki "Henry" (b. 1960)
Film star who cut his teeth in the fantasy genre, including *Message from Space* (1978), *Samurai Reincarnation* (1981) and *Legend of the Eight Samurai* (1983) for Kinji Fukasaku, and the ersatz feature *Swords of the Space Ark* (1978). Kumi Mizuno played his mother in *Thieving Ruby* (1988).

Sasaki, Katsuhiko (b. 1944)
The son of actor Minoru Chiaki, Sasaki became a star of sorts during the lean 1970s, toplining such mediocre fare as *Godzilla vs.*

Megalon (1973), *Evil of Dracula* (1975), and *Terror of Mechagodzilla* (1975). In recent years he appeared in *Godzilla vs. Biollante* (1989) and *Godzilla vs. King Ghidorah* (1991).

Sato, Makoto (b. 1934)
Intense, wide-mouth star of war and spy movies who occasionally appeared in fantasy films. He was the villain in *The H-Man* (1958), the Black Pirate in *The Lost World of Sinbad* (1963), and the pathetic Urocco in *Message from Space* (1978). Sato also starred in one of Honda's last non-fantasy features, *The Man in Red* (1961). Better remembered in Japan as the star of Toho's "Three Guys" film series.

Satsuma, Kenpachiro (b. 1948)
The actor inside Godzilla for seven films, from *Godzilla 1985* (1984) through *Godzilla vs. Destroyer* (1995). Satsuma also played the Smog Monster in *Godzilla vs. the Smog Monster* (1971) and Gigan in *Godzilla On Monster Island* (1972) as a warm-up.

Sawaguchi, Yasuko (b. 1965)
Fawn-like pop star who played—badly—the ingenue in *Godzilla 1985* (1984). Sawaguchi's acting has improved somewhat with age, however, she was fine in the otherwise tepid *Yamato Takeru* (1994). In between she made a cameo as the scientist's daughter in *Godzilla vs. Biollante* (1989), and appeared opposite Toshiro Mifune in Kon Ichikawa's largely unseen-in-the-West fantasy *Princess of the Moon* (1987).

Sawamura, Ikio (1905–1975)
Short, little old man with an almost falsetto voice, and a favorite of both Ishiro Honda and Akira Kurosawa. For the latter he was memorable as the bell ringer in *Yojimbo* (1961). For Honda he played the railway man seen at the start of *Battle in Outer Space* (1959), the cabby in *Gorath* (1962), a witch doctor in *King Kong vs. Godzilla* (1962), a priest in *Godzilla vs. the Thing* (1964), the guy who fishes the princess out of the water in *Ghidrah—The Three-Headed Monster* (1964), a dog owner in *Frankenstein Conquers the World* (1965), an Infant Island slave in *Godzilla versus the Sea Monster* (1966), a frightened fisherman in *War of the Gargantuas* (1966), a native shot by Dr. Who in *King Kong Escapes* (1967), a farmer who finds a Kilaak transmitter in *Destroy All Monsters* (1968), a street vendor in *Godzilla's Revenge* (1969), and Mafune's manservant in *Terror of Mechagodzilla* (1975). He died of cancer.

Hiroshi Sekita (b. 1932)
The third regular opponent of monster suit actor Haruo "Godzilla" Nakajima (following Katsumi Tezuka and Shoichi Hirose), Sekita played Sanda, the Brown Gargantua, in *War of the Gargantuas* (1966), Ebirah, the giant prawn, in *Godzilla versus the Sea Monster* (1966), Mechani-Kong and Gorosaurus in *King Kong Escapes* (1967), Angilas in *Destroy All Monsters* (1968), and Gaborah in *Godzilla's Revenge* (1969). Sekita was also one

of the actors (and led by Nakajima) in the extra-large Mothra costume in the original *Mothra* (1961).

Sekizawa, Shinichi (1920–1993)
Screenwriter who alternated with Takeshi Kimura as Toho's main fantasy film scribe. Sekizawa's screenplays were notably lighter, often satirical, less psychological and more upbeat than Kimura's, often eschewing logic for visually striking imagery. He directed Tadao Takashima in the presumed lost Shintoho film *Fearful Invasion of the Flying Saucers* (1955) prior to his first *kaiju eiga*, *Varan the Unbelievable*, in 1958. This was followed by *Battle in Outer Space* (1959), *The Secret of the Telegian* (1960), *Mothra* (1961), *King Kong vs. Godzilla* (1962), *Atragon* (1963), *The Lost World of Sinbad* (written with Kimura, 1963), *Godzilla vs. the Thing*, *Dagora the Space Monster*, *Ghidrah—The Three-Headed Monster* (all 1964), *Monster Zero* (1965), *Godzilla versus the Sea Monster* (1966), *Son of Godzilla* (1967), *Latitude Zero*, *Godzilla's Revenge* (both 1969), and *Godzilla on Monster Island* (1972). Sekizawa also contributed the stories to *Godzilla vs. Megalon* (1973) and *Godzilla vs. the Cosmic Monster* (1974), and wrote several animated films (including *Gulliver's Travels Beyond the Moon*, 1965, and *Jack and the Beanstalk*, 1967), and episodes of "Ultraman."

Senda, Koreya (b. 1904)
Grey-haired character actor who essayed Takashi Shimura-esque elder scientist roles in *The H-Man* (1958), *Varan the Unbelievable* (1958), and *Battle in Outer Space* (1959).

Shimura, Takashi (1905–1982)
One of Japan's finest actors, Shimura was the leader of the *Seven Samurai* (1954) and unforgettable as the dying government worker in *Ikiru* (1952), both for Akira Kurosawa, two of 22 films he made for the director. Shimura was also a staple of the fantasy film genre, beginning with *Godzilla, King of the Monsters!* (1954), in which he played elder scientist Kyohei Yamane. He reprised the role in *Gigantis the Fire Monster* (1955), and played similar roles in *The Mysterians* (1957), *Gorath* (1962), *Ghidrah—The Three-Headed Monster* (1964), *Frankenstein Conquers the World* (1965), and *Prophecies of Nostradamus* (1974). He also appeared in *Mothra* (as a newspaper editor, 1961), *The Whale God* (as a priest, 1962), *The Lost World of Sinbad* (as the king, 1963), and *Kwaidan* (as a priest, 1964). Alas, one of his last roles, in Kurosawa's *Kagemusha* (1980), was cut from the U.S. version. Shimura died of complications from emphysema.

Shirakawa, Yumi (b. 1936)
Kaiju eiga star of the 1950s, Shirakawa starred opposite Kenji Sahara in *Rodan* (1956), *The Mysterians* (1957), and *The H-Man* (1958), and later appeared in *The Secret of the Telegian* (1960), *Gorath* (1962), and *Adventures of Takla Makan* (1966). She also appears in Ozu's *Early Autumn* (1961), and starred opposite Akira Takarada and Jerry (*Mothra*) Ito in the satire *Wall-Eyed Nippon* (1964). Shirakawa also starred in several non-fantasy films directed by Ishiro Honda.

Shishido, Jo (b. 1933)
Puffy-cheeked actor who played Captain Joe in *Fugitive Alien* and *Star Force: Fugitive Alien II* (both 1978) for Tsuburaya Productions. Shishido was a big star at Nikkatsu Studios in the 1960s, and is better remembered for his crime films with director Seijun Suzuki, notably *Tokyo Drifter* (1965) and *Branded to Kill* (1967). The still-active prolific actor appeared in at least 13 features in 1960 alone.

Stanford, Leonard "Len" (b. 1920?)
Amateur actor living in Japan featured prominently as astronaut Roger Richardson in *Battle in Outer Space* (1959).

Suzuki, Kazuo (b. 1937)
Peter Lorre-esque bit player at Toho, specializing in slimy thugs, notably the short, bumbling bank robber in

Godzilla's Revenge (1969). His fantasy film credits include *Godzilla vs. the Thing* (1964), *Ghidrah—The Three-Headed Monster* (as an assassin, 1964), *Monster Zero* (as an X-ite henchman, 1965), *Godzilla versus the Sea Monster* (as an Infant Island slave, 1966), *King Kong Escapes* (as a Who henchman, 1967), *Son of Godzilla* (as a plane's radio operator, 1967), *Destroy All Monsters* (as a Kilaak henchman, 1968), and *Terror of Mechagodzilla* (as yet another alien henchman, 1975).

Tajima, Yoshifumi (b. 1918)
Frequent supporting player in Toho's *kaiju eiga*, memorable as villain Kenji Sahara's slimy, patheic agent in *Godzilla vs. the Thing* (1964). Though very talented, for some reason it appears the actor rarely played anything beyond tiny walk-ons and bit parts in other genres. His other genre credits include *Rodan* (1956), *The H-Man* (as a detective melted by an H-Man, 1958), *Varan the Unbelievable* (1958), *The Secret of the Telegian* (1960), *The Human Vapor* (1960), *Mothra* (1961), *King Kong vs. Godzilla* (1962), *Atragon* (1963), *Dagora the Space Monster* (as a jewel thief, 1964), *Ghidrah—The Three-Headed Monster* (as a ship's captain, 1964), *Frankenstein Conquers the World* (as the sub commander, 1965), *Monster Zero* (leading the army, also 1965), *War of the Gargantuas* (as a detective,

1966), *King Kong Escapes* (as a Who henchman, 1967), *Destroy All Monsters* (as a general, 1968), *Godzilla's Revenge* (as a detective, 1969), and *Godzilla 1985* (blink and you'll miss him, 1984).

Takada, Minoru (1899–1977)
Severe, *shacho* type actor, utilized in every genre since the 1920s, often cast as government officials by Honda, notably *Battle in Outer Space* (1959), *The Last War* (1961), and *Ghidrah—The Three-Headed Monster* (as the official to whom the Peanuts address their plan to defeat Ghidrah, 1964). He also played the main villain in the obscure *The Invisible Man* (1954).

Takashima, Masanobu (b. 1966)
Son of actor Tadao Takashima and the brother of Masahiro Takashima (q.v.), Masanobu starred in *Godzilla vs. Biollante* (1989). His other credits include *Rainbow Bridge* (1993).

Takashima, Masahiro (b. 1965)
Older brother of Masanobu Takashima, and the son of Tadao Takashima, Masahiro starred in *Gunhed* (1989), *Zipang* (1990), and *Godzilla vs. Mechagodzilla* (1993). His other credits include *Bu Su* (1987), *Love and Action in Osaka* and *Stay Gold* (both 1988).

Takashima, Tadao (b. 1930)
Comedy star often teamed with Yu Fujiki; together they starred in *King Kong vs. Godzilla* (1962) and *Atragon* (1963). Prior to this Takashima starred in Shinichi Sekizawa's *Fearful Invasion of the Flying Saucers* (1955), and after played Nick Adams' colleague in *Frankenstein Conquers the World* (1965) and the project leader in *Son of Godzilla* (1967). He recently made a cameo in *Godzilla vs. Mechagodzilla* (1993).

Takemitsu, Toru (1930–1996)
Important film composer of the Japanese New Wave who scored Masaki Kobayashi's *Kwaidan* (1964). He career was the subject of the excellent "Music for the Movies" documentary series, which is available on home video.

Tamba, Tetsuro (b. 1922)
Durable Yakuza star who has made sporadic fantasy film appearances. He's in *Kwaidan* (1964), *Black Lizard* (1968), *Submersion of Japan, Prophecies of Nostradamus* (as Dr. Nishiyama, 1974), *Message from Space* (as Noguchi, 1978), and *Samurai Reincarnation* (1981). Probably best known in the West as "Tiger" Tanaka, the head of the Japanese Service in the Bond picture *You Only Live Twice* (1967).

怪獣 東京大攻撃

Tamblyn, Russ (b. 1932)
Star of *War of the Gargantuas* (1966), the versatile actor had already starred in several fantasies for producer George Pal. He was *tom thumb* (1958), and appeared in the Cinerama anthology *The Wonderful World of the Brothers Grimm* (1962). He was also used to great effect in the best ghost story ever filmed, *The Haunting* (1963). After this he appeared in dreck like *Frankenstein vs. Dracula* (1971) before returning to some measure of overdue prominence in David Lynch's "Twin Peaks" teleseries. He also starred in several classic musicals, including *Seven Brides for Seven Brothers* (1954) and *West Side Story* (1961).

Tanaka, Kunie (b. 1932)
Popular character actor with Robert Mitchum features. Best known during the 60s as "Young Guy's" friend/rival in the popular series, before turning to juicy Yakuza and *jidai-geki* supporting roles during the 1970s. His fantasy credits include *Kwaidan* (1964) and *Evil of Dracula* (1975).

Tanaka, Tomoyuki "Yuko" (1910–1997)
Toho producer who, along with director Ishiro Honda, special effects man Eiji Tsuburaya, and composer Akira Ifukube, essentially created the *kaiju eiga* genre. And while Honda, Tsuburaya, and Ifukube went on to do several dozen genre films for Toho, only Tanaka is credited with every Godzilla feature until his death (though his frail health prevented him from taking a more active role in recent years). Though he did not produce every Toho-made fantasy, he came awfully close, producing or co-producing nearly all its sci-fi films through the early-1990s, as well as most of its war movies and crime films (as opposed to Sanezumi Fujimoto, who did most of Toho's "women's" pictures and light comedies). Tanaka also co-produced many of Kurosawa's films, including *The Hidden Fortress* (1958), *The Bad Sleep Well* (1960), *Yojimbo* (1961), *Sanjuro* (1962) and *High and Low* (1963). In all, he produced some 200+ films during his 51-year career. He died of a stroke at 86, and is survived by his wife, former actress Chieko Nakakita, who played the crying mother in *Godzilla versus the Sea Monster* (1966).

Taniguchi, Senkichi (b. 1912)
Routine Toho director in the low-"A"/high-"B" range whose credits include *The Lost World of Sinbad* (1963), *The Killing Bottle* (1967), and *International Secret Police: Key of Keys* (1965), the film that became Woody Allen's *What's Up, Tiger Lily?* (1966). Married to actress Kaoru Yachigusa.

Tazaki, Jun (1910–1985)
Stern-looking supporting player, often cast as project leaders and generals in Toho monster epics. He was the main scientist in both *Monster Zero* (1965) and *Destroy All Monsters* (1968), and played generals in *King Kong vs. Godzilla* (1962), *Frankenstein Conquers the World* (1965) and *War of the Gargantuas* (1966). Tazaki's best roles, however, were as the doomed-but-dedicated spaceship captain in *Gorath* (1962) and as the stubborn, long-lost Captain Jinguji in *Atragon* (1963). His other genre credits include *The Lost World of Sinbad* (as a lusty, frog-eating guard, 1963), *Godzilla vs. the Thing* (as a newspaper editor, 1964), *Dagora, the Space Monster* (as an investigator, also 1964), *Kwaidan* (as a guard in the "In a Cup of Tea" story, 1964), *Godzilla versus the Sea Monster* (as a Red Bamboo leader), and *The Killing Bottle* (as the president of Buddabal, 1967). His non-genre credits include *Tokyo File 212* (the first US/Japanese co-production, 1950), *Gate of Hell* (1953), *Seven Samurai* (as a foolish *samurai* challenger), *High and Low* (as a shoe company executive, 1963), *Ran* (as a general, 1985), and lots of Toho-produced war movies. The actor looked quite a bit like Toshiro Mifune, and cleverly spoofed Mifune's *Yojimbo* role in at least one Crazy Cats comedy.

Tezuka, Katsumi (b. 1912)
Minor supporting player and occasional monster suit actor, Tezuka played Godzilla, at least for one sequence, in the original *Gojira* (1954), and shared monster duties with Nakajima again as *Varan the Unbelievable* (1958). He also played Godzilla's first opponent, Angilas, in *Gigantis the Fire Monster* (1955), and appears in human form in *Rodan* (1956) and *The H-Man* (1958) before disappearing from view.

Togin, Chotaro (b. 1941) Boyish supporting player, best seen as the SY-3 co-pilot in *Destroy All Monsters* (1968). Togin also appeared in many Toho fantasies, including *Dagora, the Space Monster* (1964), *Godzilla versus the Sea Monster* (as a castaway, 1966), *Son of Godzilla* (as a surveyor, 1967), *Godzilla's Revenge* (as a detective, 1969), and *Yog—Monster from Space* (1970)

Tsuburaya, Eiji (1901–1970)
The undisputed master of special effects in Japan, Eiji Tsuburaya dominated the genre until his death, while strongly influencing new generations of artists ever since. He specialized in the construction, manipulation and photography of highly-detailed, hand-made miniatures. Alternately toy-like and amazing detailed and realistic, Tsuburaya's direction of effects sequences were consistently inventive

and kinetic. He served as special effects director or supervisor on all of Toho's fantasy and war films through 1969, including the first 10 Godzilla pictures. He also had the distinction of "sharing" director credit (his name listed second-from-last, right before the live action director) on those works where he contributed a substantial amount of effects footage. During this period, he also trained a new generation of loyal protegees, including Teisho "Sadamasa" Arikawa, Teruyoshi "Shokei" Nakano, Minoru Nakano, Koichi Takano, Kazuho "Pete" Mitsuta, and Koichi Kawakita (all q.v.). Tsuburaya formed his own production company during the 1960s, Tsuburaya Productions, and began producing sci-fi teleseries including "Ultra Q," "Ultraman," "Ultra Seven," and "Mighty Jack," while also contributing spfx for independent productions like Frank Sinatra's *None But the Brave* (1965). His sons, Hajime, Noboru, and Akira Tsuburaya, all became television producers.

Uehara, Ken (1909–1991)
Handsome leading player in films spanning 55 years, and the father of popular actor-singer Yuzo Kayama (q.v.). Uehara played one of the leading scientists in *Gorath* (1962), and virtually reprised his title role from the film *The Story of Tank Commander Nishizumi* in *Atragon* (1963) for director Ishiro Honda.

Utsui, Ken (b. 1931) Shintoho and later Daiei star who won immortality as Starman (known as Supergiant in Japan) in nine films reedited into four, longer features for release on American television: *Atomic Rulers*, *Invaders from Space* (1957), *Attack from Space*, and *Evil Brain from Outer Space* (1958). Still active in show business.

Wakabayashi, Akiko (b. 1939)
Exotic star, often cast as mysterious foreigners, Wakabayashi played the princess-turned-Martian in *Ghidrah—The Three-Headed Monster* (1964), Mie Hama's neighbor in *King Kong vs. Godzilla* (1962), Hama's maid in *The Lost World of Sinbad* (1963), and a diamond-obsessed moll in *Dagora, the Space Monster* (1964). She also turns up in Woody Allen's *What's Up, Tiger Lily?* (1966), and played the Japanese spy Aki in the James Bond adventure *You Only Live Twice* (also with Mie Hama, 1967).

Wakayama, Tomisaburo (1929–1992)
Brother of "Zatoichi" star Shintaro Katsu, Wakayama starred, memorably, as "Lone Wolf" in the popular film and television series. He appeared in numerous Daiei ghost stories, as well as Jun Fukuda's *ESPY* (1974), *Hinotori* (1978), and Kinji Fukasaku's

Samurai Reincarnation (1981). He also appeared in American-made films like *The Bad News Bears Go to Japan* (1978) and *Black Rain* (1989).

Yachigusa, Kaoru (b. 1931)
Wife of director Senkichi Taniguchi, Yachigusa is best-known in this country as Musashi Miyamoto's faithful love interest in Hiroshi Inagaki's *Samurai* trilogy (1954–56). However, she is also known to fantasy film fans as the dancer Yoshio Tsuchiya is obsessed with in *The Human Vapor* (1960). Still active in films and on television, she was memorable as Tatsuya Nakadai's husband in *Hachi-ko* (1987).

Yamamoto, Ren (b. 1930)
Doomed, older brother in *Godzilla, King of the Monsters!* (1954), Yamamoto seemed to specialize playing working class monster victims. He's the sailor nearly killed by two monsters in *War of the Gargantuas* (1966). He also appears in *Half Human* (1955), *Gigantis the Fire Monster* (as the commander of landing craft, 1955), *Rodan* (as a soldier, 1956), *The H-Man* (as a gangster, 1958), *Mothra* (as a sailor, 1961), *King Kong vs. Godzilla* (as a helicopter pilot, 1962), and *Godzilla vs. the Thing* (as a sailor, 1964).

Yamashita, Kensho (b. 1944)
Teen idol director tapped to helm *Godzilla vs. Space Godzilla* (1994), not one of the series' finest.

Yasuda, Kimiyoshi (1911–1983)
Daiei house director who helmed many "Zatoichi" and "Kyoshiro Nemuri" films. For our purposes he directed the first *Majin* film (1966), as well as the memorable *100 Monsters* (1968) and its sequel, *Along with Ghosts* (1969).

Yuseph Osman "Johnny" (1920?–1982)
Turkish actor and manager of the Kokusei Agency, which handled Western amateur actors in Japanese movies. Yuseph played an astronaut in *Battle in Outer Space* (1959), a villain in *The Last Death of the Devil* (a Moon Mask Rider featurette, 1959), Jerry Ito's Western henchman in *Mothra* (1961), a victim of Magma the Walrus in *Gorath* (1962), a naval officer in *Son of Godzilla* (1967) and "King Stone" in *The Streetfighter* (1974).

RATINGS

★ = poor
★★ = fair
★★★ = good
★★★★ = excellent
✹ = not available for review

FILMOGRAPHY

Atomic Rulers ★★ (MEDALLION TV, 1964)
Kotetso no kyojin—Supa Jyaiantsu "The Steel Giant—Super Giant I & II" ✹ (FUJI/SHINTOHO, 1957)
Director: Teruo Ishii **Screenplay:** Ichiro Miyagawa, Shinsuke Niegishi **Director of Photography:** Takashi Watanabe
Special Effects: Akira Watanabe **Music:** Chumei Watanabe
Producer: Mitsugi Okura **Cast:** Ken Utsui, Junko Ikeuchi.

First of four "Starman" feature adaptations released directly to television in the U.S. In Japan, these fast-paced, goofy superhero adventures were released serial style, though in two, longer halves rather than broken up into 12 or more shorts like American chapterplays. Starman (known as Supergiant in Japan, and played by beefy, charming Ken Utsui) is the Japanese equivelent of Superman, and the films (there were nine hour-long featurettes in Japan) are even more intensely-paced than the best American serials of the 30s and 40s. Though one quickly tires of the mindless action, Starman himself is rather charming and the films have admirably ambitious art direction (Ken Adam on a shoestring) and a plethora of cheap but imaginative effects. In this adventure, often referred to as *Atomic Rulers of the World,* Starman battles gangsters from "Magolia" seeking a nuclear device. Followed by *Attack from Space* (1957).

Atragon ★★★ (AIP, 1965)
Kaitei gunkan "Undersea Battleship" ★★★ ½ (TOHO, 1963)
Director: Ishiro Honda **Special Effects Director:** Eiji Tsuburaya **Screenplay:** Shinichi Sekizawa, based on the novels *Kaitei gunkan* by Shunro Oshikawa, and *Kaitei okoku* by Shigeru Komatsuzaki
Director of Photography: Hajime Koizumi **Art Director:** Takeo Kita **Special Effects Photography:** Teisho Arikawa, Mototaka Tomioka **Music:** Akira Ifukube **Producer:** Tomoyuki Tanaka **Cast:** Tadao Takashima, Yoko Fujiyama, Yu Fujiki, Kenji Sahara, Ken Uehara, Hiroshi Koizumi, Jun Tazaki, Yoshifumi Tajima, Akihiko Hirata, Eisei Amamoto, Susumu Fujita, Minoru Takada, Hisaya Ito, Ikio Sawamura, and Tetsuko Kobayashi.

AMERICAN INTERNATIONAL presents in COLORSCOPE
ATRAGON

Ride the JUGGERNAUT of destruction from the depths of the Seven Seas to the Outer Limits of Space!

An adventure beyond your wildest dreams - as a Super-weapon meets Super-Force with the fate of the Universe at stake!

SEE: the terror swath of the deadly Astral Disks.
SEE: the Exotic Rites and Grotesque Passions of the Kingdom of MU.
SEE: underwater Juggernauts of destruction!

Produced by TOHO CO. Ltd.

One of Toho's best fantasies, and one of the very few Japanese sci-fi films to actually put characterization ahead of its special effects. Centering on a mysterious Captain Nemo-like figure, the film was the career highlight of longtime supporting player Jun Tazaki, who brings to the role just the right balance of stand-offishness and vulnerability. The story involves a disparate band looking for a long-lost submarine commander when the Atlantian-like Mu Empire threatens the Surface Earth. Takashima and Fujiki reprise their characters from *King Kong vs. Godzilla* in all but name, but it is the late Setsuko Kobayashi who steals the film as the wicked Mu Empress. The rest of the cast is excellent, too, as is Ifukube's score. Producer Tanaka added a giant monster, the sea serpent Manda, to boost box office sales; it would return—more effectively—in *Destroy All Monsters* a half-decade later.

Attack from Space ★ 1/2 (MEDALLION TV, 1964)

Supa Jyaiantsu: jinko eisei to jinrui no hametsu/uchusen to jinko eisei no gekitotsu "Super Giant: Satellites and the Destruction of Mankind/The Spaceships and Satellites Duel" ✹ (FUJI/SHINTOHO, 1957 AND 1958)
Director: Teruo Ishii **Screenplay:** Ichiro Miyagawa, Shinsuke Niegishi **Director of Photography:** Takashi Watanabe **Special Effects:** Akira Watanabe **Music:** Chumei Watanabe **Producer:** Mitsugi Okura **Cast:** Ken Utsui, Junko Utako Mitsuda.

Starman adventure #2, and set almost entirely in outer space. Not as good as *Atomic Rulers*, despite some nice artwork, because it's even more mindless than the previous entry, and just goes on and on. The picture is worth watching, however, for its complete disregard of science, as characters walk around space platforms in open space with no protective clothing, to say nothing of oxygen masks, while others "fall" off the platform (to where?). Followed by *Invaders from Space* (1958).

Attack of the Monsters ★★ (AIP-TV, 1969)

Gamera tai daiakuju Giron "Gamera vs. the Giant Evil Beast Guiron" ★★ 1/2 (DAIEI, 1969)
Director: Noriaki Yuasa **Special Effects Director:** Kazufumi Fujii **Screenplay:** Nisan Takahashi **Director of Photography:** Akira Kitazaki **Producer:** Hidemasa Nagata **Cast:** Nobuhiro Kajima, Christopher Murphy, Miyuki Akiyama, Yuko Hamada, Eiji Funakoshi, Kon Omura, Edith Hanson.

A dream-like kid's fantasy: two preteens, one Japanese (Kajima), one American (Murphy), are kidnapped by a UFO, almost have there brains eaten by evil alien women on a remote planet, and watch giant turtle monster Gamera and steak knife monster Guiron duke it out. Nearly plotless, with the two kids simply wandering around the spartan alien base admiring the scenery as they watch the monsters from the sidelines. AIP-TV's version has since replaced by a much inferior international version, *Gamera vs. Guiron* (★), whose dubbing is among the very worst ever, and distracting in the extreme. The widescreen image is also horrendously panned and scanned. These new "Sandy Frank" versions do have one advantage over the AIP editions,

however: scenes of quasi-graphic violence, previously cut by AIP, have been restored. Especially bizarre is a duel between Guiron and "Space Gyaos" (the bat-like monster from *Return of the Giant Monsters*, painted silver). Reminiscent of a sequence in *Monty Python and the Holy Grail*, Gyaos is chopped literally limbed from limbed, and the sequence ends with Gyaos' limbless trunk diced like a sausage by the chortling Guiron. Followed by *Gamera vs. Monster X* (1970).

Attack of the Mushroom People ★★½

(AIP-TV, 1965)

Matango "Matango" ★★★½ (TOHO, 1963)

Director: Ishiro Honda **Special Effects Director:** Eiji Tsuburaya **Screenplay:** Takeshi Kimura, suggested by the short story "The Voice of the Night," by W.H. Hodgson **Director of Photography:** Hajime Koizumi **Music:** Sadao Bekku **Producer:** Tomoyuki Tanaka **Cast:** Akira Kubo, Kumi Mizuno, Kenji Sahara, Hiroshi Koizumi, Yoshio Tsuchiya, Miki Yashiro, Hiroshi Tachikawa, Eisei Amamoto, Yutaka Oka, Haruo Nakajima.

It's a shame that screenwriter Kimura and director Honda made so few horror films, because this is a superb, much-underrated picture, though its unfortunate title has delegated it to late-night TV, and now it's hard to even find it there. The story, about a group of shipwrecked vacationers (great performances all) slowly succumbing to the poisonous yet alluring mushrooms is fascinating and multi-layered. Although the performances are all but lost in the dubbed version, and faded, panned-and-scanned TV prints shown here lose most of director Honda and cinematoragpher Koizumi's pictoral design, it still holds up amazingly well. It's unsettling, superbly plotted, and a must-see.

Attack of the Super Monsters, The ★

(ASSOCIATES ENTERTAINMENT INTERNATIONAL, 1992)

Kyoryu sentai Koseidon "Dinosaur Fighting Team Koseidon" ✺ (TSUBURAYA PRODUCTIONS, 1978–9) [TV]

Directors: Toru Sotoyama and Hiroshi Jinzeni **Special Effects Director:** Shoei Tojo **Teleplay:** Masaki Tsuji, based on the story by Hiroyasu Yamaura **Music:** Toshiaki Tsushima **Series Creator:** Ifumi Uchiyama **Producer:** Akira Tsuburaya **Cast:** none.

Unusual but dreary feature adaptation of a Japanese TV show mixing suitmation effects with cartoon animation. Odd, but ineffective.

Battle in Outer Space ★★½ (COLUMBIA, 1960)

Uchu dai senso "Great War in Space" ★★★½ (TOHO, 1959)

Director: Ishiro Honda **Special Effects Director:** Eiji Tsuburaya **Screenplay:** Shinichi Sekizawa, based on a story by Jotaro Okami **Director of Photography:** Hajime Koizumi **Special Effects Photography:** Teisho Arikawa **Art Director:** Teruaki Abe **Music:** Akira Ifukube **Producer:** Tomoyuki Tanaka **Cast:** Ryo Ikebe, Kyoko Anzai, Minoru Takada, Koreya Senda, Len Stanford, Harold S. Conway, Hisaya Ito, Yoshio Tsuchiya, Kozo Nomura, Fuyuki Murakami, Nadao Kirino, Ikio Sawamura.

Superior invasion epic rivaled only by George Pal's *War of the Worlds* (1953), *Earth vs. the Flying Saucers* (1955), and *Independence Day* (1996) in terms of scale. A treat in Toho Scope and on big, movie screens, where films like this belong. The film has almost no story—it's one big battle from beginning to end—and neatly divided into two parts: part one has two rocketships flying to the moon to destroy the alien base, while the much shorter Act Two is the climatic

battle between the saucers and futuristic jets capable of leaving the Earth's atmosphere. Best of all are the alien's remote controlled meteors [reminiscent of similar devices used in *This Island Earth,* Universal-International, 1955], which destroy Manhattan and the Golden Gate Bridge. Meanwhile, an even more impressive mothership sucks up Tokyo like a giant vacuum cleaner—incredible! Yoshio Tsuchiya's possessed astronaut stands out among the human cast. The American version deletes about 15 minutes worth of footage, making the already breathlessly-paced film move even faster, though at the cost of much of the human drama. Moreover, a good deal of Ifukube's great score has been replaced with forgettable American stock themes, which really hurt the rhythm of the final battle.

The Bermuda Depths ★ ½
(ABC-TV, 1978)
Bamyuda no nazo
"Mystery of Bermuda" ✹
(RANKIN-BASS, IN
ASSOCIATION WITH
TSUBURAYA PRODUCTIONS, 1979)
Director: Tsugunobu "Tom" Kotani
Screenplay: William Overgard, based on a story by Arthur Rankin, Jr.
Director of Photography: Jeri Sopanen **Music:** Maury Laws
Producers: Arthur Rankin, Jr. and Jules Bass **Cast:** Leigh McCloskey, Carl Weathers, Connie Selleca, Burl Ives.
Confused, illogical, and ultimately boring Rankin-

Bass/Tsuburaya co-production about a giant sea turtle which plays more like a Harlequin romance than a Gamera movie. *Zzzzzz.*

Black Lizard ★ ★ ★ ½ (CINEVISTA, 1985)
Kurotokage "Black Lizard" ★ ★ ★ ½ (SHOCHIKU, 1968)
Director: Kinji Fukasaku **Screenplay:** Masashige Narusawa and Kinji Fukasaku, based on the play by Yukio Mishima and the novel by Rampo Edogawa
Director of Photography: Hiroshi Dowaki **Art Director:** Kyohei Morita **Music:** Isao Tomita **Cast:** Akihiro Maruyama, Isao Kimura, Keiko Matsuoka, Jumya Usami, Yusuke Kawazu, Ko Nishimura, Tetsuro Tamaba, Yukio Mishima.
Wonderfully campy thriller in the John Waters vein with very slight fantasy elements. The notorious thief Black Lizard (Maruyama, in drag) matches wits with a brilliant detective (Kimura) in this stylish film superbly directed by Fukasaku. An obscure quasi-sequel, *Black Rose* (1969) followed, also with Maruyama.

Catastrophe: 1999 see *Prophecies of Nostradamus*

Daigoro vs. Goliath
(UNRELEASED IN THE UNITED STATES)
Kaiju daifunsen—Daigoro tai Goriasu
"The Monster's Desperate Battle: Daigoro vs. Goliath" ★ ★ ½ (TOHO, 1972)
Producer: Noboru Tsuburaya
Cast: Hiroshi Inuzuka.
A co-production between Tsuburaya Productions and Toho, this is a colorful giant monster movie for kids too little for even a Gamera movie.

Strangely, it was never released in this country; its modest but reasonably successful efforts give it a measure of class missing even from the Godzilla films of this period. Hiroshi Inuzuka of the Crazy Cats stars.

Dagora, the Space Monster ★ (AIP-TV, 1965)

Uchu daikaiju Dogora "Space Monster Dogora" ★★★ (TOHO, 1964)

Director: Ishiro Honda **Special Effects Director:** Eiji Tsuburaya **Screenplay:** Shinichi Sekizawa, based on the short story "Space Mons," by Jojiro Okami **Director of Photography:** Hajime Koizumi **Special Effects Photography:** Teisho Arikawa and Mototaka Tomioka **Art Director:** Takeo Kita **Music:** Akira Ifukube **Producer:** Tomoyuki Tanaka **Cast:** Yosuke Natsuki, Yoko Fujiyama, Akiko Wakabayashi, Hiroshi Koizumi, Seizaburo Kawazu, Jun Tazaki, Jun Funato, Dan Yuma (Robert Dunham), Susumu Fujita, Nobuo Nakamura, Yoshifumi Tajima, Eisei Amamoto, Haruya Kato.

This underrated *kaiju eiga* is the least-known of the Honda-Tsuburaya cannon. Unfortunately, the horribly dubbed, dark and grainy (and, almost thankfully, quite obscure) home video version makes the mistake of thinking that its mix of jewel thieves and sprawling space jellyfish was meant to be taken seriously. It isn't. When seen as a satire (and in Japanese), however, the film is often hilarious, while the effects (the monster is achieved via cartoon animation and a marionette manipulated in water, and not a guy in a suit) are unique and colorful. Best of all are the performances, especially by American Robert Dunham as a "diamond G-Man," more Japanese than the Japanese!

Deathquake ★1/2 (SHOCHIKU FILMS OF AMERICA, 1982)

Jishin retto "Earthquake Islands" ✹ (TOHO, 1980)

Director: Kenjiro Omori **Special Effects Director:** Teruyoshi Nakano **Screenplay:** Kaneto Shindo **Director of Photography:** Rokuro Nishigaki **Special Effects Photography:** Takeshi Yamamoto and Mitsuhiro Hasegawa **Art Director:** Iwao Akune **Music:** Toshiaki Tsushima **Producer:** Tomoyuki Tanaka **Cast:** Hiroshi Katsuno, Toshiyuki Nagashima, Yumi Takigawa, Kayo Matsuo, Shuji Otaki, Eiji Okada, Shin Saburi, Norihei Miki, Tsutomu Yamazaki.

Boring disaster film in the *Submersion of Japan* vein. Despite an all-star cast and some impressive effects work by Nakano, it's a pretty mindless picture, poorly received in Japan, and barely shown in the United States.

Destroy All Monsters ★★★ (AIP, 1969)

Kaiju soshingeki "All Monsters Attack" ★★★ 1/2 (TOHO, 1968)

Director: Ishiro Honda **Special Effects Director:** Teisho Arikawa **Special Effects Supervisor:** Eiji Tsuburaya **Screenplay:** Kaoru Mabuchi (Takeshi Kimura) and Ishiro Honda **Director of Photography:** Taiichi Kankura **Art Director:** Takeo Kita **Music:** Akira Ifukube **Producer:** Tomoyuki Tanaka **Cast:** Akira Kubo, Jun Tazaki, Yoshio Tsuchiya, Kyoko Ai, Yukiko Kobayashi, Kenji Sahara, Andrew Hughes, Chotaro Togin, Yoshifumi Tajima, Hisaya Ito, Henry Okawa, Ikio Sawamura, Yutaka Sada, Nadao Kirino, Wataru Omae, Susumu Kurobe, Kazuo Suzuki, Toru Ibuki, Saburo Iketani, Haruo Nakajima, Little Man Machan, Hiroshi Sekita, Susumu Utsumi.

As the Golden Age of *kaiju eiga* drew to a close,

Toho threw all its eggs in one basket for this highly satisfying if unoriginal monster epic. Essentially merging *Battle in Outer Space* with multi-monster bashes of the last few entries, *Destroy All Monsters* (or, as it is affectionately known, DAM), is notable for the sheer number of monsters which appear: Godzilla, Minya, Rodan, Ghidrah, Mothra (larvae form), Gorosaurus, Manda, Angilas, Baragon, Spiga, and Varan (the latter three appearing fleetingly). None of it is new, though so superbly crafted by all concerned (Ifukube's score, Arikawa's effects direction, the ensemble cast, Honda's editing), who cares? Officially unavailable for many years, the picture resurfaced in a Toho-approved international edition (★★1/2) which is letterboxed, but

with new dubbing (by William Ross) twice as bad and badly written as AIP's version. The AIP version, incidentally, featured the voices of Hal Linden and AMC host Bob Dorian. Followed by *Godzilla's Revenge* (1969).

Destroy All Planets ★ 1/2 (AIP-TV, 1968)
Gamera tai uchu kaiju Bairasu "Gamera vs. the Outer Space Monster Virus" ★★ (DAIEI, 1968)
Director: Noriaki Yuasa **Special Effects Directors:** Kazufumi Fujii and Yuzo Kaneko **Screenplay:** Nisan Takahashi **Director of Photography:** Akira Kitazaki **Music:** Kenjiro Hirose **Cast:** Kojiro Hongo, Toru Takatsuka, Peter Williams, Carl Clay, Michiko Yaegaki, Mari Atsumi, Junko Yashiro, Mary Morris.

The first Gamera movie successfully told from a child's perspective, this one finds two kids—one Japanese, the other American—fiddling with a mini-sub before being kidnapped by aliens and taken aboard a spaceship which can only be described as looking like a bunch of striped ping pong balls glued together. The kids fool around the ship nonchalantly, before a giant squid-like creature with a face like a parakeet (Bairasu) threatens Gamera. Undone by a bevy of stock footage to pad out the running time. Though frequently shown on television 20 years ago, this and *Gamera vs. Monster X* (1970) were not part of the "Sandy Frank" package of poorly-redubbed home video releases, making the film somewhat more obscure than other entries. Followed by *Attack of the Monsters* (1969).

Don't Call Me a Con Man ★★★ 1/2
(TOHO INTERNATIONAL, 1966)
Daiboken "Big Adventure" ★★★ 1/2 (TOHO, 1965)
Alternate title: *Don't Call Me a Crime Man*
Director: Kengo Furusawa **Special Effects Director:**

Eiji Tsuburaya **Screenplay:** Ryozo Kasahara and Yasuo Tanami **Director of Photography:** Tadashi Iimura **Producers:** Shin Watanabe and Sanezumi Fujimoto **Cast:** The Crazy Cats (Hitoshi Ueki, Hajime Hana, Kei Tani, Hiroshi Inuzuka, Senri Sakurai, Eitaro Ishibashi, Shin Yasuda), Reiko Dan, Fubuki Koshiji, The Peanuts (Emi and Yumi Ito), Andrew Hughes, Harold S. Conway, Nadao Kirino, Hisaya Ito.

Crazy Cats comedy with special effects by Eiji Tsuburaya. Filmed at the height of the James Bond craze, Ueki, Hana, Tani, et. al. uncover a plot by Nazis to create a Fourth Reich and restore Hitler (still alive and played by Andrew Hughes) to power. Clearly Toho hoped this mix of brand name special effects (a miniature sub, an exploding island, etc.), Bond-esque opulence, and Japan's Number One comedy team would translate well overseas. Sadly, it was barely released in the U.S., though a big hit in Japan. The Peanuts, regulars on The Crazy Cats' TV show, do a number; it and the film's other songs are enjoyable. A funny picture, too.

Ebirah, Horror of the Deep see *Godzilla versus the Sea Monster*

ESPY ★1/2 (TOHO INTERNATIONAL, 1975)
Esupai "Espy" ✹ (TOHO, 1974)
Director: Jun Fukuda **Special Effects Director:** Teruyoshi Nakano **Screenplay:** Ei Ogawa, based on a story by Sakyo Komatsu **Director of Photography:** Masaharu Ueda **Art Director:** Shinobu Muraki **Music:** Masaaki Hirao **Producers:** Tomoyuki Tanaka and Fumio Tanaka **Cast:** Hiroshi Fujioka, Kaoru Yumi, Masao Kusakari, Yuzo Kayama, Tomisaburo Wakayama, Katsumasa Uchida, Steve Green, Eiji Okada, Robert Dunham, Goro Mutsumi.

Also known as *E.S.P./Spy,* this routine thriller mixes telekinesis with an international assassination plot with ho-hum results. Though featuring an all-star cast (including "Young Guy" Yuzo Kayama, *Woman in the Dunes'* Eiji Okada, and Tomisaburo Wakayama from the "Lone Wolf and Cub" films), solid direction from Fukuda and decent effects by Nakano, the picture, similar to George Pal's *The Power* (1968) is pretty mediocre, at least in the edited and badly-dubbed home video version available in the U.S. from UPA.

Evil Brain from Outer Space
★★ (MEDALLION TV, 1964)
Supa Jyaiantsu: uchu kaijin shutsugen "Super Giant: Mysterious Spacemen Appear" ✹ (FUJI/ SHINTOHO, 1958)
Director: Akira Miwa **Screenplay:** Ichiro Miyagawa, Shinsuke Niegishi **Director of Photography:** Takashi Watanabe **Special Effects:** Akira Watanabe **Music:** Chumei Watanabe **Producer:** Mitsugi Okura **Cast:** Ken Utsui, Chisako Tahara.

Last of the "Starman" films finds our hero battling wildly-designed mutants and miscellaneous hoods wearing the "Batman" emblem, all for the want of the title brain. Wild, tiresome, and insanely nonsensical.

怪獣 東京大攻撃

Evil of Dracula ★1/2 (UPA, 1980)
Chi o suu bara "The Blood-Sucking Rose" ✹
(TOHO, 1975)
Director: Michio Yamamoto **Screenplay:** Ei Ogawa
and Masaru Takasue **Director of Photography:**
Kazutami Hara **Art Director:** Kazuo Satsuya **Music:**
Riichiro Manabe **Producer:** Fumio Tanaka **Cast:**
Toshio Kurosawa, Kunie Tanaka, Mariko Mochizuki,
Katsuhiko Sasaki, Shin Kishida, Yunosuke Ito.

By far the least interesting of Yamamoto's vampire
trilogy, this time set at a university between semesters.
Yamamoto didn't want to make it and his lack of
enthusiasm shows in this lackluster production.

The Final War ✹ (SAM LAKE ENTERPRISES, 1962)
Daisanji sekai taisen—yonju-ichi jikan no kyofu "World
War III: 41 Hours of Fear" ✹
(TOEI, 1960)
Director: Shigeaki Hidaka
Screenplay: Hisataka Kai **Director
of Photography:** Tadashi Arakami
Cast: Tatsuo Umemiya, Yoshiko
Mita, Yayoi Furusato, Noribumi
Fujishima, Yukiko Nikaido,
Michiko Hoshi.

No one I know, Japanese or
American, has seen this
frustratingly obscure end of the
world tale, made before Toho's *The
Last War* (1961) and in black and
white instead of color. Though this
film seems to have actually existed at one time—the
lavish destruction scenes in *Invasion of the Neptune
Men* (1961) may have even been lifted from this
production—but as this book went to press it was not

**"Frankenstein Conquers
the World"**

available on tape or laserdisc here or in Japan, and may
never have actually been shown in this country.

Frankenstein Conquers the World ★★1/2
(AIP, 1966)
Furankenshutain tai chitei kaiju Baragon "Frankenstein
vs. the Subterranian Monster Baragon" ★★★
(TOHO/UPA, 1965)
Director: Ishiro Honda **Special Effects Director:** Eiji
Tsuburaya **Screenplay:** Kaoru Mabuchi (Takeshi
Kimura), based on a treatment by Reuben Bercovitch
Director of Photography: Hajime Koizumi **Special
Effects Photography:** Teisho Arikawa and Mototaka
Tomioka **Art Director:** Takeo Kita **Music:** Akira
Ifukube **Producers:** Tomoyuki Tanaka and Henry G.
Saperstein **Cast:** Tadao Takashima, Kumi Mizuno,
Nick Adams, Yoshio Tsuchiya, Kenji Sahara, Susumu
Fujita, Nobuo Nakamura, Takashi Shimura, Yoshifumi
Tajima, Yoshio Kosugi, Nadao Kirino, Peter Mann,
Hisaya Ito, Haruya Kato, Senkichi Omura, Keiko
Sawai, Ikio Sawamura, Yutaka Sada, Koji Furuhata,
Haruo Nakajima.

A giant-sized Frankenstein (Furuhata) battles a
tubby, Boston Terrier-like lizard (Nakajima) as
American scientist Adams woos beautiful Kumi
Mizuno in this, the first Japanese/U.S. *kaiju eiga*. The
picture's opening is incredible: the heart of the
Frankenstein monster smuggled out of Nazi Germany
via submarine to Hiroshima just as the atomic bomb is
dropped, all to Akira Ifukube's eerie, ominous music.
Unfortunately, the rest of the film doesn't measure up;
the monster scenes (or rather, the search and confusion
about the monsters' whereabouts) go on and on,
though the relationship between Adams and Mizuno is
interesting and there are several impressive effects

sequences. An alternate ending, not used in either version, in which Frankenstein battles a giant "devil-fish" (i.e., big octopus) is more foreboding and downbeat, and would've made a better ending. Baragon returned—briefly—in the all-star *Destroy All Monsters* (1968).

Fugitive Alien ★½ (KING FEATURES, 1988)
Suta-urufu ✹ (TSUBURAYA PRODUCTIONS, 1978) [TV]
Directors: Kiyosumi Kukazawa and Minoru Kanaya
Teleplay: Keiichi Abe, Bunko Wakatsuki, Yoshihisa Araki, Hiroyasu Yamamura, Hideyoshi Nagasaka, and Toyohiro Ando **Music:** Norio Maeda **Producer:** Noboru Tsuburaya **Cast:** Tatsuya Azuma, Jo Shishido, Miyuki Tanigawa, Choei Takahashi, Tsutomu Yukawa, Hiro Tateyama, Akihiko Hirata.

Shoestring TV production-turned pseudo-feature has mindless action and pacing of 30s serial, but isn't very good and the dubbing is as cheap as the dime-store costumes. Nikkatsu star Jo Shishido (*Branded to Kill*) co-stars, and Akihiko Hirata appears briefly.

Gamera see *Gammera the Invincible*

Gamera Super Monster see *Super Monster*

Gamera—The Guardian of the Universe
★★★½ (A.D. VISION, 1995)
Gamera—daikaiju kuchu kessen "Gamera—Decisive Air Battle" ★★★½ (DAIEI/NIPPON TV/HAKUHODO, 1995)
Director: Shusuke Kaneko **Special Effects Director:** Shinji Higuchi **Screenplay:** Kazunori Ito **Director of Photography:** Junichi Tozawa **Special Effects Photography:** Hiroshi Kidokoro **Art Director:** Toshio Miike **Music:** Ko Otani **Producer:** Tsutomu

Tsuchikawa **Cast:** Tsuyoshi Ihara, Akira Onodera, Ayako Fujitani, Shinobu Nakayama, Yukijiro Hotaru, Kojiro Hongo, Akira Kubo, Takateru Manabe, Yumi Kameyama.

The best giant monster movie since at least *Destroy All Monsters* (1968) is, in its original, subtitled version, both wildly imaginative while paying tribute to *kaiju eiga* triumphs of the past. In theaters, it's also scary and unsettling, something never expected from a Gamera movie. Gamera battles several Gyaoses (from *Return of the Giant Monsters*) in this superbly directed, edited and scored feature, whose effects (directed by the then-28-year-old Higuchi) reveals just how lacking Toho's films had become. The film has several scenes that, again in a theater, are simply breathtaking: Gyaos' swooping toward a baseball dugout, Gamera's first flight before astonished onlookers, Gamera and Gyaos chasing one another outside the earth's atmosphere then free-falling back to earth. Made for a tiny fraction of the cost of *Jurassic Park* ($4 million vs. $70 million), yet many times better. Hongo and Kubo have cameos as ship's captains during the prologue. Followed by *Gamera 2: Advent of Legion* (1996).

Gamera 2: Advent of Legion
(UNRELEASED IN THE UNITED STATES)
Gamera 2: Region shurai "Gamera 2: Attack of Legion" ★★★ (DAIEI/NIPPON TV/ HAKUHODO, 1996)
Director: Shusuke Kaneko **Special Effects Director:** Shinji Higuchi **Screenplay:** Kazunori Ito **Director of Photography:** Junichi Tozawa **Special Effects Director of Photography:** Hiroshi Kidokoro **Art Director:** Toshio Miike **Music:** Ko Otani **Producers:** Yasuyoshi Tokuma, Tsutomu Tsuchikawa, Naoki Sato, Miyuki Nanri **Cast:** Toshiyuki Nagashima, Miki Mizuno,

Tamotsu Ishibashi, Mitsuru Fukikoshi, Ayako Fujitani, Yusuke Kawazu.

Okay sequel to *Gamera: The Guardian of the Universe* is more ambitious production-wise, but lacking in strong characterizations and a compelling storyline. This time Gamera battles a giant crab-like creature, and lots of little one-eyed crab critters which swarm over the big turtle like thousands of cockroaches. Kaneko's direction is solid, and he uses the Hokkaido locations to good effect, while Higuchi's effects work is continually inventive and surprising. And while Ito's script nicely brings children back into the series, the material simply isn't up to the picture's technical achievements. Highlight: an entire city is blown up, with Gamera at ground zero. A sequel has been announced.

Gamera vs. Barugon see *War of the Monsters*

Gamera vs. Guiron see *Attack of the Monsters*

Gamera vs. Gyaos see *Return of the Giant Monsters*

Gamera vs. Monster X ★★ (AIP-TV, 1970)
Gamera tai maju Jaiga "Gamera vs. the Demon Beast Jaiga" ★★1/2 (DAIEI, 1970)
Director: Noriaki Yuasa **Special Effects Director:** Kazufumi Fujii **Screenplay:** Nisan Takahashi **Director of Photography:** Akira Kitazaki **Music:** Shunsuke Kikuchi **Producer:** Hidemasa Nagata **Cast:** Tsutomu Takakuwa, Cary Barris, Katherine Murphy, Kon Omura, Junko Yashiro.

Fun Gamera picture with elements from *Fantastic Voyage* (1966) as two kids in a mini-sub travel through Gamera's ailing body, having been surrogately impregnated by the four-legged dinosaur Monster X. The rest of the film isn't much, however, as the two monsters clash at Expo 70, though there's less stock footage and more scenes of destruction than most Gamera movies. Like *Destroy All Planets*, *Gamera vs. Monster X* has not yet turned up on home video, and hasn't been seen much since the late-70s. Followed by *Gamera vs. Zigra* (1971).

Gamera vs. Zigra ★ (KING FEATURES, 1987)
Gamera tai shinkai kaiju Jigura "Gamera vs. the Deep Sea Monster Zigra" ★1/2 (DAIEI, 1971)
Director: Noriaki Yuasa **Special Effects Director:** Kazufumi Fujii **Screenplay:** Nisan Takahashi **Director of Photography:** Akira Kitazaki **Art Director:** Tomohisa Yano **Music:** Shunsuke Kikuchi **Producer:** Hidemasa Nagata **Cast:** Eiko Yanami, Reiko Kasahara, Mikiko Tsubouchi, Koji Fujiyama, Isamu Sakagami, Arlene Zoellner, Gloria Zoellner.

The weakest of the Gamera pictures (even *Super Monster* is better), and the last produced before Daiei's bankruptcy, *Gamera vs. Zigra* is cheap and uninspired, and its Sandy Frank-dubbed version (it was the only "Classic Gamera" movie not picked up for television showings in the 1970s) is virtually unwatchable. Gamera battles a shark-line alien in this thrillless, unoriginal adventure. The two children, a Japanese boy and a Western girl, are vexatious as hell and all the adults are dolts. Followed by *Super Monster* (1980).

Gammera the Invincible ★★
(WORLD ENTERTAINMENT CORP., 1966)
Daikaiju Gamera "Giant Monster Gamera" ★★
(DAIEI, 1965)
Director: Noriaki Yuasa **Special Effects Director:**

GAMMERA THE INVINCIBLE

STARRING ALBERT DEKKER **Cast of thousands!**
BRIAN DONLEVY
DIANE FINDLAY DIST. BY WORLD ENT. CORP.
A HARRIS ASSOCIATES PRESENTATION

Yonesaburo Tsukiji **Screenplay:** Nisan Takahashi, based on an idea by Yonejiro Saito **Director of Photography:** Nobuo Munekawa **Music:** Tadashi Yamauchi **Cast:** Eiji Funakoshi, Harumi Kiritachi, Junichiro Yamashiko, Yoshiro Uchida, Michiko Sugata, Yoshiro Kitahara, Jun Hamamura, George Hirose, Bokuzen Hidari. With Brian Donlevy, Albert Dekker, Diane Findlay, John Baragrey, Ed O'Neill, Alan Oppenheimer.

The first Gamera movie (and originally released with that extra "m" in the title) was, like *Godzilla, King of the Monsters!* (1956), filmed in black and white and released here with extensive footage of American actors inserted into the action. Unlike the original *Gojira*, however, Daiei's filmmakers were just making a giant monster movie to rival Toho's box office champ. The fire-breathing, flying turtle is impressive if improbable (though its later opponents would be even more outlandish); more problematic is the film's central human character, a turtle-loving boy obsessed with the giant beast, despite the latter's propensity to roast fleeing extras. *Gammera the Invincible,* featuring Donlevy, Dekker, et. al. appearing in a goodly amount of new footage directed by Sandy Howard, was widely syndicated in the 1970s, then disappeared for a time only to be released to home video as *Gamera* (★). This new version removed all the footage with the American cast while reinserting vaguely similar footage featuring Western—a-hem!—actors that were in the original Japanese version, but cut from *Gammera the Invincible.* Though much closer to the original, Japanese edition, the shorter, heavily Americanized *Gammera's* pacing is much better, and the dubbing is infinately better. Followed by *War of the Monsters* (1966)

Ghidrah—The Three-Headed Monster ★★★
(CONTINENTAL, 1965)
San daikaiju chikyu saidai no kessen "Three Giant Monsters Battle on Earth" ★★★½ (TOHO, 1964)
Director: Ishiro Honda **Special Effects Director:** Eiji Tsuburaya **Screenplay:** Shinichi Sekizawa **Director of Photography:** Hajime Koizumi **Special Effects Photography:** Teisho Arikawa, Mototaka Tomioka **Art Director:** Takeo Kita **Music:** Akira Ifukube **Producer:** Tomoyuki Tanaka **Cast:** Yosuke Natsuki, Yuriko Hoshi, Hiroshi Koizumi, Takashi Shimura, The Peanuts (Emi and Yumi Ito), Akiko Wakabayashi, Hisaya Ito, Akihiko Hirata, Kenji Sahara, Ikio Sawamura, Yoshifumi Tajima, Minoru Takada, Eisei Amamoto, Yoshio Kosugi, Haruya Kato, Senkichi Omura, Toru Ibuki, Kazuo Suzuki, Susumu Kurobe, Someshō Matsumoto, Haruo Nakajima, Shoichi "Solomon" Hirose.

Lively monster mash pits Godzilla, Rodan, and Mothra against the magnificent three-headed winged dragon Ghidrah (called King Ghidorah in Japan) in this first all-star monster rally. Mixed into the narrative is a subplot about a group of assassins trying to kill an exotic princess (Wakabayashi) possessed (or something) and convinced she's from a planet ravaged by Ghidrah eons earlier. The monster scenes are spectacularly done, though some *kaiju eiga* fans dislike the fact that Rodan, in his second appearance, had become an essentially comical character. But they also win our affection; when I saw this at a revival theater several years ago the initially blasé audience gasped when Mothra is zapped into the air several times by Ghidrah's electric bolts, and cheered the monsters on during the big finale. As usual, Honda, Ifukube, Hajime Koizumi, et. al. do a fine job, as does the ensemble cast. Followed by *Monster Zero* (1965).

The Ghost of Yotsuya ★★★

(SHIMOTO ENTERPRISES, 1960)

Tokaido Yotsuya kaidan "Ghost Story of Yotsuya in Tokaido" ★★★ (SHINTOHO, 1959)

Director: Nobuo Nakagawa **Screenplay:** Masayoshi Onuki and Yoshihiro Ishikawa, based on the Kabuki play by Nanboku Tsuruya **Director of Photography:** Tadashi Nishimoto **Art Director:** Haruyasu Kurosawa **Producer:** Mitsugu Okura **Cast:** Shigeru Amachi, Noriko Kitazawa, Kazuko Wakasugi, Shuntaro Emi, Junko Ikeuchi, Ryozaburo Nakamura, Jun Otomo.

One of many film versions of Japan's most famous ghost story. This version, the only one commercially available on home video (and even it's extremely obscure) is colorful and lively. It's very "Japanese" but filmed in a manner not unlike Hammer's classic horror films from the same period.

Gigantis the Fire Monster ★★

(WARNER BROS., 1959)

Gojira no gyakushu "Godzilla's Counterattack" ★★ (TOHO, 1955)

Director: Motoyoshi Oda **Special Effects Director:** Eiji Tsuburaya **Screenplay:** Takeo Murata and Shigeaki Hidaka, based on a treatment by Shigeru Kayama **Director of Photography:** Seiichi Endo **Art Director:** Takeo Kita **Music:** Masaru Sato **Producer:** Tomoyuki Tanaka

Cast: Hiroshi Koizumi, Setsuko Wakayama, Minoru Chiaki, Takashi Shimura, Yukio Kasama, Mayuri Mokusho, Sonosuke Sawamura, Masao Shimizu, Takeo Oikawa, Seijiro Onda, Yoshio Tsuchiya, Minnosuke Yamada, Ren Yamamoto, Senkichi Omura, Haruo Nakajima, Katsumi Tezuka.

A quickie sequel to *Godzilla, King of the Monsters!* (1954), *Gigantis* (aka *Godzilla Raids Again*) is structurally flawed, with the highlight, a battle between Godzilla (called Gigantis because the American distributor thought people would confuse this with a reissue of the first film) and Angilas, an Anklyosaur-type dinosaur coming in the middle, not at the end. Initially, the American version was supposed to be heavily reworked, (as "The Volcano Monsters," with a script by Ib Melchior) and Toho even sent new rubber suits to America for new special effects sequences to be shot. All this was followed by *King Kong vs. Godzilla* (1962).

Godzilla, King of the Monsters! ★★½

(GODZILLA RELEASING COMPANY, 1956)

Gojira "Godzilla" ★★★½ (TOHO, 1954)

Director: Ishiro Honda **Screenplay:** Takeo Murata and Ishiro Honda, based on a treatment by Shigeru Kayama **Director of Photography:** Masao Tamai **Art Director:** Satoshi Chuko **Music:** Akira Ifukube **Special Effects Director:** Eiji Tsuburaya **Producer:** Tomoyuki Tanaka **Cast:** Akira Takarada, Momoko Kochi, Akihiko Hirata, Takashi Shimura, Fuyuki Murakami, Sachio Sakai, Toranosuke Ogawa, Ren Yamamoto, Kin Sugai, Kokuten Kodo, Haruo Nakajima.

The original, Japanese version of *Godzilla, King of the Monsters!*—minus Raymond Burr and known in Japan as *Gojira*—has been stubbornly elusive in the U.S., until several bootlegging operations did what

Toho should have done many years ago: they have released gorgeous, crystal-sharp, English subtitled editions. In short, the Japanese version is more serious, more ambitious than the American version, though the stateside version, directed by Terry Morse, is decent for what it is. Unlike *Varan the Unbelievable* (1958), *King Kong vs. Godzilla* (1962) and other Americanized monster movies, *Godzilla, King of the Monsters!* was actually done with considerable care and ingenuity. It's respectful, not contemptuous, of the Japanese footage, and plays with it as best as can be expected. The Japanese version has surprises here and there, but as it was, admittedly, a Japanized version of *The Beast from 20,000 Fathoms* (1953) and *King Kong* (1933), more than a direct Japanese reaction to The Bomb and nuclear testing. It's also not the revelation subsequently mutilated works like *Gorath* (1962), *Dagora, the Space Monster* (1964) and *King Kong vs. Godzilla* are when seen in their original form. Certainly this first of 22 Godzilla features to date is the most serious, probably the most ambitious, and it has a freshness and energy which inevitably declined over time. And yet the best and most original and most audacious Japanese *kaiju eiga* were yet to come. Only after they felt secure in their own abilities and international marketability did the Japanese pay less attention to American tastes and turned to their own unique and very real strengths. Godzilla is, however, an interesting beginning, with its superb blend of "suitmation" techniques, puppetry (yes, puppetry), and even a limited amount of stop motion and rotoscope animation. Akira Ifukube's score (to say nothing of Godzilla's roar, which he also created) is ominous and unforgettable (portions of which Ifukube later adapted into, of all things, Kon Ichikawa's *The Burmese Harp*), and there are fine performances from Takarada, Kochi, Hirata, and Shimura. Naturally, the subtitled performances work in a way they never could in the dubbed version. But, of course, it is Eiji Tsuburaya painstaking special effects that truly beguile the senses: we admire his ingenuity, but also his keen eye for those haunting images that stay with you forever. Followed by *Gigantis the Fire Monster* (1955).

Godzilla 1985 ★½ (NEW WORLD, 1985)
Gojira "Godzilla" ★★½ (TOHO, 1984)
Director: Koji Hashimoto **Special Effects Director:** Teruyoshi Nakano **Screenplay:** Shuichi Nagahara, based on a story by Tomoyuki Tanaka **Director of Photography:** Kazutani Hara **Special Effects Photography:** Takeshi Yamamoto and Toshimitsu Oneda **Art Director:** Akira Sakuragi **Music:** Reijiro Koroku **Producers:** Tomoyuki Tanaka and Fumio Tanaka **Cast:** Keiju Kobayashi, Ken Tanaka, Yasuko Sawaguchi, Shin Takuma, Yosuke Natsuki, Tetsuya Takeda, Eitaro Ozawa, Takeshi Kato, Yoshifumi Taijma, Hiroshi Koizumi, Kei Sato, Kenpachiro Satsuma, Raymond Burr, Warren Kemmerling, Travis Swords.

After a nine-year abscence, the King of the Monsters returned to the screen in this big budget (about $10 million) reworking of the Godzilla legend. Both a remake and direct sequel to the first film—and ignoring all the sequels in between—Godzilla once again becomes a metaphor of nuclear terror, and this time Cold War tensions are added into the mix in a major way. The result is an ambitious and generally admirable monster epic, though there are major scripting flaws (scientists figure out how to stop Godzilla barely one-third into the film), and the special effects are uneven, though often impressive.

However, the film was badly Americanized by New World, which cheaply inserted scenes featuring Raymond Burr (reprising his role of journalist Steve Martin) with none of the care of *Godzilla, King of the Monsters!* These new scenes cued audiences to laugh at the picture, and shamelessly pitched soda pop as various military personnel huddle around Dr Pepper machines. New World also rearranged scenes, cut others out, and edited the picture in such a way that the Soviets become the bad guys. They also inserted Marv Newland's one-joke short *Bambi Meets Godzilla* (1969) before the feature. Too bad. Followed by *Godzilla vs. Biollante* (1989).

Godzilla on Monster Island ★

(DOWNTOWN DISTRIBUTION CO., 1977)
Chikyu kogeki meirei: Gojira tai Gaigan "Earth Destruction Directive: Godzilla vs. Gigan" ★½
(TOHO, 1972)
Director: Jun Fukuda **Special Effects Director:** Teruyoshi Nakano **Screenplay:** Shinichi Sekizawa **Director of Photography:** Kiyoshi Hasegawa **Special Effects Photography:** Mototaka Tomioka **Art Director:** Yoshifumi Honda **Music:** Akira Ifukube (stock themes only) **Producer:** Tomoyuki Tanaka **Cast:** Hiroshi Ishikawa, Yuriko Hishimi, Tomoko Umeda, Minoru Takashima, Kunio Murai, Zan Fujita, Wataru Omae, Gen Shimizu, Haruo Nakajima, Kenpachiro Satsuma, Kanta Ina, Yukietsu Omiya.

One of the very worst Godzilla movies, *Monster Island,* known today as *Godzilla vs. Gigan,* is just a rehash of the evil aliens vs. humans/alien monsters vs. Earth monsters formula. This travesty, however, was made on a fraction of the budget of the 60s G-films, and it shows. King Ghidorah, in his 4th appearance,

looks stiff and disheveled, and the film relies heavily on stock footage from earlier entries (*Ghidrah—The Three-Headed Monster*, etc.). Angilas is also back; he and Godzilla talk to one another in heavily distorted, synthesizer tones, while an wholly unimpressive *kaiju,* Gigan, an outer space whatsit, makes its debut. Even the very impressive Ifukube score was lifted from another movie: *Birth of the Japanese Islands.* Terrible.

Godzilla Raids Again see *Gigantis the Fire Monster*

Godzilla vs Biollante ★★

(HBO HOME VIDEO, 1992)
Gojira tai Biorante "Godzilla vs. Biollante" ★★½
(TOHO, 1989)
Director: Kazuki Omori **Special Effects Director:** Koichi Kawakita **Screenplay:** Kazuki Omori, based on a story by Shinichiro Kobayashi **Director of Photography:** Yudai Kato **Special Effects Photography:** Kenichi Eguchi **Music:** Koichi Sugiyama, with Godzilla themes by Akira Ifukube **Producers:** Tomoyuki Tanaka and Shogo Tomiyama **Cast:** Kunihiko Mitamura, Yoshiko Tanaka, Masanobu Takashima, Megumi Odaka, Toru Minegishi, Ryunosuke Kaneda, Koji Takahashi, Yasuko Kawaguchi, Toshiyuki Nagashima, Yoshiko Kuga, Katsuhiko Sasaki, Kenpachiro Satsuma

Just as *Godzilla 1985,* at least in its original version, proved a giant leap from the cheapie Godzilla movies of the 1970s, *Godzilla vs. Biollante* takes the series into a dramatic new cycle, filmed in a completely new (though not always better) style, a style which would remain relatively consistent through the present. Written and directed by Omori, it makes more wrong turns than right ones, and it's often boring, poorly acted and scored, but when it comes alive—at least when it was new—it was an impressive show indeed. Seen today, Biollante is pretty clunky; the series got better before getting worse again, but to fans who were floored to learn the film even existed it was a real treat. *Godzilla vs. Biollante* went straight to cable television and home video, making it the first Godzilla film to forgo a theatrical release since *Son of Godzilla* (1967). Followed by *Godzilla vs. King Ghidorah* (1991).

Godzilla vs. Destroyer

(UNRELEASED IN THE UNITED STATES)
Gojira tai Desutoroiya "Godzilla vs. Destroyer" ★★
(TOHO, 1995)
Director: Takao Okawara **Special Effects Director:** Koichi Kawakita **Screenplay:** Kazuki Omori **Special Effects Photography:** Kenichi Eguchi **Music:** Akira Ifukube **Producers:** Tomoyuki Tanaka and Shogo Tomiyama **Cast:** Tatsumi Takuro, Yoko Ishino, Yasufumi Hayashi, Megumi Odaka, Momoko Kochi, Akira Nakao, Masahiro Takashima, Kenpachiro Satsuma, Ryo Hariya, Hariken Ryu.

Reputed to be the last Japanese-made Godzilla film for quite some time, *Godzilla vs. Destroyer* isn't the worst of the new series, but it's nevertheless a weary, noisy, souless little picture. Omori's script admirably (or exploitatively, its hard to tell) tries to link this, the 22nd entry with the original, 41-year-old *Gojira,* and this certainly maintains the viewer's interest for the reasonably impressive first half-hour. Even Emiko Yamane (Kochi) has been brought back, though both her character and the actress are wasted in a mostly thankless and minor role. There are also other nice touches, but the more intriguing references to the first film are underdeveloped or forgotten about along the way. Moreover, new scenes with the clumsy-looking

Destroyer monsters overwhelm the last two-thirds of the picture. Sequences featuring these creatures make more than a passing nod to *Predator* and *Aliens* (indeed the film is as much an "homage" to the Alien films as the original *Gojira*). They're also hopelessly hokey and their footage ploddingly edited, particularly where clunky full-size props are used. Okawara's direction of these scenes are surprisingly stiff and thunderously dull. The miniature and optical special effects are equally sloppy, with several laughably bad composite shots showing blasé crowds leisurely strolling/driving/flying toward the battling monsters; in another scene, Kawakita used plastic *Destroyer* toys for a mass attack sequence (painfully obvious on the big screen). The effects director's work seems to get colder and less inspired with each film—*Destroyer's* effects sequences have the look of something designed by a machine, they're so bereft of humanity. Akira Ifukube's score is also a disappointment. Not bad, really, but in light of his superb work on *Godzilla vs. Mechagodzilla* it is a sizable letdown. However, his cue for Godzilla's much-touted death is moving, even if the sequence isn't. Followed by TriStar's all-American *Godzilla* (1998).

Godzilla vs. Gigan see *Godzilla on Monster Island*

Godzilla vs. King Ghidorah

(UNRELEASED IN THE UNITED STATES)
Gojira tai Kingugidora "Godzilla vs. King Ghidorah" ★★★1/2 (TOHO, 1991)
Director/Screenplay: Kazuki Omori **Special Effects Director:** Koichi Kawakita **Director of Photography:** Yoshinoru Sakiguchi **Special Effects Photography:** Kenichi Eguchi **Art Director:** Ken Sakai **Music:** Akira

Ifukube **Producers:** Tomoyuki Tanaka and Shogo Tomiyama **Cast:** Anna Nakagawa, Megumi Odaka, Kosuke Toyohara, Kiwako Harada, Tokuma Nishioka, Shoji Kobayashi, Yoshio Tsuchiya, Richard Berger, Chuck Wilson, Kenji Sahara, Robert Scottfield, Koichi Ueda, Kenpachiro Satsuma.

Though it borrows heavily from *The Terminator* and its time travel logic is a bit skewered, this is the best Godzilla film of the new series. It's cleverly-written, with solid, human characters. Best among these is a WWII veteran-turned corporate executive, passionately played by Tsuchiya, whose connection to Godzilla becomes the very symbol of Japan's postwar success. In addition to the title monsters, Godzilla is seen in his pre-Atomic exposure dinosaur state (the Godzillasaurus), while Ghidorah mutates into Mecha-Ghidorah for the grand finale, set against the towering skyscrapers of Shinjuku. Ifukube returned for the impressive, if not terribly original score (e.g., the title theme is music from *King Kong vs. Godzilla*, the march from *Destroy All Monsters*, etc.). Followed by *Godzilla vs. Mothra* (1992).

Godzilla vs. Mechagodzilla (1974) see *Godzilla vs. the Cosmic Monster*

Godzilla vs. Mechagodzilla
(UNRELEASED IN THE UNITED STATES)
Gojira tai Mekagojira "Godzilla vs. Mechagodzilla" ★★1/2 (TOHO, 1993)
Director: Takao Okawara **Special Effects Director:** Koichi Kawakita **Screenplay:** Wataru Mimura **Director of Photography:** Yoshinori Sekiguchi **Special Effects Photography:** Kenichi Eguchi **Art Director:** Ken Sakai **Music:** Akira Ifukube **Producers:**

Tomoyuki Tanaka and Shogo Tomiyama **Cast:** Masahiro Takashima, Ryoko Sano, Daijiro Harada, Megumi Odaka, Ichirota Miyagawa, Kenji Sahara, Akira Nakao, Tadao Takashima, Leo Mengetti, Keiko Imamura, Sayaka Osawa, Kenpachiro Satsuma, Wataru Fukuda, Hariken Ryu.

Despite Kawakita's splendid effects work, decent direction from Okawara, and Akira Ifukube's majestic, poignant music—his best score since the 60s—this 40th anniversary film (a year early, actually, but that's how it was promoted) is nonetheless a letdown. The human characters are colorless ciphers and the script is sketchy and underdeveloped. Sequences cut out of the film but available on Toho's CAV laserdisc version flesh the characters out dramatically and should have been left in. The monster sequences are impressive but go on too long. This time Mechagodzilla is on our side, built by the Japanese from the remains of Mecha-Ghidorah to defeat Godzilla. A revamped Rodan, in its first major appearance since the 60s, also looks good, if more conventional and *pterodactyl*-like. The Son of Godzilla also returns, this time called "Baby Godzilla," and darn cute, though nothing like little Minira of 25 years earlier. Followed by *Godzilla vs. Space Godzilla* (1994).

Godzilla vs. Megalon ★ (CINEMA SHARES, 1976)
Gojira tai Megaro "Godzilla vs. Megalon" ★1/2 (TOHO, 1973)
Director: Jun Fukuda **Special Effects Director:** Teruyoshi Nakano **Screenplay:** Jun Fukuda, based on a treatment by Shinichi Sekizawa **Director of Photography:** Yuzuru Aizawa **Music:** Riichiro Manabe **Producer:** Tomoyuki Tanaka **Cast:** Katsuhiko Sasaki, Hiroyuki Kawase, Yutaka Hayashi, Kotaro Tomita, Wolf Hotsuke, Robert Dunham, Shinji Takagi,

Kenpachiro Satsuma, Tsugutoshi Komada.

The cheapest of all Godzilla movies, Megalon looks more like an episode of "Ultraman Leo" than the classic G-films of the 1960's. Everything looks shoddy, from the special effects to the costumes and music (again done by *Smog Monster's* Manabe). Like *Monster Island,* the film is overloaded with special effects stock footage from the glory days, and the new stuff, featuring Gigan and the beetle-like Megalon are inadequete. Ironically, this was the only Godzilla film to get an airing on network television (hosted by John Belushi wearing a Godzilla suit, and edited down to 60 minutes), and it actually received a rave (if condescending) review from *The New York Times*! Followed by *Godzilla vs. the Cosmic Monster* (1974).

Godzilla vs. Monster Zero see *Monster Zero*

Godzilla vs. Mothra (1964) see *Godzilla vs. the Thing*

Godzilla vs. Mothra
(UNRELEASED IN THE UNITED STATES)
Gojira tai Mosura "Godzilla vs. Mothra" ★★★
(TOHO, 1992)
Director: Takao Okawara **Special Effects Director:** Koichi Kawakita **Screenplay:** Kazuki Omori **Special Effects Photography:** Kenichi Eguchi **Music:** Akira Ifukube **Producers:** Tomoyuki Tanaka and Shogo Tomiyama **Cast:** Tetsuya Bessho, Satomi Kobayashi, Takehiro Murata, Makoto Otake, Megumi Odaka, Akira Takarada, Keiko Imamura, Sayaka Osawa, Shoji Kobayashi, Kenpachiro Satsuma.

Follow-up to *Godzilla vs. King Ghidorah* (1991) is as fun as its predecessor, though not nearly as original. In fact, this is basically a remake of both *Mothra* (1961) and *Godzilla vs. the Thing* (1964) with a new monster, Battra (which looks like Mothra's evil twin), thrown in. What it lacks in originality—and the opening even borrows from *Raiders of the Lost Ark*!—is balanced by a simple sense of wonder as the fairy tale-like Mothra is brought into the jaded, technophelic Japan of today. Ifukube's score is lovingly arranged, and human characters aren't overwhelmed by monster footage (this soon would change). Interestingly, the story centers around a divorced couple and their young daughter; their plight is woven into the narrative quite nicely by screenwriter Omori, and well-directed by first-timer Okawara. Though Kawakita has yet to master daytime monster scenes (filmed in a soundstage; most of the new Gamera films are shot outdoors in natural light), his nighttime footage is impressive. Followed by *Godzilla vs. Mechagodzilla* (1993). A "Fairy Mothra" appears, briefly, in *Godzilla vs. Space Godzilla* (1994), while Mothra itself stars in *Mothra* (1996).

Godzilla vs. Space Godzilla
(UNRELEASED IN THE UNITED STATES)
Gojira tai Supesugojira "Godzilla vs. SpaceGodzilla" ★
(TOHO, 1994)
Director: Kensho Yamashita **Special Effects Director:** Koichi Kawakita **Screenplay:** Hiroshi Kashiwabara **Director of Photography:** Masahiro Kishimoto **Special Effects Photogaphy:** Kenichi Eguchi **Music:** Takayuki Hattori **Producers:** Tomoyuki Tanaka and Shogo Tomiyama **Cast:** Jun Hashizume, Megumi Odaka, Senkichi Yoneyama, Towako Yoshikawa, Akira Emoto, Kenji Sahara, Akira Nakao, Keiko Imamura, Sayaka Osawa, Kenpachiro Satsuma, Ryo Hariya, Wataru Fukuda, Little Frankie.

怪獣 東京大攻撃

By far the weakest of the "new" Godzilla films, Space Godzilla seems to go on forever, and in every way is inferior to *Godzilla vs. Mechagodzilla* (1993). It was at this point that effects director Kawakita began repeating himself—the Mogera opening weakly redoes the fabulous pre-title sequence to *Mechagodzilla*, etc.—while seeming to lose his enthusiasm for the series. Surprisingly, Kawakita was most proud of his Barney the Dinosaur-like reinterpretation of Godzilla's "son," now called "Little Godzilla," yet looking more cartoony and infantile than its predecessor. *Space Godzilla* itself is just a bigger Godzilla with Biollante's mouth and big, clunky crystals on its shoulders; its scenes in outer space are embarrassingly bad. Also brought back is Mogera, the giant robot from *The Mysterians* (1957), but the redesigned monster, G-Force's replacement for the defeated Mechagodzilla, has all the charm of a vacuum cleaner. Director Yamashita helms the film more like a Japanese "teen idol" film than a Godzilla movie, and the score is frequently mediocre. Followed by *Godzilla vs. Destroyer* (1995)

Godzilla vs. the Bionic Monster see *Godzilla vs. the Cosmic Monster*

Godzilla vs. the Cosmic Monster ★1/2
(CINEMA SHARES, 1977)
Gojira tai Mekagojira "Godzilla vs. Mechagodzilla" ★★
(TOHO, 1974)
Director: Jun Fukuda **Special Effects Director:** Teruyoshi Nakano **Screenplay:** Hiroyasu Yamamura and Jun Fukuda, based on a story by Shinichi Sekizawa and Masami Fukushima **Director of Photography:** Yuzuru Aizawa **Special Effects Photography:** Mototaka Tomioka and Takeshi Yamamoto **Art Director:** Kazuo

Satsuya **Music:** Masaru Sato **Producer:** Tomoyuki Tanaka **Cast:** Masaaki Daimon, Kazuya Aoyama, Akihiko Hirata, Hiroshi Koizumi, Reiko Tajima, Hiromi Matsushita, Masao Imafuku, Beru-Bera Lin, Shin Kishida, Goro Mutsumi, Kenji Sahara, Kazunari Mori, Satoru Kazumi.

A modest step up from the last several entries and known today as *Godzilla vs. Mechagodzilla*, the film pits the charcoal-gray lizard against his mechanical rival, a la *King Kong Escapes*. Created by evil space apes (inspired by the *Planet of the Apes* phenomenon of the period), Mechagodzilla is rather clunky, but combined with excellent optical work and Sato's pounding, jazzy score, the creature becomes a memorable foe. Less impressive is the *kaiju* that comes to Godzilla's aid, the Okinawan monster King Seesar, a puppy dog like creation. Angilas appears, too. The human characters and their half of the narrative aren't very interesting, though for the first time in several years familiar faces like Hirata, Koizumi, and Sahara appear. Followed by *Terror of Mechagodzilla* (1975).

Godzilla versus the Sea Monster ★★★
(WALTER READE, 1968)
Gojira, Ebirah, Mosura: nankai no daiketto "Godzilla, Ebirah, Mothra: Big Duel in the South Seas" ★★★1/2
(TOHO, 1968)
Director: Jun Fukuda **Special Effects Director:** Eiji Tsuburaya **Screenplay:** Shinichi Sekizawa **Director of Photography:** Kazuo Yamada **Special Effects Photography:** Teisho Arikawa, Mototaka Tomioka, and Taka Yuki **Music:** Masaru Sato **Producer:** Tomoyuki Tanaka **Cast:** Akira Takarada, Kumi Mizuno, Akihiko Hirata, Jun Tazaki, Hideo Sunazuka, Chotaro Togin, Toru Watanabe, Toru Ibuki, Eisei

Amamoto, Ikio Sawamura, Hisaya Ito, the Bambi Pair, Haruo Nakajima, Hiroshi Sekida.

One of the very best Godzilla films, though disliked by many fans. Castaways on a remote South Seas island must contend with Ebirah, a giant lobster, Godzilla, and the SPECTRE-like Red Bamboo, conducting heavy water experiments at a top secret base. Along the way our band of heroes, including reformed bank robber Takarada, meet up with sexy Polynesian native Mizuno, kidnapped from Infant Island and thrown into slavery by villains Hirata and Tazaki. Can Mothra save the day? Sea Monster represents a welcome change of pace and style from the Honda-Ifukube-Tsuburaya team. Fukuda brought an action director's sense of pace, versus Honda's more scientific community/documentary-influenced style, and he wisely insisted Masaru Sato score the picture. Sato's score is a refreshing change from Ifukube's grand but heavy themes, and the South Seas setting is an exotic (if budget-driven) change from the city-smashing shenanigans of previous entries. Best of all is the picture's strong narrative; it's so good you could literally remove the monsters and still have a pretty solid, entertaining picture. Followed by *Son of Godzilla* (1967).

Godzilla vs. The Smog Monster ★1/2 (AIP, 1972)
Gojira tai Hedora "Godzilla vs. Hedorah" ★★ (TOHO, 1971)
Director: Yoshimitsu Banno **Screenplay:** Yoshimitsu Banno and Kaoru Mabuchi (Takeshi Kimura) **Director of Photography:** Yoichi Manoda **Music:** Riichiro Manabe **Special Effects Director:** Teruyoshi Nakano **Producer:** Tomoyuki Tanaka **Cast:** Akira Yamaguchi, Hiroyuki Kawase, Toshie Kimura, Toshio Shibaki, Keiko Mari, Kazuo Suzuki, Haruo Nakajima, Kenpachiro Satsuma.

The most incongruous of Godzilla pictures, this was the first G-film made after the death of effects pioneer Eiji Tsuburaya, and the only fantasy film by director Banno. Series producer Tanaka was in the hospital while this was being made and was horrified with the results upon his return. It has its defenders and, to the picture's credit Hedorah (the Smog Monster) was Toho's first *kaiju* after Godzilla to consciously personify a very real threat to mankind (pollution), though by this time Godzilla's persona had, ironically, shifted 180-degrees away from atomic-bred terror to Defender of the Earth. However, the film still looks cheap (the army consists of about 10 guys), has more bad ideas than good (e.g., Godzilla flies in this one), the music is wretched, and the endless repetition of ideas, including two nearly identical climaxes, one after the other, doom the picture. The boy hero of the picture, (Kawase) played the begger's son in Kurosawa's *Dodes'ka-den* (1970). A proposed sequel, set in Africa (!) was never made. Toho rechristened the film *Godzilla vs. Hedorah* (★★), restoring a tiny amount of footage lost in AIP's badly-dubbed edition (this version's title song is in Japanese, not English). Followed by *Godzilla on Monster Island* (1972).

Godzilla vs. the Thing ★★★ (AIP, 1964)
Mosura tai Gojira "Mothra vs. Godzilla" ★★★1/2 (TOHO, 1964)
Director: Ishiro Honda **Special Effects Director:** Eiji Tsuburaya **Screenplay:** Shinichi Sekizawa **Director of Photography:** Hajime Koizumi **Special Effects Photography:** Teisho Arikawa and Mototaka Tomioka **Art Director:** Takeo Kita **Music:** Akira Ifukube **Producer:** Tomoyuki Tanaka **Cast:** Akira Takarada, Yuriko Hoshi, Hiroshi Koizumi, Yu Fujiki, Kenji

怪獣 東京大攻撃

Sahara, The Peanuts (Emi and Yumi Ito), Jun Tazaki, Yoshifumi Tajima, Kenzo Tabu, Yutaka Sada, Akira Tani, Susumu Fujita, Ikio Sawamura, Ren Yamamoto, Yoshio Kosugi, Senkichi Omura, Haruo Nakajima.

Top-notch monster epic, a candidate for the best G-film of them all, has all the right ingredients: a deft balance of straightly-done monster scenes and social satire, terrific performances, a grand score by Ifukube, and superb effects work by Tsuburaya and Co. Especially good is the Godzilla suit design, widely regarded as the best of the dozen or so variations of the costume since its debut. Standing out among the fine cast is Yoshifumi Tajima's Kumayama (villian Kenji Sahara's beard), the best role of his career. The American version contains a lengthly sequence involving the U.S. Navy's Frontier Missile Attack on the Big G; this footage was shot by Toho but for some reason omitted for the Japanese version. Otherwise, AIP's adaptation is as good as one might hope from a dubbed version, though current TV and home video prints of the film, now called *Godzilla vs. Mothra*, are blurry, faded, and panned-and-scanned, and do this fine film a major disservice. Followed by *Ghidrah—The Three-Headed Monster* (1964).

Godzilla's Revenge ★1/2 (MARON, 1971)
Oru kaiju daishingeki "All Monsters Big Attack" ★★1/2 (TOHO, 1969)
Director: Ishiro Honda **Special Effects Director:** Eiji Tsuburaya **Screenplay:** Shinichi Sekizawa **Director of Photography:** Mototaka Tomioka **Special Effects Photography:** Teisho Arikawa and Mototaka Tomioka **Art Director:** Takeo Kita **Music:** Kunio Miyaguchi **Producer:** Tomoyuki Tanaka **Cast:** Tomonori Yazaki, Kenji Sahara, Sachio Sakai, Kazuo Suzuki, Eisei

Amamoto, Yoshifumi Tajima, Chotaro Togin, Machiko Naka, Ikio Sawamura, Shigeki Ishida, Yutaka Sada, Haruo Nakajima, Little Man Machan, Hiroshi Sekita.

Inspired by Daiei's juvenile (and cheaper) Gamera movies, Toho produced this quickie Godzilla, which uses extensive footage from *Godzilla versus the Sea Monster*, *Son of Godzilla*, and others. Bridging the footage is a little boy (Yazaki) daydreaming about his friends on Monster Island. Kidnapped by desperate but bumbling bank robbers (Sakai and Suzuki), his story becomes a parable for Minya's conflict with monster bully Gabera. Badly dubbed, Minya talks like Don Knotts while the little boy, Ichiro (Yazaki), squeaks and squeals in a most annoying fashion. The film's defenders argue that if one can get past these defects the story is a charming, sad tale of a lonely latchkey boy. And it is true that the Japanese version is much, much better, coming off more as a small but personal project for director Honda and less the misguided kiddie film the American edition is. Though the title theme and a few other not-bad-though-weird cues were added to the U.S. version, most of the music was by Kunio Miyaguchi, who also scored the memorable themes for "Ultraman" and "Ultra Seven." Followed by *Godzilla vs. the Smog Monster*.

Goke, Bodysnatcher from Hell ★★★
(SHOCHIKU FILMS OF AMERICA, 1969)
Kyuketsuki Gokemidoro "Vampire Gokemidoro" ✹ (SHOCHIKU, 1968)
Director: Hajime Sato **Screenplay:** Susumu Takaku and Kyuzo Kobayashi **Director of Photography:** Shizuo Hirase **Art Director:** Tadataka Yoshino **Music:** Shunsuke Kikuchi **Producer:** Takashi Inomata **Cast:** Teruo Yoshida, Tomomi Sato, Hideo Ko, Eizo Kitamura,

Masaya Takahashi, Cathy Horlan, Kazuo Kato, Yuko Kunsunoki, Norihiko Kaneko, Harold S. Conway.

Effective, Bava-esque horror film about survivors of a plane crash in the desert stalked by a fellow passenger possessed by an alien force. Part *Invasion of the Body Snatchers,* part *Dracula,* the film has one hell of an opening and climax, and effective moments scattered throughout. Hopefully we'll see a subtitled, letterboxed edition of this almost unknown semi-classic someday.

Gorath ★★½ (BRENCO, 1964)
Yosei Gorasu "Ominous Star Gorath" ★★★★
(TOHO, 1962)

Director: Ishiro Honda **Special Effects Director:** Eiji Tsuburaya **Screenplay:** Takeshi Kimura, based on a story by Jojiro Okami **Director of Photography:** Hajime Koizumi **Special Effects Photography:** Teisho Arikawa and Mototaka Tomioka **Art Directors:** Takeo Kita and Teruaki Abe **Music:** Kan Ishii **Producer:** Tomoyuki Tanaka **Cast:** Ryo Ikebe, Yumi Shirakawa, Takashi Shimura, Kumi Mizuno, Ken Uehara, Akira Kubo, Akihiko Hirata, Jun Tazaki, Eitaro Ozawa, Seizaburo Kawazu, Ko Nishimura, Kenji Sahara, George Furness, Sachio Sakai, Ikio Sawamura, Eisei Amamoto, Nadao Kirino, Saburo Iketani, Osman Yuseph, Ed Keane, Haruo Nakajima.

Possibly the best Japanese science fiction film of them all, *Gorath* is, in its original form anyway, a sprawling epic of mankind working in tandem to move the Earth out of the path of a runaway star. Director Honda explored the theme of mankind banding together in the name of science before, in films like *The Mysterians* (1957) and *Battle in Outer Space* (1959), but here both Honda's handling of the material and the Kimura's screenplay demonstrate a

level of maturity yet to be surpassed in a Japanese sci-fi film. The picture's relative failure (compared to the huge success of the less expensive *King Kong vs. Godzilla,* made that same year) resulted in fewer ambitious, more monster-filled opuses and, in essence, signaled the end of an era. Tsuburaya's effects are among the best of his career, numerous and dramatically filmed. Producer Tanaka insisted, for box office reasons, a giant monster be added, in this case a humungous walrus named Magma; it was cut out of the U.S. version and no great loss, for its scenes stop the picture in its tracks and break the film's careful pacing. Highlights include the dramatic first act, in which spaceship commander Tazaki and his crew become trapped in the star's gravitational pull—this single sequence may be the highlight of Honda's career. Mizuno and Kubo, in their first sci-fi roles, are sexy and appealing. Also of note is Kan Ishii's score, his sole sci-fi work, which has several impressive, distinctive themes. The U.S. version does the film little good; it's poorly dubbed, while pointless astronomical gobbledygook and beeping noises have been edited in and, in possibly the most perverse decision, an optical fog has been added to much of Tsuburaya's miniature landscapes! A poor quality, hard-to-find home video version is, alas, all that presently, officially exists in the U.S., though an excellent widescreen, stereo laserdisc has been released in Japan.

The Green Slime ★★ (MGM, 1969)
Gamma sango uchu daisakusen "Gamma III's Big Outer Space Military Operation" ✹
(RAM/SOUTHERN CROSS/LUM/TOEI, 1968)
Director: Kinji Fukasaku **Screenplay:** Charles Sinclair, William Finger, Tom Rowe, and Takeo Kaneko, based

"Goke, Bodysnatcher from Hell"

"Gorath"

"The H-Man"

on a story by Ivan Reiner **Director of Photography:** Yoshikazu Yamasawa **Art Director:** Shinichi Eno **Music:** Toshiaki Tsushima **Special Effects Director:** Akira Watanabe **Special Effects Photography:** Yukio Manoda **Producers:** Ivan Reiner, Walter H. Manley, Kaname Ogisawa and Koji Ota **Cast:** Robert Horton, Richard Jaeckel, Lucianna Paluzzi, Bud Windom, Ted Gunther, Robert Dunham, David Yorston, William Ross, Cathy Horlan, Linda Miller.

Goofy space action-melodrama originally conceived as something much more ambitious with notably ludicrous monsters. Filmed in English with an all-Western cast, the picture is a lot of fun, with sometimes impressive, dramatically edited miniature work. Director Fukasaku's efforts are somewhat compromised in that an American edited the picture instead (Fukasaku's own cut of the film for Japanese release runs a brisk 77 minutes, 13 minutes shorter than the American version), the lighting is bad, and a rockin' main title theme was added. Still, Paluzzi is very sexy, and Japanese film regulars Robert *(Dagora)* Dunham, Linda *(King Kong Escapes)* Miller and Cathy *(Goke)* Horlan appear! MGM's other sci-fi release that year was *2001: A Space Odyssey.*

Gunhed (A.D. VISION, 1997)
Ganhedo "Gunhed" ★¹/₂ (TOHO, 1989)
Director: Masato Harada **Special Effects Director:** Koichi Kawakita **Screenplay:** Masato Harada and James Bannon **Director of Photography:** Junichi Fujisawa **Special Effects Photography:** Shinichi Eguchi **Music:** Toshiyuki Honda **Producers:** Tomoyuki Tanaka, Eiji Yamamura, and Tetsuhisa Yamada **Cast:** Masahiro Takashima, Brenda Bakke, Yujin Harada, Aya Enjoji, Mickey Curtis, James B.

Thompson, Doll Nguyen, Jay Kabira, Randy Reyes, Michael Yancy.

Despite some impressive effects work by Kawakita, some of it Hollywood quality at a fraction the cost, this is a cold, none-too-impressive man vs. machine adventure set in that *Blade Runner/Alien* future we've all grown so weary of.

The H-Man ★★¹/₂ (COLUMBIA, 1959)
Bijo to ekitainingen "Beauty and the Liquid People" ★★¹/₂ (TOHO, 1958)
Director: Ishiro Honda **Special Effects Director:** Eiji Tsuburaya **Screenplay:** Takeshi Kimura, based on a story by Hideo Kaijo **Director of Photography:** Hajime Koizumi **Special Effects Photography:** Hidesaburo Araki and Teisho Arikawa **Art Director:** Takeo Kita **Music:** Masaru Sato **Producer:** Tomoyuki Tanaka **Cast:** Yumi Shirakawa, Kenji Sahara, Akihiko Hirata, Makoto Sato, Koreya Senda, Yoshio Tsuchiya, Yoshifumi Tajima, Eitaro Ozawa, Ayumi Sonoda, Nadao Kirino, Hisaya Ito, Tetsu Nakamura, Senkichi Omura, Haruo Nakajima, Haruya Kato, Yutaka Sada, Ren Yamamoto, Tadao Nakamaru, Yosuke Natsuki.

Honda's horror film with sci-fi overtones is not far removed from the type of crime film hugely popular in Japan during this time. Ghostly, radioactive H-Men (and there are H-Men, despite the title) get in the way of various gangsters and seedy nightclubbers, instantly turning its victims into a pile of goo. Detective Hirata and scientist Sahara join forces to stop the human and inhuman menaces. The picture is pretty standard, but its horror sequences are not, particularly when the H-Men are first discovered, aboard a ghostly ship on a silent, fog-shrouded night. That sequence, which keenly mixes black humor with the horror, is one of

Honda's best. Sato's score is a curious and often incongruous mixture of effective and ridiculous themes. Godzilla actor Nakajima has a rare out-of-costume role as one of the doomed sailors. The first Japanese sci-fi film released in stereo in the United States (though all editions—Japanese and American—are presently mono).

Half Human: The Story of the Abominable Snowman ★ 1/2 (DCA, 1958)

Jujin yukiotako "Abominable Snowman" ✸
(TOHO, 1955)

Director: Ishiro Honda **Special Effects Director:** Eiji Tsuburaya **Screenplay:** Takeo Murata, based on a story by Shigeru Kayama **Director of Photography:** Tadashi Iimura **Art Director:** Takeo Kita **Music:** Masaru Sato **Producers:** Tomoyuki Tanaka and Minoru Sakamoto **Cast:** Akira Takarada, Momoko Kochi, Akemi Nigishi, Kenji Kasahara, Nobuo Nakamura, Yoshio Kosugi, Kokuten Kodo, Yasuhisa Tsutsumi, Sachio Sakai, Ren Yamamoto, Koji Suzuki, Akira Sera, Senkichi Omura. With John Carradine, Russell Thorsen, Robert Karnes, Morris Ankrum.

Artlessly altered Abominable Snowman picture (by Robert B. Homel and director Kenneth Crane) with endless, lengthy cutaways to filmed-in-America cast (Carridine, Ankrum, et. al.) where nothing much happens. The tiny snippets of original footage are quite interesting, but further compromised by a soundtrack which replaces the dialog, music and sound effects with yet more narration from top-billed Carradine. Unfortunately, Honda's first feature after *Godzilla, King of the Monsters!* is equally elusive in Japan: its depiction of Ainu natives is now considered politically incorrect, and the film has been unavailable for some time. Like Hammer's interesting *The Abominable Snowman of the Himalayas* (1957), *Half Human* treats its monster with sensitivity—it appears to be one of the last of an intelligent, almost-human breed. In both films, the monster has very human facial features (Honda's monster has a balding pate, no less) with hairy, ape-like bodies.

The Human Vapor ★★ (BRENCO, 1964)

Gasu ningen dai ichigo "Gas Human Being No. 1" ★★ 1/2 (TOHO, 1960)

Director: Ishiro Honda **Special Effects Director:** Eiji Tsuburaya **Screenplay:** Takeshi Kimura **Director of Photography:** Hajime Koizumi **Art Director:** Takeo Kita **Music:** Kunio Miyaguchi **Producer:** Tomoyuki Tanaka **Cast:** Tatsuya Mihashi, Keiko Sata, Kaoru Yachigusa, Yoshio Tsuchiya, Bokuzen Hidari, Hisaya Ito, Takamaru Sasaki, Kozo Nomura, Yoshifumi Tajima, Yoshio Kosugi, Tetsu Nakamura, Fuyuki Murakami, Ren Yamamoto, Tatsuo Matsumura.

Extensively reedited for American release (with some improvements, actually, but also missing several keys scenes as well) this tale of a mild-mannered librarian (Tsuchiya) who gains the ability to transform himself into a gaseous state is highly regarded by some, dismissed as a minor thriller by others. It's certainly sincerely and passionately made, and Tsuchiya's performance is excellent. Like the Phantom of the Opera, Mizuno, the Human Vapor, uses his powers in a misguided pursuit of dancer Yachigusa's affections, which reaches a dramatic climax in a theater as the authorities prepare an elaborate trap. The film would work much better in a subtitled form; for now, its Americanized edition comes off as very minor and forgettable.

Invaders from Space ★½ (Medallion TV, 1964)

Kotetso no kyojin—Supa Jyaiantsu: kaiseijin no mayo/chikyu metsubo sunzen "The Steel Giant—Super Giant: The Evil Castle of the Mysterious Planet People/The Earth Will Be Annihilated Soon" ✳ (FUJI FILM/SHINTOHO, 1957)

Director: Teruo Ishii, Koreyoshi Akasaka, and Akira Mitsuwa **Screenplay:** Ichiro Miyagawa, Shinsuke Niegishi **Director of Photography:** Takashi Watanabe **Special Effects:** Akira Watanabe **Music:** Chumei Watanabe **Producer:** Mitsugi Okura **Cast:** Ken Utsui, Minako Yamada.

The third "Starman" movie is overloaded with fight sequences as our hero battles a swarm of salamander men from outer space. The same old stuff. Followed by *Evil Brain from Outer Space* (1958).

Invasion of the Neptune Men ★★

(MEDALLION-TV, 1964)

Uchu kaizokusen "Space Pirate Ship" ✳ (NEW TOEI, 1961)

Director: Koji Ota **Screenplay:** Shin Morita **Director of Photography:** Shizuka Fuji **Producer:** Hiroshi Okawa **Cast:** Shinichi "Sonny" Chiba, Kappei Matsumoto, Mitsue Komiya, Shinjiro Ebara, Ryuko Minakami.

The Streetfighter himself, Shinichi Chiba (this was prior to his "Sonny"

days, actually), stars as superhero Space Chief ("Ironsharp" in Japan) in this familiar but well-produced alien invasion mini-epic. The special effects for this New Toei Production (a short-lived offshoot of Toei) are as good as anything Eiji Tsuburaya was doing at Toho during this period, and the impressive scenes of destruction may have been lifted from the presumably-lost *The Final War* (1960).

The Invisible Man

(UNRELEASED IN THE UNITED STATES)

Tomei ningen "Invisible Man" ★★ (TOHO, 1954)
Director: Motoyoshi Oda **Special Effects Director and Director of Photography:** Eiji Tsuburaya **Screenplay:** Shigeki Hidaka, suggested by the novel by H.G. Wells **Music:** Kyosuke Kami **Producer:** Takeo Kita **Cast:** Seizaburo Kawazu, Minoru Takada, Yoshio Tsuchiya, Yutaka Sada, Miki Sanjo, Kamatari Fujiwara, Haruo Nakajima.

Invisible man tale from the director of *Gigantis the Fire Monster*, made the same year as the first Godzilla. It's very much in the mold of Universal's Invisible Man films of the 1940s. This one stars Kawazu in the title role; he led the military in *Mothra* (1961) and was the bearded leader of the diamond circuit in *Dagora, the Space Monster* (1964). The actor spends much of the film hiding both his invisibilty and identity performing as a circus clown, a device doubtless lifted from Cecil B. DeMille's *The Greatest Show On Earth*, made two years earlier, and featuring James Stewart as a wanted man disguised as a clown who never removes his makeup. Though it appears to be very much a formula picture it's reasonably interesting, but as it's in Japanese and black and white it's also highly doubtful it'll ever be picked up for U.S. distribution.

King Kong Escapes ★★ (UNIVERSAL, 1968)

Kingukongu no gyakushu "King Kong's Counterattack" ★★★ (TOHO AND RANKIN/BASS, 1967)
Director: Ishiro Honda **Special Effects Director:** Eiji Tsuburaya **Screenplay:** Kaoru Mabuchi (Takeshi Kimura), based on the animated series **Director of Photography:** Hajime Koizumi **Special Effects Photography:** Teisho Arikawa and Mototaka Tomioka **Art Director:** Takeo Kita **Music:** Akira Ifukube Producers, Tomoyuki Tanaka, Arthur Rankin, Jr. and Jules Bass **Cast:** Akira Takarada, Mie Hama, Rhodes Reason, Linda Miller, Eisei Amamoto, Yoshifumi Tajima, Susumu Kurobe, Sachio Sakai, Nadao Kirino, Ikio Sawamura, Andrew Hughes, Cathy Horlan, Haruo Nakajima, Hiroshi Sekita.

Cartoony but enjoyable King Kong adventure (based on a forgotten American cartoon show, in fact) made by Toho in association with Rankin/Bass, the company behind all those puppet animation holiday TV specials. King Kong (less shabby but more goofy looking than in *King Kong vs. Godzilla*) battles his robot double, the impressive Mechani-Kong, as well as the allosaurus-like Gorosaurus and a rather pathetic sea serpent. Gaudy, absurd in the extreme, and nonetheless a fun picture, thanks to another great Ifukube score and a wildly theatrical performance by Amamoto as that "international Judas" Dr. Who (no relation to the British TV character). Reason and Miller spoke English during production; they were both dubbed into Japanese for release in that country, and Miller was badly dubbed by Julie Bennett for the American

version. Gorosaurs also appears in *Destroy All Monsters* (1968). Brief outtakes from the film appear in the Japanese laserdisc edition.

King Kong vs. Godzilla ★★½

(UNIVERSAL-INTERNATIONAL, 1963)
Kingukongu tai Gojira "King Kong vs. Godzilla" ★★★ (TOHO, 1962)
Director: Ishiro Honda **Special Effects Director:** Eiji Tsuburaya **Screenplay:** Shinichi Sekizawa, based on the screenplay by George Worthing Yates, from a story by Willis O'Brien **Director of Photography:** Hajime Koizumi **Special Effects Photography:** Teisho Arikawa and Mototaka Tomioka **Art Director:** Takeo Kita **Music:** Akira Ifukube **Producer:** Tomoyuki Tanaka **Cast:** Tadao Takashima, Yu Fujiki, Kenji Sahara, Mie Hama, Akiko Wakabayashi, Ichiro Arishima, Jun Tazaki, Akihiko Hirata, Tatsuo Matsumura, Senkichi Omura, Yoshio Kosugi, Akemi Negishi, Yoshifumi Tajima, Somesho Matsumoto, Ren Yamamoto, Haruo Nakajima, Shoichi "Solomon" Hirose. With Michael Keith, Harry Holcombe, and James Yagi.

The first Godzilla movie in widescreen, stereophonic sound (in Japan only) and color is basically a light-hearted satire with occasional thrills; even the battle of the titans is played for laughs. Godzilla escapes the iceberg tomb from *Gigantis the Fire Monster* while Kong is captured as a publicity stunt by a pharmaceutical company. The two clash in Tokyo (where else?) and atop Mt. Fuji. Not as good as the G-films which immediately followed, but also made with much enthusiasm and ingenuity by Toho's team of artisans. The U.S. version, produced by John Beck and directed by Thomas Montgomery, is substantially altered, with numerous and ludicrously dull scenes of Keith, Holcombe, and Yagi inserted to provide bland commentary. In so doing they cut much of the Japanese footage, hurting the film's pacing and tone while rendering scenes either too sketchy or too long. Much of Ifukube's score is replaced by stock themes from *Creature from the Black Lagoon* (1954) and other 50s U-I titles, some written by Henri Mancini but inappropriate here. And despite what you may have read elsewhere, Kong wins in both the American and Japanese version. Followed by *Godzilla vs. the Thing* (1964).

Kwaidan ★★★
(CONTINENTAL, 1965)
Kaidan "Ghost Story" ★★★½
(NINJIN CLUB/BUNGEI FOR
TOHO, 1964)

Director: Masaki Kobayashi **Screenplay:** Yoko Mizuki, based on stories by Lafcadio Hearn **Director of Photography:** Yoshio Miyajima **Art Director:** Shigemasa Toda **Music:** Toru Takemitsu **Producer:** Shigeru Wakatsuki **Cast:** Rentaro Mikuni, Michiyo Aratama, Keiko Kishi, Tatsuya Nakadai, Mariko Okada, Kazuo Nakamura, Takashi Shimura, Tetsuro Tamba, Ganaemon Nakamura, Noboru Nakaya, Jun Tazaki.

The best-known of Japanese ghost story movies was an expensive, elaborate film by standards of the time, and pretty different from the period *kaidan eiga* produced by Daiei, Toei and the other studios. It's a deliberately-

paced, satifying anthology, though beware of faded, panned-and-scanned video versions which hurt the film immeasurably. Criterion's laserdisc edition is highly recommended. Originally released in the U.S. minus "The Woman of the Snow" sequence; the since-restored version rates ★★★ ½.

Lake of Dracula ★½ (UPA, 1980)
Noroi no yakata: chi o suu me "Cursed House: Blood-sucking Eyes" ✹ (TOHO, 1971)
Director: Michio Yamamoto **Screenplay:** Ei Ogawa **Director of Photography:** Rokuro Nishigaki **Art Director:** Shigichi Ikuno **Music:** Riichiro Manabe **Producer:** Fumio Tanaka **Cast:** Midori Fujita, Choei Takahashi, Sanae Emi, Shin Kishida, Shuji Otaki, Wataru Omae.

Modern, Hammer-esque Dracula film made in Japan has its moments, but beyond the novelty, there are few thrills. In this, the second of director Yamamoto's vampire trilogy, a young woman (Takahashi) has childhood memories—or are they dreams?—of vampirism, which come back to haunt her through her paintings. Kishida makes an imposing—if 70s—Dracula, but the television and home video version is so badly dubbed and panned and scanned that it's pretty rough sledding for anyone not obsessed with the genre. Worse is UPA's inane decision to cut Dracula's gory demise (again, a la Hammer), even in the home video version! Followed by *Evil of Dracula* (1975).

The Last Days of Planet Earth see *Prophecies of Nostradamus*

The Last Dinosaur ★★★½ (ABC-TV, 1977)

Borer" ✸ (RANKIN-BASS/TSUBURAYA, 1977)
Directors: Tsugunobu "Tom" Kotani and Alex
Grasshoff **Screenplay:** William Overgard **Director of
Photography:** Shoji Ueda **Art Director:** Kazuhiko
Fujiwara **Music:** Maury Laws **Special Effects Director:**
Kazuo Sagawa **Producers:** Arthur Rankin, Jr., Jules
Bass, Noboru Tsuburaya **Cast:** Richard Boone, Joan
Van Ark, Steven Keats, Luther Rackley, Carl Hansen,
Masumi Sekiya, Tetsu Nakamura, William Ross.

Impressive B-movie, made in Japan and scheduled
for theatrical play but released directly to American
television at the last minute. A *Lost World* tale set
within the Arctic Circle, it's about a big game hunter
(well-played by craggy Richard Boone) looking for the
ultimate catch. The Tsuburaya-made man-in-suit
dinosaurs are adequete for the period, and are similar
to those seen in the Edgar Rice Burroughs film
adaptations made at the same time (*The Land That
Time Forgot,* etc.). The strong characters and solid, if
familiar storyline make this the best of the Japanese-
made giant monster movies from the 1970s.

The Last War ★★½ (BRENCO TELEVISION, 1964)
Sekai daisenso "Great World War" ★★★ (TOHO, 1961)
Director: Shue Matsubayashi **Special Effects Director:**
Eiji Tsuburaya **Screenplay:** Toshio Yasumi and Takeshi
Kimura **Director of Photography:** Rokuro Nishigaki
Special Effects Photography: Teisho Arikawa and
Mototaka Tomioka **Music:** Ikuma Dan Producers,
Sanezumi Fujimoto and Tomoyuki Tanaka **Cast:**
Frankie Sakai, Nobuko Otowa, Akira Takarada, Yuriko
Hoshi, Yumi Shirakawa, Chieko Nakakita, Chishu
Ryu, Eijiro Tono, So Yamamura, Seizaburo Kawazu,
Nobuo Nakamura, Minoru Takada, Harold S.
Conway, Jerry Ito, Saburo Iketani, Nadao Kirino,
Yutaka Sada, Wataru Omae, Kozo Nomura, Ed Keane,
Johnny Yuseph.

Grim end of the world drama, made in the wake of
American films like *On the Beach* and *The World, the
Flesh and the Devil* (both 1959), this Japanese take has
the courage to actually show us how the world ends
and pulls no punches. We witness one family's
agonizing helplessness—symbolic of Japan's fear as a
whole—as two unnamed superpowers (though clearly
intended to be the U.S. and the Soviet Union) square
off toward an inevitable holocaust. These scenes were
done with local amateur actors (such as Keane and Ito)
who are all relooped for the American version. The
film does make one concession to box office concerns,
a romantic subplot involving Takarada and Hoshi, but
this is worked well into the main narrative. The picture
was quite lavish for its day: the stars are of a higher
caliber than those usually found in *kaiju eiga*, and the
Japanese version even included an overture, suggesting
that the film premiered as a roadshow in Japan.
Tsuburaya's effects are similarly elaborate—there's a
great deal of futuristic military hardware, and the
explosive finale, in which the great capitols of the
world are blown to smithereens is spectacular. (So
spectacular, in fact, that Toho used this footage in films
as late as *The War in Space*, made more than 15 years
later!) The American version trims much footage and
rearranges the leftovers, while dubbing in—of all
things—the "It's a Small World" song from the
Disneyland ride (sung by a group of Japanese children)
as well as a speech by John F. Kennedy, heard after the
bombs have been dropped. Sakai, cast against type,
and the always fine Otowa are very good as the
parents, though everyone is, as usual, badly dubbed; an
English-subtitled edition would be nice someday.

Latitude Zero ★★½ (NATIONAL GENERAL, 1970)
Ido zero daisakusen "Latitude Zero: Great Military Battle" ✹ (TOHO/AMBASSADOR, 1969)
Director: Ishiro Honda **Special Effects Director:** Eiji Tsuburaya **Screenplay:** Ted Sherdemann and Shinichi Sekizawa **Director of Photography:** Taiichi Kankura **Special Effects Photography:** Teisho Arikawa **Art Director:** Takeo Kita **Music:** Akira Ifukube **Producers:** Tomoyuki Tanaka and Don Sharp **Cast:** Joseph Cotten, Cesar Romero, Akira Takarada, Richard Jaeckel, Masumi Okada, Patricia Medina, Linda Haynes, Akihiko Hirata, Hikaru Okada, Mari Nakayama, Tetsu Nakamura, Susumu Kurobe, Wataru Omae, Haruo Nakajima.

Eiji Tsuburaya's final sci-fi feature is this goofy, hopelessly tacky and rather wonderful underwater adventure epic filmed entirely in English. Yes, even the Japanese cast, from Takarada (a bit stiff here, but not bad) to Hirata (hopeless!), try their best and provide a rare glimpse at what these people actually sound like. Takarada, Jaeckel, and Okada stumble upon supersub commander Cotten's underwater nirvana at Latitude Zero. When the utopia is threatened by Romero and Medina, the trio joins Cotten to defeat the arch-fiends, whose arsenal includes a winged lion (Nakajima). Beset with budget problems and a seriously ill star, the filmmakers had to cut a lot of corners resulting in some pretty cheesy sets and costumes, but the finished product remains fun and involving. While often inadequate, the special effects—both on set and miniature—are plentiful, and Ifukube wrote a terrific score complete with eerie harpsichord. Due to rights problems the film is not available here or in Japan, and rarely turns up on television.

The "Legend of the Dinosaurs" ☙
(KING FEATURES, 1987)
Kyoryu—kaicho no densetsu "Legend of the Dinosaur and Monster Bird" ✹ (TOEI, 1977)
Director: Junji Kurata **Screenplay:** Masaru Igami **Director of Photography:** Sakuji Shiomi **Art Director:** Yoshimitsu Amamori **Music:** Masao Yagi **Special Effects Director:** Fuminori Obayashi **Cast:** Tsunehiko Watase, Nobuko Sawa, Shotaro Hayashi, Tomoko Kyoshima, Fuyukichi Maki, Hiroshi Nawa, Hiroshi Nawa, Kinji Nakamura.

One of the worst Japanese sci-fi films of all time, this crass travesty, about a *plesiosaur* and *pterodactyl* lurking in a Mt. Fuji-based lake, is unimaginative, derivative (from *Jaws* in particular), ineptly-made, boring in the extreme, and without redeeming values of any kind. Awful!

The Lost World of Sinbad ★★ (AIP, 1965)
Dai tozoku "The Great Thief" ★★½ (TOHO, 1963)
Director: Senkichi Taniguchi **Special Effects Director:** Eiji Tsuburaya **Screenplay:** Shinichi Sekizawa and Takeshi Kimura **Director of Photography:** Takao Saito **Music:** Masaru Sato **Producers,** Tomoyuki Tanaka and Kenichiro Tsunoda **Cast:** Toshiro Mifune, Kumi Mizuno, Akiko Wakabayashi, Mie Hama, Makoto Sato, Jun Funato, Ichiro Arishima, Jun Tazaki, Takashi Shimura, Tadao Nakamaru, Mitsuko Kusabue, Eisei Amamoto, Little Man Machan, Masaya Nihei, Tetsu Nakamura, Jerry Fujio, Yoshio Kosugi, Nadao Kirino.

A kind of Arabian Nights costume adventure, Japanese style, though in no way connected with the Sinbad stories. It certainly doesn't have Ray Harryhausen effects or even monsters of any sort. It's also pretty tepid, though the Japanese cast clearly had fun with the picture, as evidenced by the fine performances by Mizuno (as a tomboy thief), Arishima (a lusty wizard), Tazaki (he eats a live frog to illustrate his toughness) and Amamoto (as a witch). Mifune is, as almost always, electrifying, and Shimura is wasted in what amounts to a cameo role. Probably the picture's greatest asset is its terrific score by Sato; it's better than the film deserves.

The Magic Serpent
★★★ (AIP-TV, 1968)
Kai tatsu daikessen
"Decisive Battle of the Giant Magic Dragons"
★★★½ (TOEI, 1966)
Director: Tetsuya Yamauchi **Screenplay:** Masaru Igami, based on a story by Mokuami Kawatake **Director of Photography:** Mononari Washio **Art Director:** Seiji Yada **Music:** Toshiaki Tsushima **Producer:** Shigeru Okawa **Cast:** Hiroki Matsukata, Tomoko Ogawa, Ryutaro Otomo, Bin Amatsu, Nobuo Kaneko.

Delightful fantasy—somewhat obscure these days—with story elements remarkably similar to *Star Wars* (1977), and stylistically similar to the Hong Kong fantasies made 20 years later. In ancient Japan, a young man (Matsukata) is taught magic by an old wizard whose former student (Otomo) plots to take over a peaceful kingdom. Meanwhile, a young woman (Ogawa) is pursued by the former student-turned evil who's really her father. Sound familiar? Lively and imaginative, with a unique *kaiju* climax: an impressive, Reptilicus-like dragon battles a giant frog (men in suits, the dragon largely manipulated by wires a la Ghidrah) at a big, ancient castle. The clever battle of

the giants is actually more like the climatic duel between Vincent Price and Boris Karloff at the end of *The Raven* (1963) than a Godzilla movie. A giant eagle and jumbo spider also turn up. The delightful score is by Toshiaki Tsushima. A rare movie from Toei, it was released directly to American television by AIP-TV, who did such a sloppy job the "Produced by Shigeru Okada" card appears twice during the opening credits!

Majin ★★ (BERNARD LEWIS, 1968)
Dai Majin "Great Majin" ★★½ (DAIEI, 1966)
Director: Kimiyoshi Yasuda **Screenplay:** Tetsuro Yoshida **Director of Photography:** Fujio Morita **Art Director:** Hisashi Okuda **Music:** Akira Ifukube **Special Effects Director:** Yoshiyuki Kuroda **Producer:** Masaichi Nagata **Cast:** Miwa Takada, Yoshihiko Aoyama, Jun Fujimaki, Ryutaro Gomi, Tatsuo Endo, Riki Hoshimoto.

First of three films about a giant stone statue that comes to life—but not until in the final reel—to rescue pathetic peasants in this otherwise average *jidai-geki* with *kaiju eiga* influences. The special effects are impressive, however, and Ifukube wrote the ponderous but not inappropriate score. Hashimoto plays Majin. Released to television as *Majin, the Monster of Terror*, following a brief simultaneous theatrical release in both subtitled and dubbed formats. Followed by *The Return of the Giant Majin* (1966).

Majin Strikes Again
(UNRELEASED IN THE UNITED STATES)
Dai Majin gyakushu "The Great Majin's Counterattack" ★★½ (DAIEI, 1966)
Director: Issei Mori **Screenplay:** Tetsuo Yoshida **Directors of Photography:** Fujio Morita and Hiroshi

Imai **Art Director:** Hisashi Okuda **Special Effects Director:** Yoshiyuki Kuroda **Music:** Akira Ifukube **Producer:** Masaichi Nagata **Cast:** Hideki Ninoyama, Masahide Kizuka, Shinji Hori, Shiei Iizuka, Muneyuki Nagamoto, Riki Hashimoto.

Last of three Majin films is same old stuff. Clearly Daiei was hoping Majin would catch on as a kind of cross between Godzilla and their lucrative Zatoichi character. Anyway, this one features an earthquake and flood—impressively done, and seems more geared to the Gamera crowd as a trio of children figure prominently in this one. *Makalite* magazine reported in 1990 that Kevin Costner (!) had expressed interest in doing a new Majin film (to be financed by Hong Kong's Golden Harvest Ltd.), and at one time Ishiro Honda was reportedly approached to helm a remake.

The Manster ★★½ (UA, 1962)

Director: George P. Breakston and Kenneth G. Crane **Screenplay:** Walter J. Sheldon, based on a story by George P. Breakston **Director of Photography:** David Mason **Art Director:** Noboru Miyakuni **Music:** Hiroki Ogawa **Producers:** George P. Breakston, Robert Perkins, and Ryukichi Aimono **Cast:** Peter Dyneley, Jane Hylton, Tetsu Nakamura, Terri Zimmern, Norman Van Hawley, Jerry Ito, Toyoko Takechi, Alan Tarlton, Kenzo Kuroki, Shinpei Takagi, George Wyman.

An unusual film, even by Japanese *kaiju eiga* standards, this filmed-in-English production was financed by United Artists using funds tied up in Japan. Dyneley (later one of the voices on the "Thunderbirds" TV show and films) stars as a middle-aged correspondent stationed in Japan unwittingly used as a human guinea pig by a mad scientist

(Nakamura). Earlier tests had turned the scientist's brother and wife into monstrosities. An eye appears on Dyneley's shoulder and, if that weren't enough, it soon grows into a semi-formed head (resembling a hairy coconut, says *Psychotronic*). The thing with two heads commits various crimes before the creature (creatures?) split into two in the film's most daring sequence. Dyneley is more or less returned to his former state (albeit covered with drippy goo from the metamorphosis), but then must battle the pigmy-like ape-thing that grew inside him. Though dismissed by almost everybody, this is one wild picture, with admirable character development and interesting direction by Breakston and Crane.

Message from Space ★½ (UA, 1978)

Uchu no messeji "Message from Space" ☀ (TOEI, 1978) **Director:** Kinji Fukasaku **Screenplay:** Hiro Matsuda **Special Effects Director:** Nobuo Yajima **Director of Photography:** Toru Nakajima **Special Effects Photography:** Noboru Takasaki **Music:** Kenichiro Morioka **Producers:** Banjiro Uemura, Yoshinori Watanabe, and Tan Takaiwa **Cast:** Vic Morrow, Shinichi "Sonny" Chiba, Philip Casnoff, Peggy Lee Brennon, Sue Shiomi, Tetsuro Tamba, Mikio Narita, Makoto Sato, Hiroyuki "Henry" Sanada, Eisei Amamoto.

Lively but not good and overwhelming gaudy, this *Star Wars*-inspired space opera has a rotten script, generally poor special effects, and several annoying performances (Brennon in particular, though she and several other Western cast members appear to have been dubbed by others). It's basically *Seven Samurai* in space, and not unlike *Battle Beyond the Stars* (1980), that other *Seven Samurai*-influenced space opera.

MASTER SUSPENSE SHOW!

THE HORROR CHAMBER OF DR. FAUSTUS

THE MANSTER Half-Man— Half-Monster!

A killer-creature of science

"Worthy of the great horror classics of our time." —Express

A WILLIAM SHELTON PRESENTATION
DISTRIBUTED BY LOPERT PICTURES CORPORATION

Morioka's score comes precariously close to inviting a lawsuit from composer John Williams. Later a teleseries, from which the ersatz feature *Swords of the Space Ark* (1979) is derived.

Mighty Jack ★★ (KING FEATURES, 1988)
Maitei Jyaku ✹ (TSUBURAYA PRODUCTIONS, 1968) [TV]
Director: Kazuho "Pete" Mitsuda **Teleplay:** Shinichi Sekizawa **Director of Photography:** Yoshihiro Mori **Music:** Isao Tomita **Special Effects Director:** Kazuo Sagawa **Producer and Special Effects Supervisor:** Eiji Tsuburaya **Cast:** Hideaki Nitani, Naoko Kubo, Hiroshi Minami, Eisei Amamoto, Jerry Ito, Masanari Nihei, Wakako Ikeda, Akira Kasuga, Seiko Fukioka, Noriaki Inoue, Yoshitaka Tanaka, Mitsubu Oya, Eijiro Yanagi.

Tsuburaya-produced TV show in the "Mission Impossible" vein, edited into yet another mock-feature. More adult than most Tsuburaya shows; indeed, this was followed by a sequel TV program far more juvenile than its predecessor. There's plenty of action, lots of special effects (though scaled back for a TV budget), and engaging performances (badly dubbed, alas). However, like all features derived from Japanese TV shows, it doesn't really work, and would be better served subtitled and marketed for home video release.

Monster from a Prehistoric Planet ★½
(AIP-TV, 1968)
Dai kyoju Gappa "Great Giant Monster Gappa" ★★
(NIKKATSU, 1967)
Director: Haruyasu Noguchi **Screenplay:** Gan Yamazaki and Ryuzo Nakanishi **Director of Photography:** Muneo Ueda **Art Director:** Kazumi Koike **Special Effects Director:** Akira Watanabe **Music:** Seitaro Omori **Producer:** Hideo Koi **Cast:**

Tamio Kawaji, Yoko Yamamoto, Kokan Katsura, Keisuke Yukioka, Saburo Hiromatsu, Shiro Oshimi, Yuji Kotaka, Tatsuya Fuji, Koji Wada, Yuji Odaka, Mike Daning.

Gorgo, Japanese style. Mama and Papa monster comes to the aid of Baby monster kidnapped and indentured as star attraction for a greedy developer's new resort. Nikkatsu's sole *kaiju eiga*, released in some countries as *Gappa: The Triphibian Monster,* has a fascinating history but is pretty ordinary beyond the novelty of its monster family premise. These scenes, however, have a certain poignancy, particularly the teary-eyed finale. Some have praised its more satirical elements, which aren't apparent in currently available, dubbed versions. Another problem is the hazy color photography; the standard South Seas island sequences are particularly murky. *Gappa vs. Girara* has been announced by Shochiku.

Monster Zero ★★★ (MARON, 1970)
Kaiju daisenso "Great Monster War" ★★★½
(TOHO, 1965)
Director: Ishiro Honda **Special Effects Director:** Eiji Tsuburaya **Screenplay:** Shinichi Sekizawa **Director of Photoraphy,** Hajime Koizumi **Special Effects Photography:** Teisho Arikawa and Mototaka Tomioka **Art Director:** Takeo Kita **Music:** Akira Ifukube **Producers:** Tomoyuki Tanaka and Henry G. Saperstein **Cast:** Akira Takarada, Nick Adams, Kumi Mizuno, Jun Tazaki, Akira Kubo, Keiko Sawai, Yoshio Tsuchiya, Yoshifumi Tajima, Noriko Sengoku, Toru Ibuki, Kazuo Suzuki, Nadao Kirino, Saburo Iketani, Somesho Matsumoto, Kenzo Tabu, Haruo Nakajima, Shoichi "Solomon" Hirose.

Immensely entertaining Godzilla film—the sixth—

which merges elements from *Ghidrah—The Three-Headed Monster* (1964) and space operas like *Battle in Outer Space* (1959) and *The Mysterians* (1957), resulting in a visual and aural orgy. Aliens from Planet X "borrow" Godzilla and Rodan to fight the evil *Monster Zero*, who turns out to be none other than King Ghidorah (from *Ghidrah—The Three-Headed Monster*). The script is, admittedly, a mess; why, for example, do the X-ites even bother to ask for Earth's help in the first place, when they might have launched their conquest from the very beginning? Still, the film works exceedingly well in virtually every other department, from Eiji Tsuburaya's gorgeous space settings to Takeo Kita's outstanding X-ite sets. Of special note are the performances, both human and monster. Though some fans cringe at the sight of Godzilla's little jig on Planet X (known as the *Gojira Shei* in Japan), Tsuburaya and Nakajima's humanizing of Godzilla is both logical and inevitable at this point in the series—and, indeed, Godzilla's downright lovable here. More importantly, there is real chemistry among the

human cast, particularly between Adams and Takarada, and Adams and Mizuno. Tsuchiya's wonderfully eccentric alien is lost, alas in the badly-dubbed prints (with the voices especially cartoony for this outing); its worth a peak at the Japanese version for Tsuchiya's chirping, clucking, cackling alien alone. Tazaki lends considerable support as the Mission Commander, and Kubo is quite good in rare comic relief as the nerdy inventor. Retitled *Godzilla vs. Monster Zero* for television and home video release. Also known under its international title, *Invasion of Astro-Monster.* Followed by *Godzilla versus the Sea Monster* (1966).

Mothra ★★★ (COLUMBIA, 1962)
Mosura "Mothra" ★★★½ (TOHO, 1961)
Director: Ishiro Honda **Special Effects Director:** Eiji Tsuburaya **Screenplay:** Shinichi Sekizawa, based on a story by Shinichiro Nakamura **Director of Photography:** Hajime Koizumi **Special Effects Photography:** Teisho Arikawa **Art Director:** Takeo Kita **Music:** Yuji Koseki **Producer:** Tomoyuki Tanaka **Cast:** Frankie Sakai, Hiroshi Koizumi, Kyoko Kagawa, The Peanuts (Emi and Yumi Ito), Ken Uehara, Jerry Ito, Takashi Shimura, Akihiko Hirata, Seizaburo Kawazu, Yoshio Kosugi, Yoshifumi Tajima, Tetsu Nakamura, Ren Yamamoto, Haruya Kato, Osman Yuseph, Harold S. Conway, Robert Dunham, Ed Keane, Haruo Nakajima.

One of Toho's best films, *Mothra* breaks away from American monster movie cliches by abandoning the semi-documentary style used in 50s (and by Toho themselves from *Godzilla* through *Varan*) in favor of color-filled, dream-like imagery. This was also the first of Toho's monster movies to incorporate elements of satire, here directed at ugly American commercialism (albeit disguised here as "Rolisican" commercialism) in the form of Jerry Ito's snarling entrepreneur. Added to the mix are tiny twin fairies (played with great charm by the Peanuts), an appealing, light comedy star (Sakai) and you've got a preposterous, beguiling fantasy. Tsuburaya's effects are superb, in part because the caterpillar scenes were built on a much larger scale than in subsequent films. Nakajima and a bunch of college students play the larvae Mothra; in subsequent films, the larvae miniature would be but a few feet long and motorized or hand manipulated. Mothra's attack on "Newkirk City" is equally impressive, with cars strewn about the streets like flies around shit. A stereophonic laserdisc has been released in Japan. Mothra would return in *Godzilla vs. the Thing* (1964).

The Mysterians ★★1/2 (MGM, 1959)

Chikyu boeigun "Earth Defense Force" ★★1/2 (TOHO, 1957)

Director: Ishiro Honda **Special Effects Director:** Eiji Tsuburaya **Screenplay:** Takeshi Kimura, based on a treatment by Shigeru Kayama and story by Jojiro Okami **Director of Photography:** Hajime Koizumi **Special Effects Photography:** Teisho Arikawa **Art Director:** Teruaki Abe **Music:** Akira Ifukube **Producer:** Tomoyuki Tanaka **Cast:** Yumi Shirakawa, Kenji Sahara, Akihiko Hirata, Momoko Kochi, Takashi Shimura, Susumu Fujita, Hisaya Ito, Yoshio Tsuchiya, Fuyuki Murakami, Minnosuke Yamada, Harold S. Conway, George Furness, Tetsu Nakamura, Haruya Kato, Senkichi Omura, Yutaka Sada, Heiachiro "Henry" Okawa, Tadao Nakamaru, Haruo Nakajima.

The first of Toho's "Space Opera Trilogy" finds

aliens demanding Earth women and plotting to conquer the world (natch). Though clichéd in the extreme, it's also singularly Japanese in its wild, colorful, and kinetic design. There are Defense Force Super Weapons, cape-wearing aliens, ray-emitting flying saucers aplenty, and a giant, mole-like robot, Mogera (Nakajima), one of Toho's most inspired creations. Unfortunately, the film goes overboard toward the end and the final battle sequence, though an orgy of special effects and scored with tremendous energy by Ifukube, goes on forever. It also undermines the human story, in which a scientist (Hirata) naïvely joins forces with the aliens. The U.S. version, acquired by RKO shortly before shutting down its distribution arm, was released by Metro instead—Mogera's brief reappearance during the final battle was deleted, but most of the picture remained intact. The trilogy matured with the much-underappreciated *Battle in Outer Space* (1959) and peaked with *Gorath* (1962). Mogera would return—with much of its personality lost—in *Godzilla vs. Space Godzilla* (1994).

One Hundred Monsters ★★1/2

(DAIEI INTERNATIONAL FILMS, 1968)

Yokai hyaku monogatari "Story of 100 Monsters" ★★1/2 (DAIEI, 1968)

Director: Kimiyoshi Yasuda **Screenplay:** Tetsuro Yoshida **Director:** Yasukazu Takemura **Art Directors:** Yoshinobu Nishioka and Shigeru Kato

Music: Chumei Watanabe **Producer:** Yatsuhiro Yamamto **Cast:** Jun Fujimaki, Miwa Takada, Mikiko Tsubouchi, Takashi Kanda, Ryutaro Gomi, Yoshio Yoshida, Masaru Hiraizumi, Jun Hamamura, Saburo Date.

Period ghost story from Daiei about the unleashing of 100 spirits. Not seen in the United States in many years (and even then only in Japanese-American theaters) it is nonetheless spellbinding with its wide assortment of creepy apparitions, most quite unlike anything seen in the West. Standing out among them is a long-necked demon woman who wraps her neck around terrified peasants, and a Muppet-like, one-eyed umbrella critter with a long tongue. Many of the same monsters returned in another Daiei feature, *Journey Along Tokkaido Road* (1969).

Onibaba ★★★½ (TOHO INTERNATIONAL, 1965)
Oni baba "Witch" ★★★½ (KINDAI EIGA KYOKAI/TOKYO EIGA/TOHO, 1964)
Director-Screenplay: Kaneto Shindo **Director of Photography:** Kiyomi Kuroda **Art Directors:**

Kaneto Shindo and Hiroshi Matsumoto **Music:** Hikaru Hayashi **Producers:** Hisao Itoya, Setsuo Noto, and Tamotsu Minato **Cast:** Nobuko Otowa, Jitusko Yoshimura, Kei Sato, Jukichi Uno, Taiji Tonomura, Tatsuya Nakadai.

Engrossing tale of survival in Feudal Japan as a possesive, bitter old woman (Otowa) tries to terrify her daughter-in-law (Yoshimura) into submission when she becomes attracted to a mysterious wanderer (Sato). Superbly directed by Shindo (Otowa's husband), it is essentially a three-person drama (well, three people and a ghost, the latter played by Nakadai), and is a nice change from the cast-of-thousands monster epics. Love that tall grass!

Portrait of Hell ★★★
(TOHO INTERNATIONAL, 1969)
Jigokuhen "Portrait of Hell" ★★★ (TOHO, 1969)
Director: Shiro Toyoda **Screenplay:** Toshio Yasumi, based on the serial by Ryunosuke Akutagawa **Director of Photography:** Kazuo Yamada **Art Director:** Shinobu Muraki **Music:** Yasushi Akutagawa **Producers:** Tomoyuki Tanaka and Tatsuo Matsuoko **Cast:** Tatsuya Nakadai, Kinnosuke Nakamura, Yoko Naito, Jun Oide, Kichiro Nakamura, Masanobu Okubo, Eisei Amamoto, Masao Yamafuki, Ikio Sawamura, Kumeko Otoba.

Screen painter Nakadai clashes with powerful Nakamura is this pretty good *jidai-geki* with fantasy elements. This was acclaimed director Toyoda's last feature. Studio-bound and theatrical, but also colorful and interesting.

Prince of Space ★ 1/2

(WALTER H. MANLEY ENTERPRISES, 1964)
Yusei oji "Planet Prince" ✹ (TOEI, 1959)
Director: Eijiro Wakabayashi **Screenplay:** Shin
Morita, based on a story by Masaru Ito and Sanehiko
Sonoda **Director of Photography:** Masahiko Iimura
Art Director: Shuichiro Nakamura **Special Effects:**
Shozo Muroki **Music:** Katsuhisa Hattori **Cast:**
Tatsuya Umemiya, Joji Oda, Hiroko Mine, Takashi
Kanda, Nobu Yatsuna, Ken Sudo.

Toei's rival to the popular "Starman/Supergiant"
films is just as childish and cartoony, especially the
outrageously-dubbed Ambassador Phantom of the
Planet Krankor, who threatens Earth until the POS
(Umemiya) saves the day. Star Umemiya—who also
plays the POS's alter-ego, a boot-black named, in the
U.S. version, Wally!—lacks the charisma of Starman
Ken Utsui and the film is more tiresome than amusing.

Prophecies of Nostradamus ★ 1/2

(TOHO INTERNATIONAL, 1979)
Nostradamus no dai yogen Catastrophe 1999
"Great Prophecies of Nostradamus—Catastrophe
1999" ✹ (TOHO, 1974)
Director: Toshio Masuda **Special Effects Director:**
Teruyoshi Nakano **Screenplay:** Toshio Masuda and
Yoshimitsu Banno, based on a story by Tsutomu Goto
Director of Photography: Rokuro Nishigaki **Special
Effects Photography:** Mototaka Tomioka
Music: Isao Tomita **Producers:** Tomoyuki Tanaka and
Osamu (Fumio?) Tanaka **Cast:** Tetsuro Tamba, Toshio
Kurosawa, So Yamamura, Kaoru Yumi, Yoko Tsukasa,
Takashi Shimura, Akihiko Hirata, Hiroshi Koizumi,
Johnny Yuseph.

Generally weak though admirably peculiar end of
the world tale made in the wake of *Submersion of
Japan* (1973). Pollution, civil unrest, nuclear war, et.
al. all figure into this everything-but-the-kitchen-sink
disaster mishmash, supposedly based on the writings of
Nostradamus, but more akin to *Man Without a Body*
(1959). Relying heavily on stock footage (and story
ideas) from *The Last War* (1961) and *Submersion...*, the
picture is alternately odd, ludicrous, interesting and
dull. However, the post-apocalyptic coda, featuring a
pair of Elephant Man-like mutants is rather incredible.
So incredible, in fact, that a Hiroshima survivors group
has rallied against the film because of this sequence.
Also known as *Catastrophe: 1999* and released to home
video as *The Last Days of Planet Earth.*

The Return of the Giant Majin ★★

(AIP-TV, 1968)
Dai Majin ikaru "The Giant Majin Grows Angry"
★★ 1/2 (DAIEI, 1966)

*The most daring film import
ever...from Japan!*

AMERICAN
PREMIERE
TODAY

Onibaba

NOBUKO OTOWA · JITSUKO YOSHIMURA
Kei Sato · Jukichi Uno · Taiji Tonomura
A Toho release

*Extra—In Brilliant Color
"The CERAMIC ART of JAPAN"*

TOHO *cinema* 45 St. W. of B'way—LT 1-1788

Director: Kenji Misumi **Screenplay:** Tetsuro Yoshida **Director of Photography:** Fujio Morita **Art Director:** Hisashi Okuda **Special Effects Director:** Yoshiyuki Kuroda **Music:** Akira Ifukube **Producer:** Masaichi Nagata **Cast:** Kojiro Hongo, Shiho Fujimura, Taro Murui, Takashi Kanda, Tara Fujimura, Jutaro Hojo, Koji Fujiyama, Riki Hashimoto.

The second Majin film (this time starring Gamera regular Hongo) is more of the same, though this time the evil marauders show some ingenuity in trying to dispatch the great stone statue. Impressive effects work, especially Majin's parting of a lake whose effects bests *The Ten Commandments* (1956), but again Majin (Hashimoto) does little more than glower menacingly in statue form until the final reel. Followed by *Majin Strikes Again* (1966). AIP-TV's version has vanished from view, and was little-seen when it was new.

The Return of the Giant Monsters ★★
(AIP-TV, 1967)
Daikaiju kuchesen Gamera tai Gaosu "Giant Monster Air Battle: Gamera vs. Gyaos" ★★½ (DAIEI, 1967)
Director: Noriaki Yuasa **Screenplay:** Nisan Takahashi **Director of Photography:** Akira Uehara **Special Effects Directors:** Kazufumi Fujii and Yuzo Kaneko **Music:** Tadashi Yamauchi **Producer:** Hidemasa Nagata **Cast:** Kojiro Hongo, Naoyuki Abe, Kichijiro Ueda, Reiko Kasahara, Taro Marui, Yukitaro Hotaru, Yoshiro Kitahara, Shin Minatsu.

Considered by Gamera connoisseurs to be the best of the "classic" Gamera films, this second sequel once again features a little boy who figures prominently in the narrative, though it would be one more film before the mix of children and monsters was mastered by Yuasa and Takahashi. This time the big turtle battles a

Rodan-like bat creature, Gaos. The Sandy Frank redo, *Gamera vs. Gaos* (★), is horribly dubbed and notably worse than AIP's version. Followed by *Destroy All Planets* (1968) and more or less remade as *Gamera— The Guardian of the Universe* (1995).

Rodan ★★½ (DCA, 1957)
Sora no daikaiju Radon "Rodan, Giant Monster of the Sky" ★★★ (TOHO, 1956)
Director: Ishiro Honda **Special Effects Director:** Eiji Tsuburaya **Screenplay:** Takeshi Kimura and Takeo Murata, based on a story by Takashi Kuronuma **Director of Photography:** Isamu Ashida **Art Director:** Takeo Kita **Music:** Akira Ifukube **Producer:** Tomoyuki Tanaka **Cast:** Kenji Sahara, Yumi Shirakawa, Akihiko Hirata, Yasuko Nakata, Akio Koboi, Minnosuke Yamada, Yoshifumi Tajima, Fuyuki Murakami, Mike Daning, Haruo Nakajima.

Though highly regarded by some, Japan's first color monster movie is a disappointment. Coal miners are threatened first by 10-foot caterpillar monsters (called Meganuron in Japan), but these turn out to be mere morsels for the gigantic *pterodactyl* Rodan (Nakajima). Actually, there are two such creatures, and their relationship with one another provides one of the few twists in this otherwise standard *kaiju eiga*. Early scenes are heavily influenced by Warner Bros.' big ant film *Them!* (1954), while Rodan's attack on Fukuoka—though very impressive—is merely an excuse to redo ideas introduced in the first *Godzilla,* this time in color (and, mind you, only 32 of the 514 features made in Japan that year were in color). However, the final scene, in which one Rodan essentially commits suicide to join its dying mate, is intriguing and even moving. Sahara and Shirakawa carry the human story. Rodan would return in *Ghidrah—The Three-Headed Monster* (1964).

Sayonara Jupiter

(UNRELEASED IN THE UNITED STATES)
Sayonara Jyupeta "Goodbye, Jupiter" ★★
(TOHO/KABUSHIKI-KAISHA IO, 1984)
Director: Koji Hashimoto **Special Effects Director:** Koichi Kawakita **Screenplay:** Sakyo Komatsu, based on his novel **Director of Photography:** Kazutani Hara **Special Effects Photography:** Kenichi Eguchi **Art Director:** Heio Takanaka **Music:** Kentaro Haneda **Producers:** Tomoyuki Tanaka, Sakyo Komatsu, Fumio Tanaka, and Shiro Fujiwara **Cast:** Tomokazu Miura, Rachel Hugget, Diane Dangley, Miyuki Ono, Akihiko Hirata, Hisaya Morishige, Masumi Okada, Paul Taiga, Kim Bass, Marc Pinonnat, Ron Irwin, William H. Tapier.

Expensive but dull space story, despite impressive effects work, and still unreleased in the United States,

is notable mainly in that it marks the last screen appearance of character actor Hirata who died a few months after this was released.

The Secret of the Telegian ★★

(HERTS-LION, 1961)
Denso ningen "The Teleported Man" ★★
(TOHO, 1960)
Director: Jun Fukuda **Special Effects Director:** Eiji Tsuburaya **Screenplay:** Shinichi Sekizawa **Director of Photography:** Kazuo Yamada **Art Directors:** Kyoe Hamagami and Takeo Kita **Music:** Shigeru Ikeno **Producer:** Tomoyuki Tanaka **Cast:** Koji Tsuruta, Yumi Shirakawa, Tadao Nakamaru, Yoshio Tsuchiya, Akihiko Hirata, Seizaburo Kawazu, Yoshifumi Tajima, Senkichi Omura, Eisei Amamoto, Sachio Sakai, Ikio Sawamura, Fuyuki Murakami, Ren Yamamoto, Nadao Kirino, Tatsuo Matsumura.

Director Fukuda's first fantasy film is a minor crime thriller with sci-fi elements. Like *The H-Man* (1958) and *The Human Vapor* (made right after this) it involves a man whose matter is in a state of flux. In this case a bitter war veteran (Nakamaru) can turn himself into what looks like a human television signal. The back story involves stolen gold and is nothing special, and Nakamaru makes a rather bland villain. Although made in color, most of the increasingly rare TV prints are in black and white.

Solar Crisis ★★1/2 (TRIMARK, 1993)

Kuraishisu nijugoju nen "Crisis 2050" ✸
(JAPAN AMERICA, 1990)
Director: Alan Smithee (Richard C. Sarafian) **Screenplay:** Joe Gannon, Crispan Bolt, and Ted Sarafian, based on the novel by Takeshi Kawata

Director of Photography: Russ Carpenter **Art Directors:** George Jenson and John Bruce **Music:** Maurice Jarre **Special Effects Director:** Richard Edlund **Producers:** Takehito Sadamura, Takeshi Kawata, Richard Edlund, Tsuneyoshi Morishima, and James Nelson **Cast:** Tim Matheson, Charlton Heston, Annabel Schofield, Peter Boyle, Jack Palance, Tetsuya Bessho, Corin "Corky" Nemec, Paul Koslo, Scott Alan Campbell, Dorian Harewood, Brenda Bakke, Paul Williams, Michael Berryman, H.M. Wynant.

Big-budget, Japanese-financed story of attempt to avert solar flare-up which threatens earth. A fun picture barely released, despite the familiar (if not stellar) cast and impressive optical effects. The Japanese version is considered far inferior to the U.S. version, sadly released directly to home video and cable here.

Son of Godzilla ★★★ (WALTER READE, 1968)
Kaiju shima no kessen: Gojira no musuko "Monster Island's Decisive Battle: Son of Godzilla" ★★★½ (TOHO, 1967)
Director: Jun Fukuda **Special Effects Supervisor:** Eiji Tsuburaya **Special Effects Director:** Teisho Arikawa **Director of Photography:** Kazuo Yamada **Special Effects Photography:** Teisho Arikawa and Mototaka Tomioka **Art Director:** Takeo Kita **Music:** Masaru Sato **Producer:** Tomoyuki Tanaka **Cast:** Tadao Takashima, Bibari Maeda, Akira Kubo, Kenji Sahara, Akihiko Hirata, Yoshio Tsuchiya, Haruo Nakajima, Little Man Machan.

Break out the cigars, Godzilla's a daddy! The second G-film from the Fukuda/Sato/Arikawa team, and like *Godzilla versus the Sea Monster, Son of ...* eschews big city pummeling in favor of a more exotic South Seas setting (this was filmed on location in Guam). The

engaging story has reporter Kubo parachuting onto a island in the Pacific where top secret weather tests are taking place. An experiment goes awry, resulting in supersize mantises (called Kamakiras in Japan) which threaten the operation. The grasshoppers also unearth an egg from which hatches a rather homely runt Godzilla, called Minira in Japan; in the U.S. he's known as Minya though never called such in the picture. Godzilla comes to the little big critter's rescue. A giant spider, Spiga (pronounced "Spee-ga," though called Kumonga in Japan) also threatens various human and non-human characters. Though a far cry from Godzilla's persona of *Godzilla, King of the Monsters!* (1954) and even *Godzilla vs. the Thing* (1964), his relationship with Minira is sweetly and amusingly done. Certainly the film's final scene, in which Godzilla and son embrace as they drift off into hibernation, is a touching, magical moment, and completely original (Sato's music here is lovely). Jun Fukuda's direction keeps everything moving at a quick pace, and Kita's art direction is, as almost always, tops as well—even the filmed-in-the-studio sets appear insufferably hot. And what of Minira? He (it?) is first seen in the form of an inadequate puppet before growing into a midget-in-a-suit, played with great energy by Little Man Machan, a novelty wrestler. Though clumsy, somewhat dense and rather ugly, Minira is also almost irresistibly cute. Though there has been much discussion among fans regarding the implications and questions that arise from appearance of this creature (Is Godzilla male or female? If the former, where's Mrs. G? Does anyone really care?) the author has always assumed that Minya is simply a long-forgotten egg from the same species (or a similar one) that Godzilla essentially adopts. Arikawa's special

effects direction (his first such credit) are also very imaginative, though the gawky, frog-faced Godzilla costume is notably poor. Followed by *Destroy All Monsters* (1968).

Space Warriors 2000

(SPECTACULAR ENTERTAINMENT, 1985)
Uratora 6-Kyodai tai kaiju gundan "The Six Ultra-Brothers vs. the Monster Army"
(TSUBURAYA/FUJI EIGA, 1974)
Director: Sompote Sands **Producer:** Noboru Tsuburaya **Cast:** (undetermined)

Horrible, unwatchable piece of junk compiled from blurry and severely distorted episodes from several different "Ultra" shows produced by Tsuburaya Productions and a Tsuburaya-Thai co-production about the monkey god Hanuman. There's no story, and the producers of the American version have adopted a snide, condescending attitude to the whole affair. And the dubbing—as distorted as the picture is—may be the worst ever. Ghastly!

Star Force: Fugitive Alien II ★

(KING FEATURES, 1986)
Sutaurufu "Star Wolf"
(TSUBURAYA PRODUCTIONS, 1978) [TV]
Director: Kiyosumi Kukazawa and Minoru Kanaya **Teleplay:** Keiichi Abe, Bunko Wakatsuki, Yoshihisa Araki, Hiroyasu Tamamura, Hideyoshi Nagasaka, and Toyohiro Ando **Music:** Norio Maeda **Producers:** Noboru Tsuburaya, Jushichi Sano, and Akira Tsuburaya **Cast:** Tatsuma Azuma, Miyuki Tanigawa, Jo Shishido, Choei Takahashi, Tsutomu Yukawa, Hiro Tateyama.

Sequel to *Fugitive Alien* (1978), is more of the same, with even less characterization and logical

plotting than the ersatz feature that preceded it. Star Wolf Ken (Azuma) and Captain Joe (ex-Nikkatsu star Shishido) try to destroy a top secret, planet-destroying weapon on the planet Sissar in this one. Threadbare and mindless.

Super Monster ★

(SHOCHIKU FILMS OF AMERICA, 1980)
Uchu kaiju Gamera "Space Monster Gamera" ★★
(DAIEI, 1980)
Director: Noriaki Yuasa **Producers:** Masaya Tokuyama, Hirokazu Oba, and Shigeru Shinohara **Screenplay:** Nisan Takahashi **Director of Photography:** Akira Kitazaki **Art Directors:** Tomohisa Yano and Akira Inoue **Music:** Shunsuke Kikuchi **Cast:** Mach Fumiake, Yaeko Kojima, Yoko Komatsu, Keiko Kudo, Koichi Maeda, Toshie Takada.

Crass effort by the reorganized Daiei (now under the corporate thumb of Tokuma Publishing) to cash in on the series with a "new" Gamera film—the first in nine years—though composed almost entirely of footage from the earlier films. The new scenes revolve around a young boy's fascination with the big turtle and his appealing friendship with the Wonder Woman-like Fumiake, who, in turn is threatened by alien Kudo and her menagerie of old monsters (and old footage). The last Gamera movie directed by Yuasa and written by Takahashi is depressingly cheap and sometimes painful affair but, as bad as it is, *Super Monster* (aka *Gamera Super Monster*) does contain a certain childlike spirit that defined the best Yuasa-Takahashi films, and overall is a tad better than *Gamera vs. Zigra*. Followed fifteen years later by *Gamera—The Guardian of the Universe* (1995).

Terror Beneath the Sea ★ 1/2

(TELEWORLD, 1971)

Kaitei dai senso "Battle Beneath the Sea" ✸
(TOEI/K. FUJITA/RAM FILMS, 1966)

Director: Hajime Sato **Screenplay:** Koichi Otsu, based on an original story by Masami Fukushima **Director of Photgraphy:** Kazuo Shimomura **Art Director:** Shinichi Eno **Music:** Shunsuke Kikuchi **Special Effects Director:** Nobuo Yajima **Producers:** Masafumi Soga, Ivan Reiner, Walter Manley, Koji Kameda, Seiichi Yoshino and William Ross **Cast:** Shinichi "Sonny" Chiba, Peggy Neal, Andrew Hughes, Eric Nielsen, Mike Daning, Franz Gruber, Hans Hornef.

Cheap production conceived for syndication in the United States stars a pre-Streetfighter Shinichi "Sonny" Chiba and a cast of Western amateur actors living in Tokyo. Baddie Nielsen is turning human beings into Creature from the Black Lagoon-like slaves at his underwater hideout. Very minor and cheap, worth a look only for the sequence where our heroes are turned into monstrosities. The American version has been redubbed, despite the mostly-English-speaking cast, and the opening titles for the U.S. version are perhaps the most ineptly done in the history of motion pictures. Heroine Neal also faced Nielsen in the Crazy Cats comedy *Las Vegas Free-for-All* (1967).

Terror of Godzilla, The see *Terror of Mechagodzilla*

Terror of Mechagodzilla ★ 1/2

(BOB CONN, 1978)

Mekagojira no gyakushu "Mechagodzilla's Counterattack" ★★ 1/2 (TOHO, 1975)

Director: Ishiro Honda **Special Effects Director:** Teruyoshi Nakano **Screenplay:** Yukiko Takayama

THE MIGHTY TITAN OF TERROR in his MOST INCREDIBLE ADVENTURE!

ALL NEW! NEVER BEFORE SEEN!

KING of the MONSTERS

The Terror of GODZILLA

a TOHO PRODUCTION in association with TOHO EIZO COMPANY LTD.
Distributed by BOB CONN ENTERPRISES   In COLOR and WIDESCREEN   G

Director of Photography and Effects Photography, Mototaka Tomioka **Art Director:** Yoshifumi Honda **Music:** Akira Ifukube **Producer:** Tomoyuki Tanaka **Cast:** Katsuhiko Sasaki, Tomoko Ai, Akihiko Hirata, Katsumasa Uchida, Goro Mutsumi, Kenji Sahara, Tomoe Mari, Shin Roppongi, Tadao Takamaru, Kotaro Tomita, Masaaki Daimon, Ikio Sawamura, Kazuo Suzuki, Toru Kawane, Kazunari Mori, Tatsumi Fuyamoto.

Ishiro Honda's last film (and the 15th Godzilla feature) is the best of the 70s Godzilla films. Takayama's script and Honda's direction is darker and more pessimistic than any of the Godzilla sequels that proceeded it. Of course by now the series had become so ritualized that Honda and Takayama's ambitions had to work around the usual monster fist a' cuffs and cartoonish alien villains, but in some respects *Terror of Mechagodzilla*, while generally mediocre, mirrors Honda's original Godzilla. Significantly, both center around a tormented scientist played in both films by Hirata, and both have downbeat endings. Godzilla's robotic foe has been reconstructed by aliens with the help of a discredited scientist (Hirata) and his mysterious daughter (Ai). The aliens dispatch Mechagodzilla 2 (Mori) and a new monster, Titanosaurus (Fuyamoto), to conquer the world just as father and daughter begin to have second thoughts about what they've unleashed. The special effects are extremely limited and modest but unlike *Godzilla on Monster Island* (1972) and *Godzilla vs. Megalon* (1973), *Terror of Mechagodzilla* doesn't rely on the shameless use of stock footage from previous works, either. The Godzilla suit is pretty bad (though not as awful as the last few films, and inhabited this time by Kawane), the Mechagodzilla costume is worn and shabby, and the seahorse-like Titanosaurus is unmemorable. The dubbing, as usual, is terrible. A 35mm English-subtitled print has turned up in recent years, and it's amazing how much better the darker elements of the story play in this format. Strangely, the cheap sets and limited effects work actually look better on a big theater screen than on home video, though one would think the opposite would be true. Several notably different home video and television versions exist, and the film may have also been released theatrically under at least one alternate title: *The Terror of Godzilla* (ad art was prepared, as had been done with *Godzilla vs. the Bionic Monster*). The most recent home video version is singularly inept, an edited-for-content version that apparently played the kiddie matinee circuit back in late-1970s; other scenes are schitzophrantically edited about for no apparent reason. This editing wreaks havoc with Akira Ifukube's ominous score, and ironically, previous home video and television versions featured most of the cut footage. Followed by *Godzilla 1985* (1984).

Tetsuo: The Iron Man ★★

(ORIGINAL CINEMA, 1991)

Tetsuo "Tetsuo" ★★ (KAIJU THEATRE, 1988)

Producer-Director-Screenwriter-Art Director: Shinya Tsukamoto **Directors of Photography:** Shinya Tsukamoto and Kei Fujiwara **Music:** Chu Ishikawa **Cast:** Tomoro Taguchi, Kei Fujiwara, Nabu Kanaoko, Shinya Tsukamoto, Naomasa Musaka, Renji Ishibashi.

Low budget, filmed in 16mm featurette from jack-of-all-trades Tsukamoto (see above). Various metal fetishists have sex, turn into monstrosities and fight one another. Vastly overrated, more an inspired student film from a talented beginner than the daringly original cult film it has often been mistaken for. Followed by a 35mm in-name-only sequel, *Tetsuo II: Body Hammer*. The name Tetsuo means, literally, "iron man."

The Three Treasures ★★★

(TOHO INTERNATIONAL, 1960)

Nippon tanjo "Birth of Japan" ★★★ (TOHO, 1959)

Director: Hiroshi Inagaki **Special Effects Director:** Eiji Tsuburaya **Screenplay:** Toshio Yasumi and Ryuzu Kikushima, based on the legends and the origin of the Shinto **Director of Photography:** Kazuo Yamada **Special Effects Photography:** Teisho Arikawa **Art Music:** Akira Ifukube **Cast:** Toshiro Mifune, Yoko Tsukasa, Kyoko Kagawa, Koji Tsuruta, Takashi Shimura, Misa Uehara, Kinuyo Tanaka, Nobuko Otowa, Akira Kubo, Ganjiro Nakamura, Akira Takarada, Yu Fujiki, Eijiro Tono, Akihiko Hirata, Jun Tazaki, Hisaya Ito, Yoshio Kosugi, Yoshifumi Tajima, Akira Tani, Ikio Sawamura, Senkichi Omura, Yutaka Sada, Eisei Amamoto, Keiju Kobayashi, Ichiro Arishima, Kenichi "Enoken" Okomoto.

When Japanese films first became popular in the United States, director Inagaki was nearly as well known as Kurosawa. His *Miyamoto Musashi* (1954) was released here as *Samurai* (with added narration by William Holden), and won the Academy Award for Best Foreign Film. Even today more of Inagaki's movies are available on home video than virtually any other Japanese filmmaker after Kurosawa. One that hasn't surfaced in many years is *The Three Treasures*, which was Japanese equivalent of Cecil B. DeMille's *The Ten Commandments* (1956). This epic runs three hours (plus intermission), and, typical of Inagaki's films, has gorgeous photography and an all-star cast.

(If you want to get a sense of this film's scale, rent Inagaki's similarly huge *Chushingura,* 1962.) It has strong fantasy elements, including a multi-headed dragon star Mifune battles during Act II. Though actually pretty unimpressive technically—it looks like just what it is, a marionette—it nevertheless can be viewed as the embryonic inspiration for one of Toho's best monsters, King Ghidorah. Moreover, Tsuburaya's other effects are very impressive, though without the benefit of subtitles you'll wonder what's going on half the time. The U.S. version, possibly shown only in Los Angeles, was heavily cut, and the varying picture quality of the home video version in Japan suggests that it, too was heavily edited for general release. Remade, more or less, as *Yamato Takeru* (1993).

Tidal Wave ★ (NEW WORLD, 1975)
Nippon chiubotsu "Submersion of Japan" ★★★ (TOHO, 1973)
Director: Shiro Moritani **Special Effects Director:** Teruyoshi Nakano **Screenplay:** Shinobu Hashimoto, based on the novel by Sakyo Komatsu **Directors of Photography:** Hiroshi Murai and Daisuke Kimura **Special Effects Photography:** Mototaka Tomioka **Art Director:** Yoshiro Muraki **Music:** Masaru Sato **Producers:** Tomoyuki Tanaka and Osamu Tanaka **Cast:** Keiju Kobayashi, Hiroshi Fujioka, Tetsuro Tamba, Ayumi Ishida, Shogo Shimada, Nobuo Nakamura, Tadao Nakamaru, Yusuke Takita, Andrew Hughes, Isao Natsuyagi, Hideaki Nitani, Lorne Greene, Rhonda Leigh Hopkins, John Fujioka, Marvin Miller.

By far the most commercially successful genre film of the 1970s, *Submersion of Japan* was given a limited, subtitled release in its original form, but was much more widely seen as the bastardized *Tidal Wave,* with almost all of the human interest footage cut and new, annoying scenes of Lorne Greene (fresh from his other disaster epic, *Earthquake*) cut in. As *Tidal Wave,* it comes off as a very mediocre disaster pic; it died quickly and is almost forgotten today. In its original form, *Submersion...* is, like *The Last War* (1961), an intelligent depiction of Japan's postwar feelings of helplessness and isolationism. The few American writers who saw the complete, subtitled version when it was new praised it highly, but in hindsight the picture also marked the beginning of a disturbing trend. As writer Guy Tucker rightly points out in his book *Age of the Gods,* the picture's huge reception in Japan resulted in a number of pseudo-Hollywood-style all-star spectacles which emphasized vastness over intimacy, the Big Picture over characterization. The films that followed it—*ESPY, Prophecies of Nostradamus* (both 1974), *Deathquake* (1980), and even *Godzilla 1985* (1984)—aped *Submersion's* formula. The special effects by Nakano are outstanding, and the best of his career.

Time of the Apes ★½ (SANDY FRANK, 1987)
"Ape Corps" ✸ (TSUBURAYA PRODUCTIONS, 1974) [TV]
Directors: Atsuo Okunaka and Kiyasumi Fukuzawa **Teleplay:** Keiichi Abe, based on a story by Sakyo Komatsu, Koji Tanaka, and Aritsume Toyoda **Director of Photography:** Yoshihiro Mori **Music:** Toshiaki Tsushima **Producers:** Mataichi Takahashi and Masashi Tadakuma **Cast:** Reiko Tokunaga, Hiroko Saito, Masaaki Kaji, Hitoshi Omae, Tetsuya Ushida, Baku Hatakeyama, Kazue Takita, Noboru Nakaya.

Planet of the Apes, Japanese style. Yet another teleseries adapted, badly, into feature film format for U.S. television release. Unlike the Apes series, however, the man-apes in this time travel story are just a gimmick, and the cheaply-done teleseries, as can best be determined, has none of the intelligence of Fox's films, though its wit and spotty but sometimes vivid imagination helps somewhat. The ending, however, is a terrible, gobbledy-goop-filled mess.

The Vampire Doll ★★★

(TOHO INTERNATIONAL, 1971)
Yureiyashiki no kyofu: chi o su ningyo "Fear of the Ghost House: Blood-Sucking Doll" ★★★ (TOHO, 1970)
Director: Michio Yamamoto **Screenplay:** Ei Ogawa and Hiroshi Nagano **Director of Photography:** Kazutani Hara **Art Director:** Yoshifumi Honda **Music:** Riichiro Manabe **Special Effects:** Toho Special Effects Group **Cast:** Kayo Matsuo, Yukiko Kobayashi, Yoko Minazake, Atsuo Nakamura, Junya Usami, Akira Nakao, Sachio Sakai, Jun Hamamura.

It's unforunate that the best of Yamamoto's vampire trilogy is the least accessible in the United States. It was released subtitled 25 years ago and has since vanished; for some reason UPA's Henry Saperstein never leased it even though he released the latter two to television and home video. It's a moody, effective chiller with several really good moments, and about on par with the later Hammer films which this so clearly was trying to imitate. Followed by *Lake of Dracula* (1971).

Varan the Unbelievable ★1/2

(CROWN INTERNATIONAL, 1962)
Daikaiju Baran "Giant Monster Varan" ★★
(TOHO, 1958)
Director: Ishiro Honda **Special Effects Director:** Eiji Tsuburaya **Screenplay:** Shinichi Sekizawa, based on a story by Takeshi "Ken" Kuronuma **Director of**

Photography: Hajime Koizumi **Special Effects Photography:** Teisho Arikawa **Art Director:** Kiyoshi Suzuki **Music:** Akira Ifukube **Producer:** Tomoyuki Tanaka **Cast:** Kozo Nomura, Ayumi Sonoda, Fumio Matsuo, Koreya Senda, Akihiko Hirata, Fuyuki Murakami, Akira Sera, Yoshio Tsuchiya, Minnosuke Yamada, Hisaya Ito, Yoshifumi Tajima, Nadao Kirino, Fumiko Homma, Haruo Nakajima, Katsumi Tezuka. With Myron Healey, Tsuruko Kobayashi.

Disappointing *kaiju eiga* which began as a Japanese-American co-production for U.S. television (ABC), and became a full-fledged feature when the American company backed out. The result is a cheap-looking, minor film with little to offer beyond Ifukube's great score, which was deleted from American prints anyway. And if the original, Japanese version looks cheap and uninspired, the American version is many times worse, with much footage spliced out and dull, condescending footage of "star" Healey spliced in. The story concerns a giant monster (called Baran in Japan) hiding in a remote lake who crankily wakes up and destroys an Ainu village before flying jet-like to Haneda airport. The hard-to-see creature is nothing special save for its unique, flying squirrel-like aeronautics, also excised—senselessly—from domestic prints. Did American producer/director Jerry Baerwitz actually think audiences would rather see spliced-in-star Myron Healey rambling on and on about desalination levels ("All I get is sand! Nothing but sediment!") than a giant monster in flight? In fact, there's very little of the Japanese footage at all: the American version runs 17 minutes shorter than the Japanese cut, and at least half of that consists of Myron Healey being condescending to his Japanese-American wife (Kobayashi). Incidentally, the opening titles fail to credit a single

member of the Japanese cast and crew. Also, the Japanese footage is badly printed, and the monster, for the most part, is difficult to make out in the domestic version. Even the effects sequences are unambitious, and incorporate much stock footage from the first *Godzilla.* That and its second-tier cast (top-lined by the familiar but hardly bankable Nomura) confirm its B-movie status. Varan himself (played by Nakajima and Tezuka) is undistinguished, a Godzilla wannabe, who returned for an extremely brief cameo in the all-star *Destroy All Monsters* ten years later.

Virus ★★★ (BROADWOOD PRODUCTIONS, 1980)

Fukkatsu no hi "Resurrection Day" ★★★1/2
(HARUKI KADOKAWA FILMS/TBS, 1980)
Director: Kinji Fukasaku **Screenplay:** Koji Takada, Gregory Knapp, and Kinji Fukasaku, based on the novel by Sakyo Komatsu **Director of Photography:** Daisaku Kimura **Art Director:** Yoko Yoshinaga **Music:** Teo Macero **Producer:** Haruki Kadokawa **Cast:** Glenn Ford, George Kennedy, Henry Silva, Robert Vaughn, Chuck Conners, Ken Ogata, Stuart Gillard, Bo Svenson, Masao Kusakari, Isao Natsuki, Shinichi "Sonny" Chiba, Olivia Hussey, Cec Linder, Edward James Olmos.

Superbly directed by Fukasaku, and light years ahead of his other sci-fi efforts (*The Green Slime*, *Message from Space*), this horrifying, still relevant end-of-the-world drama was an expensive international production but sadly ignored here, dismissed (generally by those who hadn't bothered to see it) as yet another 70s era disaster picture. Most of the world dies when chemical weapons are unleashed in a botched smuggling operation, but the deadly virus never makes it to Antarctica whose diverse, international

inhabitants survive. But that's only the beginning of this bleak and haunting film, which deserves much more attention than it has ever received. The Japanese version is considerably longer (mainly sequences set in Japan, for obvious reasons, but there are other differences here and there), and there were several versions released stateside as well (the 108-minute home video version is what's reviewed above).

Voyage into Space ★1/2 (AIP-TV, 1970)

Jiyanto robo "Giant Robot" ★★★
(NET-TV, ASAHI, 1967)
Director: Minoru Yamada **Teleplay:** Masaru Igami **Music:** Takeo Yamashita **Producer:** Mitsuru Yokoyama **Cast:** Mitsunobu Kaneko, Akio Ito

Adapted from the "Johnny Socko and His Flying Robot" tv show, and one of the first instances of a Japanese teleseries adapted to feature length for television release in the U.S. Admirably wild with weird, out-of-this-world monsters (about a dozen of them, in fact) threatening Giant Robot (a man in a flimsy costume that suggests an Egyptian Pharaoh) and his pal Johnny Socko (Kaneko). Though bootlegs of this "movie" have been a much sought after item at sci-fi conventions (*Voyage into Space* rarely, if ever, turns up on television anymore), as a feature it quickly grows tiresome; interested parties are advised to scan individual episodes of the juvenile but entertaining series instead.

The War in Space ★

(GOLD KEY ENTERTAINMENT, 1980?)
Wakusei daisenso "Great Planet War" ★1/2
(TOHO, 1977)
Director: Jun Fukuda **Special Effects Director:**

Teruyoshi Nakano **Screenplay:** Ryuzo Nakanishi and Shuichi Nagahara, based on an idea by Hachiro Jinguji **Director of Photography:** Yuzuru Aizawa **Art Director:** Kazuo Satsuya **Music:** Toshiaki Tsushima **Producers:** Tomoyuki Tanaka and Fumio Tanaka **Cast:** Kensaku Morita, Ryo Ikebe, Akihiko Hirata, Yuko Asano, Hiroshi Miyauchi, Goro Mutsumi, Shuji Otaki, Shoji Nakayama, David Perrin, William Ross.

Conceived by producer Tanaka as "Battle in Outer Space 2" this terrible film was an acknowledged effort to cash in on *Star Wars* prior to that film's release in Japan. In fact, the picture is more a pathetic remake of *Atragon* (1963), this time set in outer space with stoic Ryo Ikebe substituting for Jun Tazaki and evil Venusians standing in for the Mu Empire. Though highly regarded by a tiny contingient of Japanese fans, *The War in Space* is cheap, blatantly derivative, and not remotely amusing. The last of Toho's 70s-style special effects features, and the last in anamorphic wide screen. The films that followed, from a technical standpoint, would be much more up to date and in the Hollywood style, but their unique "Japaneseness" would largely end with this film, pathetic though it is. Sadly, this would also be director Fukuda's last feature.

War of the Gargantuas ★★½

(MARON, 1970)
Furankenshutain no kaiju—Sanda tai Gaira
"Frankenstein Monsters—Sanda vs. Gaira" ★★★
(TOHO, 1966)
Director: Ishiro Honda **Special Effects Director:** Eiji Tsuburaya **Associate Producer:** Henry G. Saperstein **Screenplay:** Ishiro Honda and Kaoru Mabuchi (Takeshi Kimura) **Director of Photography:** Hajime Koizumi **Art Director:** Takeo Kita **Music:** Akira Ifukube

Producer: Tomoyuki Tanaka **Cast:** Kenji Sahara, Kumi Mizuno, Russ Tamblyn, Jun Tazaki, Nobuo Nakamura, Kipp Hamilton, Yoshifumi Tajima, Hisaya Ito, Nadao Kirino, Kozo Nomura, Ikio Sawamura, Ren Yamamoto, Haruo Nakajima, Hiroshi Sekita.

Outrageous *kaiju eiga*, *War of the Gargantuas* is a sequel to *Frankenstein Conquers the World* (1965), though American dubbing obscures this. Next to the original *Godzilla,* this was probably the most influential *kaiju eiga* for Japanese audiences—at the time it was considered horrifying—and its influence can be seen in films as recent as *Gamera—The Guardian of the Universe* (1995). Tamblyn and sexy Mizuno star as scientists trying to save their kindly Brown Gargantua (Sanda, essayed by stuntman/actor Sekita) from his evil half-brother, Green Gargantua (Gaira, played by Nakajima). Unlike the Godzilla films, where the giant reptile is deliberately lumbering, the Gargantuas are jarringly agile; that combined with the fact that we can actually see the actors eyes beneath their overstuffed costumes adds much. There's also lots of futuristic hardware, and a giant octopus monster in the admirably unsettling prologue. Tamblyn lacks the chemistry with Mizuno that Nick Adams had in *Frankenstein Conquers the World* and *Monster Zero* (both 1965), though his performance is all right, if a bit flip and sleepily underplayed. "Special Guest Star" Kipp Hamilton warbles—quite embarrassingly—a stop-the-show number entitled "Feel in My Throat," (later affectionately adapted by Devo). Much more impressive is Toho's stock company of actors, including the durable Tazaki leading the troops, Tajima and Ito investigating the strange goings-on, and Nakamura offering sage advice as the requisite elderly scientist. Sahara is top-billed in the Japanese edition, though his role remains fairly minor in both versions. Little snippets have been deleted in the American version, while alternate takes have been edited in, but generally this is unintrusive. What is intrusive is the removal of one of Ifukube's finest marches in favor of cheap library music—played over and over—which gives the film at times the feel of a Republic serial. Russ Tamblyn, who replaced Tab Hunter during preproduction, speaks English in the film, though his dialogue had to be relooped and is often out of synch. The rest of the dubbing is poor; even exterior scenes sound as if they were recorded in a shoe box. "Godzilla vs. Gargantua," proposed around 1980, was never filmed.

War of the Monsters ★½ (AIP-TV, 1967)

Daikaiju ketto Gamera tai Barugon "Great Monster Duel: Gamera vs. Barugon" ★★ (DAIEI, 1966)

Director: Shigeo Tanaka **Special Effects Supervisors:** Noriaki Yuasa and Kazufumi Fujii **Screenplay:** Nisan Takahashi **Director of Photography:** Michio Takahashi **Music:** Chuji Kinoshita **Producer:** Hidemasa Nagata **Cast:** Kojiro Honda, Kyoko Enami, Akira Natsuki, Koji Fujiyama, Yuzo Hayakawa, Ichiro Sugai.

The second Gamera movie has a much larger budget and, like the rest of the series, is in color, but resoundingly dull. It's also thoroughly ludicrous, even though the script asks us to take the increasingly absurd chain of events seriously. This time Gamera battles Barugon (not to be confused with Baragon, the monster from *Frankenstein Conquers the World*), a four-legged whatsit, with a rhino-like head, deadly rainbow rays emitting from its spiny back and deadly, darting tongue. Add to this an exasperatingly boring subplot about jewell thieves and you've got 100 minutes of sheer boredom. The badly-redubbed home video version, renamed *Gamera vs. Barugon,* is even worse (★). Followed by the much better *The Return of the Giant Monsters* (1967).

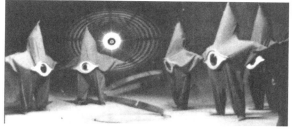

Warning from Space ★★½ (AIP-TV, 1960)

Uchujin Tokyo ni arawaru "Spaceman Appears in Tokyo" ✹ (DAIEI, 1956) aka The Mysterious Satellite

Director: Koji Shima **Screenplay:** Hideo Oguni, based on the novel by Gentaro Nakajima **Director of Photography:** Kimio Watanabe **Art Director:** Shigeo Muno **Special Effects Supervisor:** Noriaki Yuasa (?) **Producer:** Masaichi Nagata **Cast:** Toyomi Karita, Keizo Kawasaki, Isao Yamagata, Buntaro Miake, Shozo Nanbu, Mieko Nagai, Kyoko Hirai, Bin Yagasawa.

Charming feature from director Shima and the late screenwriter Hideo Oguni, who penned many of Kurosawa's best films. Also known as *The Mysterious Satellite,* this was the very first Japanese sci-fi picture in color. Cautiously friendly aliens try to warm mankind of its reckless use of nuclear power (a la *Day the Earth Stood Still*) and a runaway comet with Earth *(When Worlds Collide).* Though probably inspired by both American pictures, this work shows an inventiveness and style characteristic of Toho's Honda-Tsuburaya team, only they hadn't quite reached that level of maturity yet (*Rodan,* made that same year is, by contrast, far more conventional). The special effects and art direction are quite good, too, which begs the question: Why didn't Daiei make more sci-fi movies?

"Warning from Space"

The X from Outer Space ★★½

(AIP-TV, 1968)

Uchu daikaiju Girara "Giant Space Monster Girara" ★★★ (SHOCHIKU, 1967)

Director: Kazui Nihonmatsu **Screenplay:** Kazui Nihonmatsu, Hidemi Motomoshi, and Moriyoshi Ishida **Director of Photography:** Shizuo Hirase **Art Director:** Shigemori Shigeta **Music:** Taku Izumi **Special Effects Director:** Hiroshi Ikeda **Producer:** Akihiko Shimada **Cast:** Toshinari Kazusaki, Eiji Okada, Peggy Neal, Itoko Harada, Shinichi Yanagisawa, Franz Gruber, Keisuke Sonoi, Mike Daning, Torahiko Hamada, Ryuji Kita, Takanobu Hozumi.

Shochiku's sole *kaiju eiga* to date is an appealing, if utterly absurd tale of a giant reptilian space chicken thingamajig, Girara, accidentally hatched when brought back to Earth. The film's first half, set mostly in outer space, is most bemusing, with light, happy-happy music on the soundtrack (Izumi's Django Reinhardt-esque score seems to define the word "quirky"), while various astronauts, male and female, seem more concerned about the action at the Moon Base's cocktail lounge than scientific study. This gaiety is so bizarre and unexpected the film acquires a tremendous likability, even when the far more conventional monster stuff gets down to business in the second half, and misplays a straight face. Neal plays the requisite Western actor with tremendous charm, and acclaimed thespian Okada plays the Jun Tazaki role. Girara returned, via stock footage, in Yoji Yamada's *Tora-san's Forbidden Love* (1984), in a sequence which hilariously satirizes the genre, and Shochiku announced *Gappa vs. Girara* in 1997.

Yog—Monster from Space ★½

(AIP, 1971)

Kessen! Nankai no daikaiju Gezora, Ganime, Kameba "Decisive Battle! Giant Monsters of the South Seas: Gezora, Ganime, and Kameba" ★★ (TOHO, 1970)

Director: Ishiro Honda **Special Effects Director:** Teisho Arikawa **Screenplay:** Ei Ogawa **Director of Photography:** Taiichi Kankura **Art Director:** Takeo Kita **Music:** Akira Ifukube **Producers:** Tomoyuki Tanaka and Fumio Tanaka **Cast:** Akira Kubo, Atsuko Takahashi, Yoshio Tsuchiya, Kenji Sahara, Noritake Saito, Yukiko Kobayashi, Tetsu Nakamura, Chotaro Togin, Wataru Omae, Sachio Sakai, Yu Fujiki, Yuko Sugihara, Haruo Nakajima.

Pretty wretched film—when even Ifukube's score is mediocre you know you're in trouble—about a trio of monsters (see above) possessed by unseen aliens on a South Seas isle. They also possess Sahara's slimy villian, and his against-type performance is one of the films few redeaming values—it's all been done before, and Ogawa's screenplay has it all done before again and again. The monsters, are particularly colorless and more annoying than threatening, save perhaps for the goofy but likeable Gezora the Cuttlefish. Though released in 1970, this was really the last *kaiju eiga* filmed in the Classic style; that's it's so terrible makes it all the more painful to watch.

Zeram ★★★ (FOX LORBER, 1994)

Zeiramu "Zeram" ★★★ (GAGA/GROWD, 1991)

Director: Keita Amamiya **Screenplay:** Keita Amamiya and Hajime Matsumoto **Director of Photography:** Hiroshi Kidokoro **Producers:** Yoshinori Chiba and Koichi Sugisawa **Cast:** Yuko Moriyama, Yukijiro Hotaru, Kunihiko Iida, Mizuho Yoshida, Sachi Kashino, Satoko Kurenai.

Exciting, funny sci-fi thriller, originally released subtitled, about renegade 8-feet-tall alien (Zeram), the sexy female bounty pursuing him (Moriyama), and two Tokyo cable TV guys who are accidentally placed in the center of the action. The performances (especially Hotoru, later the reluctant investigator in *Gamera—The Guardian of the Universe*) are lively and amusing. Followed by *Zeram 2*. Dubbed version gets (★★ ½) rating.

怪獣 東京大攻撃

Selected Bibliography

Interviews

Chiba, Shinichi By Chris D. in Tokyo, Japan 15 November 1997.

Dunham, Robert By telephone 3 December 1995.

Fujiki, Yu At the Tokyu Inn, Shibuya (Tokyo, Japan) 24 January 1996.[1]

Fukasaku, Kinji At the Tokyu Inn, Ginza (Tokyo, Japan) 27 January 1996.[1]

Fukuda, Jun At Toho Studios (Tokyo, Japan) 2 February 1996.[1]

Funakoshi, Eiji At the Akasaka Tokyu Hotel (Tokyo, Japan) 26 January 1996.[1]

Hama, Mie At the Seiyo Hotel (Tokyo, Japan) 31 January 1996.[1]

Honda, Ishiro By James Bailey at his home (Tokyo, Japan) c.1991.

Honda, Kimi At her home (Tokyo, Japan) 27 January 1996.[1]

Horton, Robert At his home (Encino, California) 9 September 1997.

Hoshi, Yuriko At Toho Geino (Tokyo, Japan) 29 January 1996.[1]

Ifukube, Akira At his home (Tokyo, Japan). 18 December 1994.[2]

Ishii, Teruo At the Keio Plaza Hotel (Tokyo, Japan) 2 February 1996.[1]

Kochi, Momoko Near Tokyo Broadcasting System Studios (Tokyo, Japan) 29 January 1996.[1]

Kotani, Tsugunobu "Tom." By fax 11 March 1996.[3]

Kubo, Akira At the Tokyo Hilton, Shinjuku (Tokyo, Japan) 25 January 1996.[1]

Kurosawa, Akira By fax 13 March 1996.[3]

Matsubayashi, Shue At the Tokyo Hilton, Shinjuku (Tokyo, Japan) 27 January 1996.[1]

Matsumura, Tatsuo At the Tokyo Hilton, Shinjuku (Tokyo, Japan) 27 January 1996.[1]

Medina, Patricia At her home (Los Angeles, California) 28 March 1994.

Mitsuta, Kazuho "Pete" At Tsuburaya Productions (Tokyo, Japan) 26 January 1996.[4]

Mizuno, Kumi By telephone 16 July 1996.[3]

Nakanishi, Ryuzo and Gan Yamazaki At the Tokyo Hilton, Shinjuku (Tokyo, Japan) 27 January 1996.[1]

Nakano, Minoru In Tokyo, Japan 18 December 1994.[2]

Nakano, Teruyoshi By Steve Ryfle and Stuart Galbraith IV at the Tokyo Hilton (Tokyo, Japan) 25 January 1996.

Natsuki, Yosuke By telephone 11 March 1997.[3]

Okamoto, Kihachi At the Hollywood Roosevelt Hotel (Hollywood, California) 28 June 1997.[5]

Omura, Kon By telephone 7 March 1997.[3]

Reason, Rhodes By telephone 23 Mar. 1996.

Ross, William By Steve Ryfle at the Tokyo Hilton (Tokyo, Japan) 26 January 1996.

Sahara, Kenji At the Tokyo Hilton, Shinjuku (Tokyo, Japan) 29 January 1996.[4]

Saperstein, Henry G. At UPA Production of America (Sherman Oaks, California) 12 January 1994.

Sato, Masaru At the Tokyo Hilton, Shinjuku (Tokyo, Japan) 27 January 1996.[1]

Suzuki, Seijun At the Hotel Nikko (Beverly Hills, California) 20 March 1997.[3]

Takano, Koichi At Tsuburaya Productions (Tokyo, Japan) 26 January 1996.[4]

Takarada, Akira At the Imperial Hotel (Tokyo, Japan) 25 January 1996.[1]

Tsuburaya, Akira At Tsuburaya-Eizo (Tokyo, Japan) 30 January 1996.[4]

Tsuburaya, Kazuo At Tsuburaya Productions (Tokyo, Japan) 26 January 1996.[4]

Tsuchiya, Yoshio At Keio Plaza Hotel (Tokyo, Japan) 20 December 1994.[2]

Ueki, Hitoshi At Watanabe Production (Tokyo, Japan) 30 January 1996.[1]

Yamamoto, Michio At Tokyu Inn, Ginza (Tokyo, Japan) 31 January 1996.[1]

Yuasa, Noriaki By Mail 10 February 1996.[3]

Translated by:
1. Atsushi Sakahara
2. Yoshihiko Shibata
3. Yukari Fujii
4. Atsushi Saito
5. Kurando Mitsutake

Books

Bock, Audie. *Japanese Film Directors*. Tokyo, New York and San Francisco: Kodansha International, 1978.

Buehrer, Beverley Bare. *Japanese Films: A Filmography and Commentary, 1921–1989*. Jefferson, NC: McFarland, 1990.

Carr, Robert E. and R.M. Hayes. *Wide Screen Movies: A History and Filmography of Wide Gauge Filmmaking*. Jefferson, NC: McFarland, 1988.

Cowie, Peter, gen ed. *World Filmography*. London: The Tantivy Press, 1977. Two volumes.

Film Literature Index (volumes 1-19). Albany: State University of New York at Albany, 1973–1991.

Galbraith, Stuart, IV. *The Japanese Filmography, 1900–1994*. Jefferson, NC: McFarland & Company, 1996.

_____. *Japanese Science Fiction, Fantasy and Horror Films: A Critical Analysis of 103 Features Released in the United States, 1950–1992*. Jefferson, NC: McFarland, 1993.

Goble, Alan, ed. *The International Film Index, 1895–1990*. London: Bowker-Saur, 1991.

Hanson, Patricia King and Stephen L., eds. *The Film Review Index* (volume 2). Phoenix, AZ: Oryx, 1987.

Isemura, Yoshifumi and Hiroshi Nakamitsu. *Cinema Club 1994*. Tokyo: Pia Corp., 1993.

Katz, Ephraim. *The Film Encyclopedia*. New York: Cromwell, 1979.

Krafsur, Richard P., ex. ed. *The American Film Institute Catalog of Motion Pictures: Feature Films, 1961–1970*. New York: Bowker, 1976.

Kuroda, Toyoji, ed. *UniJapan Film and Japanese Film*. Tokyo: UniJapan Film, 1960–1992. Annual and quarterly volumes.

_____, ed. *Japanese Film 1992–1993*. Tokyo: UniJapan Film, 1991.

Kurosawa, Akira. *Something Like an Autobiography*. New York: Random House, 1982.

Lee, Walt, comp. *Reference Guide to Fantastic Films: Science Fiction, Fantasy and Horror*. Los Angeles: Chelsea-Lee Books, 1972–1974. Three volumes.

Lent, John A. *The Asian Film Industry*. London: Christopher Helm, Publishers, 1990.

Mellen, Joan. *Voices from the Japanese Cinema*. New York: Liveright, 1979.

New York Times Film Reviews: 1913–1968. The New York Times and Arno Press, 1970.

Nolletti, Anthony Jr., and David Desser, eds. *Reframing Japanese Cinema: Authorship, Genre, History*. Bloomington and Indianapolis, IN: Indiana University Press., 1992.

Re-Thinking the Emergence of Wide-Screen in Japan. unpublished essay. No date given and author undetermined.

Richie, Donald. *The Films of Akira Kurosawa*. Berkeley and Los Angeles: University of California Press, 1985.

Sato, Tadao. *Currents in Japanese Cinema*. Trans. Gregory Barrett. New York: Harper & Row, 1982.

Slide, Anthony. *The American Film Industry*. Westport, CT: Greenwood, 1986.

_____. *The International Film Industry*. Westport, CT: Greenwood, 1989.

Svensson, Arne. *Screen Series: Japan*. New York: A.S. Barnes & Co., 1971.

Thomas, Nicholas, ed. *International Dictionary of Films and Filmmakers: Actors and Actresses*. Chicago and Lond: St. James Press, 1990. Second Edition.

_____, ed. *International Dictionary of Films and Filmmakers: Directors*. Chicago and London: St. James Press, 1990. Second Edition.

Tucker, Guy Mariner. *Age of the Gods—A History of the Japanese Fantasy Film*. New York: Daikaiju Publishing, 1996

Tsushinsha, Jiji, ed. *Japanese Motion Picture Almanac 1957*. Tokyo: Promotion Council of the Motion Picture Industry of Japan, Inc., 1957.

Warren, Bill. *Keep Watching the Skies!*. Jefferson, NC: McFarland, 1982, 1986. Two volumes.

Variety Film Reviews, 1905–1992. New York and London: Garland, 1989–1994.

Variety Obituaries, 1905–1986. New York and London: Garland, 1989.

Selected Periodicals

Asian Trash Cinema, Boxoffice, Cinefantastique, CinemaScore, Cult Movies, Filmfax, G-Fan (fomerly G-Force), The Hollywood Reporter, The Japanese Fantasy Film Journal, Japanese Giants, The Kaiju Review, Kinema Jumpo, Markalite, Monster International, Monthly Film Bulletin, Monster Attack Team, Outré, Sight and Sound, Variety, (Nihon rando no) Yumei Kaiju

FILM	STUDIO	RELEASE DATE	DIRECTOR	SPFX DIRECTOR	LENGTH	COLOR/B&W	SCREEN SHAPE	SOUND SYSTEM	MONSTER(S)
Godzilla, King of the Monsters!	Toho	November 3, 1954	Ishiro Honda	Eiji Tsuburaya	98 mins.	Black and white	Academy ratio (1.33:1)	monophonic	Godzilla
Gigantis the Fire Monster	Toho	April 24, 1955	Motoyoshi Oda	Eiji Tsuburaya	82	Black and white	Academy ratio	monophonic	Godzilla, Angilas
Half Human: The Story of the Abominable Snowman	Toho	August 14, 1955	Ishiro Honda	Eiji Tsuburaya	95	Black and white	Academy ratio	monophonic	Abominable Snowman and Son
The Mysterious Satellite (aka Warning from Space)	Daiei	January 29, 1956	Koji Shima	Yonesaburo Tsukiji	87	Eastman Color	Academy ratio	monophonic	starfish-like aliens
Rodan	Toho	December 26, 1956	Ishiro Honda	Eiji Tsuburaya	82	Eastman Color	Academy ratio	monophonic	Rodans (2) and Meganurons
Atomic Rulers	Shintoho	July 30 and August 16, 1957	Teruo Ishii	undetermined	49 and 52	Black and white	Academy ratio	monophonic	none
Invaders from Space	Shintoho	October 1 and October 8, 1957	Teruo Ishii	undetermined	48 and 39	Black and white	Academy ratio	monophonic	evil aliens
The Mysterians	Toho	December 28, 1957	Ishiro Honda	Eiji Tsuburaya	89	Eastman Color	Toho Scope (2.35:1)	Perspecta Stereophonic Sound	Mogera
Attack from Space	Shintoho	December 18, 1957 and January 3, 1958	Teruo Ishii	undetermined	39 and 39	Black and white	Academy ratio	monophonic	evil aliens
The H-Man	Toho	July 24, 1958	Ishiro Honda	Eiji Tsuburaya	87	Eastman Color	Toho Scope	Perspecta Stereophonic Sound	H-Men
Varan the Unbelievable	Toho	October 14, 1958	Ishiro Honda	Eiji Tsuburaya	87	Black and white	Toho Pan Scope (some footage converted from Academy ratio)	Perspecta Stereophonic Sound	Varan
Prince of Space	Toei	March 19, and May 26, 1959	Eijiro Wakabayashi	Shozo Muroki	57 and 64	Black and white	ToeiScope (2.35:1)	monophonic	evil aliens
Evil Brain from Outer Space	Shintoho	March 27, and April 24, 1959	Chogi Akasaka	undetermined	57 and 57	Black and white	Academy ratio	monophonic	evil aliens
Battle in Outer Space	Toho	December 26, 1959	Ishiro Honda	Eiji Tsuburaya	93	Eastman Color	Toho Scope	Perspecta Stereophonic Sound	midget aliens
The Secret of the Telegian	Toho	April 10, 1960	Jun Fukuda	Eiji Tsuburaya	85	Eastman Color	Toho Scope	Perspecta Stereophonic Sound	electrically-transmitted man
The Human Vapor	Toho	December 11, 1960	Ishiro Honda	Eiji Tsuburaya	92	Eastman Color	Toho Scope	Perspecta Stereophonic Sound	The Vapor Man

FILM	STUDIO	RELEASE DATE	DIRECTOR	SPFX DIRECTOR	LENGTH	COLOR/B&W	SCREEN SHAPE	SOUND SYSTEM	MONSTER(S)
Mothra	Toho	July 30, 1961	Ishiro Honda	Eiji Tsuburaya	101 mins.	Eastman Color	Toho Scope	Perspecta Stereophonic Sound	Mothra (larve and winged form)
The Last War	Toho	October 8, 1961	Shue Matsubayashi	Eiji Tsuburaya	108	Eastman Color	Toho Scope	Perspecta Stereophonic Sound	none
Gorath	Toho	March 21, 1962	Ishiro Honda	Eiji Tsuburaya	89	Eastman Color	Toho Scope	Perspecta Stereophonic Sound	Magma
King Kong vs. Godzilla	Toho	August 11, 1962	Ishiro Honda	Eiji Tsuburaya	98	Eastman Color	Toho Scope	Perspecta Stereophonic Sound	Godzilla, King Kong, giant octopus
Attack of the Mushroom People	Toho	August 11, 1963	Ishiro Honda	Eiji Tsuburaya	89	Eastman Color	Toho Scope	monophonic	Mushroom People
The Lost World of Sinbad	Toho	October 26, 1963	Senkichi Taniguchi	Eiji Tsuburaya	97	Eastman Color	Toho Scope	monophonic	witch
Atragon	Toho	December 22, 1963	Ishiro Honda	Eiji Tsuburaya	96	Eastman Color	Toho Scope	Perspecta Stereophonic Sound	Manda
Godzilla vs. The Thing (aka Godzilla vs. Mothra)	Toho	April 29, 1964	Ishiro Honda	Eiji Tsuburaya	89	Eastman Color	Toho Scope	monophonic	Godzilla, Mothra (winged) and offspring (two larvae)
Dagora, the Space Monster	Toho	August 11, 1964	Ishiro Honda	Eiji Tsuburaya	83	Eastman Color	Toho Scope	monophonic	Dagora,
Ghidrah—The Three-Headed Monster	Toho	December 20, 1964	Ishiro Honda	Eiji Tsuburaya	92	Eastman Color	Toho Scope	monophonic	Godzilla, Rodan, Mothra (lavra form)
Kwaidan	Ninjin Club/ Bungei (and released by Toho)	February 27, 1965	Masaki Kobayashi	[none credited]	164	Eastman Color	Toho Scope	monophonic	ghosts
Frankenstein Conquers the World	Toho, in association with UPA Productions of America	August 8, 1965	Ishiro Honda	Eiji Tsuburaya	95	Eastman Color	Toho Scope	monophonic	Frankenstein's Monster, Baragon
Gammera the Invincible (aka Gamera)	Daiei	November 27, 1965	Noriaki Yuasa	Noriaki Yuasa	78	Black and white	DaieiScope (2.35:1)	monophonic	Gamera
Monster Zero (aka Godzilla vs. Monster Zero)	Toho, in association with UPA Productions of America	December 20, 1965	Ishiro Honda	Eiji Tsuburaya	94	Eastman Color	Toho Scope	monophonic	Godzilla, King Ghidorah, Rodan

FILM	STUDIO	RELEASE DATE	DIRECTOR	SPFX DIRECTOR	LENGTH	COLOR/B&W	SCREEN SHAPE	SOUND SYSTEM	MONSTER(S)
The Magic Serpent	Toei	March 5, 1966	Tetsuya Yamauchi and Kunio Kunisada	Shigeru Akutsuka	87 min.	Eastman Color	ToeiScope	monophonic	Froggo (giant frog), Draggo (giant dragon)
War of the Monsters (aka Gamera vs. Barugon)	Daiei	April 17, 1966	Shigeo Tanaka	Noriaki Yuasa	100	Eastman Color	DaieiScope	monophonic	Gamera, Barugon
Majin (aka Majin, the Hideous Idol)	Daiei	April 17, 1966	Kimiyoshi Yasuda	Yoshiyuki Kuroda	84	Eastman Color	DaieiScope	undetermined	Majin
War of the Gargantuas	Toho	July 31, 1966	Ishiro Honda	Eiji Tsuburaya	93	Eastman Color	Toho Scope	monophonic	Sanda, the Brown Gargantua, and Gairah, the Green Gargantua
The Return of the Giant Majin	Daiei	August 13, 1966	Kenji Misumi	Yoshiyuki Kuroda	79	Eastman Color	DaieiScope	monophonic	Majin
Majin Strikes Again	Daiei	December 10, 1966	Issei Mori	Yoshiyuki Kuroda	87	Eastman Color	DaieiScope	monophonic	Majin
Godzilla versus the Sea Monster	Toho	December 17, 1966	Jun Fukuda	Eiji Tsuburaya	87	Eastman Color	Toho Scope	monophonic	Godzilla, Ebirah, Mothra, giant condor
Return of the Giant Monsters (aka Gamera vs. Gyaos)	Daiei	March 15, 1967	Noriaki Yuasa	Noriaki Yuasa	87	Eastman Color	DaieiScope	monophonic	Gamera, Gyaos
The X from Outer Space	Shochiku	March 25, 1967	Kazui Nihonmatsu	Hiroshi Ikeda	88	Eastman Color	Shochiku GrandScope (2.35:1)	monophonic	Girara
Monster from a Prehistoric Planet	Nikkatsu	April 22, 1967	Haruyasu Noguchi	Akira Watanabe	84	Eastman Color	NikkatsuScope (2.35:1)	monophonic	Baby Gappa, Mama Gappa, Papa Gappa
King Kong Escapes	Toho, in association with Rankin-Bass Productions	July 22, 1967	Ishiro Honda	Eiji Tsuburaya	104	Eastman Color	Toho Scope	monophonic	King Kong, Mechani-Kong, Gorosaurus
Son of Godzilla	Toho	December 16, 1967	Jun Fukuda (director), Eiji Tsuburaya (supervisor)	Teisho Arikawa	86	Eastman Color	Toho Scope	monophonic	Godzilla, Minya, gimantises (3), Spiga
Kuroneko	Nichei Shinsha/Kindai Eiga Kyokai (and released by Toho)	February 24, 1968	Kaneto Shindo	[none credited]	99	Black and white	Toho Scope	monophonic	ghosts
Destroy All Planets	Daiei	March 20, 1968	Noriaki Yuasa	Noriaki Yuasa	81	Eastman Color	DaieiScope	monophonic	Gamera, Bairusu [aka Virus] (with Barugon and Gyaos, via stock footage)

FILM	STUDIO	RELEASE DATE	DIRECTOR	SPFX DIRECTOR	LENGTH	COLOR/B&W	SCREEN SHAPE	SOUND SYSTEM	MONSTER(S)
Destroy All Monsters	Toho	August 1, 1968	Ishiro Honda	Teisho Arikawa (director), Eiji Tsuburaya (supervisor)	89 mins.	Eastman Color	CinemaScope (2.35:1)	monophonic	Godzilla, King Ghidorah, Rodan, Mothra, Angilas, Minya, Gorosaurus, Spiga, Manda, Baragon, Varan
Attack of the Monsters (aka Gamera vs. Guiron)	Daiei	March 21, 1969	Noriaki Yuasa	Noriaki Yuasa	83	color	DaieiScope	monophonic	Gamera, Giron, Space Gyaos
Latitude Zero	Toho, in association with Don Sharp Productions	July 26, 1969	Ishiro Honda	Eiji Tsuburaya	108	Eastman Color	CinemaScope	monophonic	winged lion, batmen, giant rats
Godzilla's Revenge	Toho	December 20, 1969	Ishiro Honda	Eiji Tsuburaya and Ishiro Honda	70	Eastman Color	CinemaScope	monophonic	Godzilla, Minya, Gabara, gimantis (with Ebirah, Spiga et. al via stock footage)
Gamera vs. Monster X	Daiei	March 21, 1970	Noriaki Yuasa	Noriaki Yuasa	83	Eastman Color	DaieiScope	monophonic	Gamera, Monster X, baby Monster X
The Vampire Doll	Toho	July 4, 1970	Michio Yamamoto	Teruyoshi Nakano	93	Eastman Color	CinemaScope	monophonic	vampire
Yog—Monster from Space	Toho	August 1, 1970	Ishiro Honda	Teisho Arikawa	84	Eastman Color	CinemaScope	monophonic	Gezora, Ganime, Kameba, alien spores
Lake of Dracula	Toho	June 16, 1971	Michio Yamamoto	Teruyoshi Nakano	82	Eastman Color	CinemaScope	monophonic	vampires
Gamera vs. Zigra	Daiei	July 17, 1971	Noriaki Yuasa	Noriaki Yuasa	88	DaieiColor	DaieiScope	monophonic	Gamera, Zigra
Godzilla vs. The Smog Monster (aka Godzilla vs. Hedorah)	Toho	July 24, 1971	Yoshimitsu Banno	Teruyoshi Nakano	85	Eastman Color	CinemaScope	monophonic	Godzilla, Hedora (The Smog Monster)
Godzilla on Monster Island (aka Godzilla vs. Gigan)	Toho	March 12, 1972	Jun Fukuda	Teruyoshi Nakano	89	Eastman Color	CinemaScope	monophonic	Godzilla, Gigan, King Ghidorah, Angilas
Daigoro vs. Goliath	Tsuburaya Productions (and released by Toho)	December 17, 1972	Toshihiro Iijima	Tsuburaya Productions	85	Eastman Color	Academy ratio	monophonic	Daigoro, Goliath
Godzilla vs. Megalon	Toho	March 17, 1973	Jun Fukuda	Teruyoshi Nakano	81	Eastman Color	CinemaScope	monophonic	Godzilla, Megalon, Gigan, Jet Jaguar
Submersion of Japan/Tidal Wave	Toho	December 29, 1973	Shiro Moritani	Teruyoshi Nakano	140	Eastman Color	Panavision	magnetic stereo	none

FILM	STUDIO	RELEASE DATE	DIRECTOR	SPFX DIRECTOR	LENGTH	COLOR/B&W	SCREEN SHAPE	SOUND SYSTEM	MONSTER(S)
Godzilla vs. the Cosmic Monster (aka Godzilla vs. Mechagodzilla)	Toho	March 21, 1974	Jun Fukuda	Teruyoshi Nakano	84 mins.	Eastman Color	CinemaScope	monophonic	Godzilla, Mechagodzilla, Angilas (with King Ghidorah, et al via stock footage)
Evil of Dracula	Toho	July 20, 1974	Michio Yamamoto	Teruyoshi Nakano	87	Eastman Color	CinemaScope	monophonic	vampire
The Last Days of Planet Earth (aka Prophecies of Nostradamus & Catastrophe: 1999)	Toho	August 3, 1974	Toshio Masuda	Teruyoshi Nakano	114	Eastman Color	Panavision	monophonic	post-apocalyptic mutants
ESPY (aka ESP/SPY)	Toho	December 28, 1974	Jun Fukuda	Teruyoshi Nakano	94	Eastman Color	CinemaScope	monophonic	none
Terror of Mechagodzilla (aka The Terror of Godzilla)	Toho	March 15, 1975	Ishiro Honda	Teruyoshi Nakano	83	Eastman Color	CinemaScope	monophonic	Godzilla, Mechagodzilla Titanosaurus
The War in Space	Toho	December 17, 1977	Jun Fukuda	Teruyoshi Nakano	90	color	CinemaScope	monophonic	furry giant
Super Monster (aka Gamera Super Monster)	Daiei	March 20, 1980	Noriaki Yuasa	[none credited]	91	DaieiColor	Wide Screen (1.85:1)	monophonic	Gamera (with Barugon, Gyaos, Viras, Guiron, Monster X, and Zigra via stock ftg.)
Deathquake	Toho	August 30, 1980	Kenjiro Omori	Teruyoshi Nakano	127	color	Wide Screen	Dolby Stereo (?)	none
Godzilla 1985	Toho	December 15, 1984	Koji Hashimoto	Teruyoshi Nakano	103	color	Wide Screen	Dolby Stereo	Godzilla
Godzilla vs. Biollante	Toho	December 16, 1989	Kenjiro Omori	Koichi Kawakita	104	color	Wide Screen	Dolby Stereo	Godzilla, Biollante
Zeram	Gaga/Crowd	August 1991	Keita Amamiya	undetermined	96	color	Wide Screen	Dolby Stereo	Zeiram
Godzilla vs. King Ghidorah	Toho	December 14, 1991	Kenjiro Omori	Koichi Kawakita	103	color	Wide Screen	Dolby Stereo	Godzilla, King Ghidorah, Mecha-Godzilla, Godzillasaurus
Godzilla vs. Mothra	Toho	December 12, 1992	Takao Okawara	Koichi Kawakita	104	color	Wide Screen	Dolby Stereo	Godzilla, Mothra (lavrae and winged), Battra (larvae and winged)
Godzilla vs. Mechagodzilla	Toho	December 11, 1993	Takao Okawara	Koichi Kawakita	108	color	Wide Screen	Dolby Stereo	Godzilla, Mechagodzilla, Rodan, Fire Rodan, Baby Godzilla?

FILM	STUDIO	RELEASE DATE	DIRECTOR	SPFX DIRECTOR	LENGTH	COLOR/B&W	SCREEN SHAPE	SOUND SYSTEM	MONSTER(S)
Godzilla vs. Space Godzilla	Toho	December 10, 1994	Kensho Yamashita	Koichi Kawakita	105 mins.	color	Wide Screen	Dolby Stereo	Godzilla, Space Godzilla, M.O.G.E.R.A., Little Godzilla
Gamera: The Guardian of the Universe	Daiei/ Tokuma Publishing/Nippon TV Network/Hakuhodo for Toho release	March 1995	Shusuke Kaneko	Shinji Higuchi	95	color	Wide Screen	Dolby Stereo	Gamera, Gyaos
Godzilla vs. Destroyer	Toho	December 9, 1995	Takao Okawara	Koichi Kawakita	103	color	Wide Screen	Dolby Stereo	Godzilla, Destroyer, Junior Godzilla
Gamera 2	Daiei/ Tokuma Publishing/Nippon TV Network/Hakuhoden for Toho release	July 13, 1996	Shusuke Kaneko	Shinji Higuchi	100	color	Wide Screen	Dolby Stereo	Gamera, Legion

About the Author

This is Stuart Galbraith IV's third book on Japanese cinema, following *Japanese Science Fiction, Fantasy and Horror Films* (McFarland & Co., 1994) and *The Japanese Filmography* (McFarland, 1996). He is also the author of *Motor City Marquees* (McFarland, 1995), interviewed cinematographer Vilmos Zsigmond for the DVD of *The Sadist*, and has written for *Filmfax, Outré, RetroVision*, and *Cult Movies*. Galbraith was a film critic and columnist for the *Ann Arbor News* and is now a curator at the USC Warner Bros. Archives. He recently made his feature film acting debut as Tabby, a catatonic has-been in Joal Ryan's *Former Child Star* (1997) and as an interview subject in the documentary *Birds of a Feather* (1998). He lives in Hollywood with his cat, Chibi-san.

Also from Feral House

Sex, American Style
AN ILLUSTRATED ROMP THROUGHOUT THE GOLDEN AGE OF HETEROSEXUALITY
Jack Boulware

The 70s was a time saturated with sex: singles's bars, nudism, porn theatres, hot tubs, couple-swapping, swingers' retreats, compliant stewardesses and mass market titillation. The lavishly illustrated *Sex, American Style* revisits the charmingly naïve but sex-crazed period of American history.

8 × 11 ◆ 250 pages ◆ illustrated ◆ $16.95 ◆ ISBN0-922915-46-6

Nightmare of Ecstasy
THE LIFE AND ART OF EDWARD D. WOOD, JR.
Rudolph Grey

The credited basis for the Tim Burton movie *Ed Wood* is far more intriguing and revealing in print. "Finally the Ed Wood story told in all its naked wonder. *Nightmare of Ecstasy* is and hilarious but heartbreaking portrayal of a brave, eccentric and sometimes insane film director. I stayed up all night reading it with my mouth hanging open."—John Waters

6 × 9 ◆ 232 pages ◆ illustrated ◆ $14.95 ◆ ISBN0-922915-24-5

Grossed-Out Surgeon Vomits Inside Patient!
AN INSIDER'S LOOK AT SUPERMARKET TABLOIDS
Jim Hogshire

The papers that occupy supermarket checkout stands are no longer the object of derision; they're the mainstay of American media. How do they work? How did they start? Who's behind them, and why? Former tab writer Jim Hogshire turns the tables on the papers that shape how and what America thinks with an important and entertaining book.

6 × 9 ◆ 160 pages ◆ illustrated ◆ $12.95 ◆ ISBN0-922915-42-3

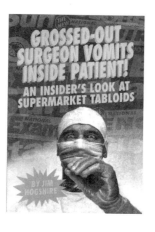

Order from Feral House with check or money order plus $3 for the first book and for 50¢ each additional book ordered. For a free catalogue of publications, send a SASE.

FERAL HOUSE ◆ 2532 LINCOLN BLVD., ◆ SUITE 359 ◆ VENICE, CA 90291

Visit our website: www.feralhouse.com